THE MOST
BEAUTIFUL
VILLAGES
OF FRANCE®

French Edition
Editorial Director: Clélia Ozier-Lafontaine,
assisted by Héloïse Moulard
Design and Typesetting: Alice Leroy

English Edition
Editorial Director: Kate Mascaro
Editor: Helen Adedotun
Translated from the French by Anne McDowall,
Kate Ferry-Swainson, and Kate Robinson
Proofreading: Nicole Foster
Production: Caroline Lhomme
Color Separation: IGS-CP, L'Isle d'Espagnac
Printed in Bosnia and Herzegovina by GPS

Simultaneously published in French as
Les Plus Beaux Villages de France:
180 destinations de charme à découvrir
© Éditions Flammarion, Paris, 2025
First English-language edition
© Flammarion, S.A., Paris, 2016
This revised and updated English-language edition
© Éditions Flammarion, Paris, 2025

editions.flammarion.com
@flammarioninternational

25 26 27 3 2 1
ISBN: 978-2-08-046255-8
Legal Deposit: 02/2025

Les Plus Beaux Villages de France®
association

THE MOST
BEAUTIFUL
VILLAGES
OF FRANCE®

Discover 180 Charming Destinations

Flammarion

Preface

From the shores of Lake Geneva to the coast of the English Channel, from the vineyards of Alsace to the volcanos of Auvergne, and from the châteaux of Val de Loire to the island of La Réunion, The Most Beautiful Villages of France reveal all of the charm and diversity of the country. The variety of its landscapes, architecture, and heritage, as well as its history, traditions, terroir, and savoir faire make for places that are never identical, but are always enchanting.

In addition to the visual delights in store, The Most Beautiful Villages of France offer unique experiences in exceptional settings to visitors in search of the good life, simple pleasures, and enriching encounters with locals.

Bringing together 180 jewels of French rural tourism that have been awarded the prestigious national label of excellence, this guide provides a multitude of destinations for your next getaway and extends an invitation to take "the road less traveled." These localities are also—and perhaps above all—vibrant communities that the residents are committed to preserving and keeping alive, in order to share with you a little of what makes them happy and proud to call their village home.

Alain Di Stefano
President of Les Plus Beaux Villages de France association
Deputy Mayor of Yèvre-le-Châtel, in the Loiret

Foreword

Over the past thirteen years, I have traveled all over France in search of the country's most beautiful villages, some of which aspire to be voted the Best Loved Village of France on the show I present on France Télévisions. Saint-Cirq-Lapopie, Eguisheim, Cordes-sur-Ciel, Ploumanac'h, Rochefort-en-Terre, Kaysersberg, Cassel, Saint-Vaast-la-Hougue, Hunspach, Sancerre, Bergheim, Esquelbecq, Collioure—those may be the thirteen villages that have received the honor, yet there are so many others, just as splendid, which continually elicit the same reaction from viewers: "France is so beautiful!" What other country can boast such diverse landscapes, such a wealth of villages and countryside, on the coast and in the mountains, and such a variety of built, natural, and culinary heritage?

Of course, France has changed over the last thirteen years. Its administrative regions have been restructured, but the spirit of its villages has remained intact and vibrant across the country. Year after year, I discover with the same delight, and in each village, an incredible historical, touristic, architectural, and gastronomic heritage, not to mention the women and men who champion this legacy. These villages speak volumes about French identity and roots; the feeling of belonging to a tight-knit community; an attachment to several acres of land, a built heritage, historical monuments, local traditions, carefully preserved time-tested flavors, and, most of all, the conviviality and solidarity of a collectivity whose destiny we share. Some villages are picture-perfect landscapes where time seems to have stopped, offering visitors the idyllic image they came to see. Others have carefully maintained whatever brought them fame in the past while adapting to the changing times to avoid turning into an open-air museum. Let us not forget that these French villages also represent a culture—often a heritage—within everyone's reach, which generates tourism and contributes to the economy. These villages are undoubtedly a treasure for posterity.

As you read this book and discover France's most beautiful villages, I am sure you will have only one desire: to take the byways leading to these unspoiled destinations that restore our hope in the future.

Stéphane Bern

The Most Beautiful Villages of France

The association of Les Plus Beaux Villages de France® was founded in the early summer of 1981, after one man encountered a certain book. That man was Charles Ceyrac, mayor of the village of Collonges-la-Rouge in Corrèze, and the book was *Les Plus Beaux Villages de France*, published by Sélection du Reader's Digest. This book gave Ceyrac the idea of harnessing people's energy and passion to protect and promote the exceptional heritage of France's most beautiful villages. Sixty-six mayors signed up to Charles Ceyrac's initiative, which was made official on March 6, 1982 at Salers in Cantal, France. Today, this national network of 180 villages works to protect and enhance the heritage of these exceptional locations in order to increase their renown and promote their economic development.

Three steps to becoming one of The Most Beautiful Villages of France

THREE PRELIMINARY CRITERIA

In the first instance, the village looking to join the association must submit an application showing that it meets the following criteria:
- a total population of no more than 2,000 inhabitants
- at least two protected sites or monuments (historic landmarks, etc.)
- proof of mass support for the application for membership via public debate

THIRTY-TWO EVALUATION CRITERIA

If the application is accepted, the village then receives a site visit. After an interview with the local council and a photographic report have been completed, a table of thirty-two criteria is used to evaluate the village's historical, architectural, urban, and environmental attributes, as well as its own municipal initiatives to promote the village.

THE VERDICT OF THE QUALITY COMMISSION

The finished evaluation report is put before the Quality Commission, which alone has the power to make decisions on whether a village should be accepted (an outcome requiring a two-thirds majority in the vote). About ten villages apply each year, and about 20% of applications are successful. The approved villages are also subject to regular reevaluation in order to guarantee each visitor an outstanding experience.

A concept that has traveled the globe

Interest in preserving and enhancing rural heritage transcends national boundaries, and several initiatives throughout Europe and the rest of the world have given rise to other associations on the French model, in Wallonia (Belgium), Quebec (Canada), Italy, Japan, Spain, Switzerland, Saxony (Germany), Lebanon, Bosnia and Herzegovina, and China. Collaborating with the **Federation of the Most Beautiful Villages of the World**, these associations are now taking their expertise to emerging networks.

To read more about the association, visit:
les-plus-beaux-villages-de-france.org

Save the date
- **Journées Européennes des Métiers d'Art® (European Artistic Craft Days):** 1st weekend in April
- **La Nuit Romantique dans Les Plus Beaux Villages de France® (The Most Beautiful Villages of France Romantic Evening):** 3rd Saturday in June
- **Journées Européennes du Patrimoine® (European Heritage Days):** 3rd weekend in September

To reserve your next trip, take part in events, or keep up with the latest news, visit our website at:
les-plus-beaux-villages-de-france.org
or follow us on social media

The 180 Most Beautiful Villages of France by geographical region

Bar-le-Duc
Metz
Nancy
Strasbourg
Épinal
Colmar
Chaumont
Belfort
Dijon Vesoul
Besançon
Lons-le-Saunier
Mâcon
Bourg-en-Bresse
Annecy
Lyon Chambéry
Grenoble
Valence
Gap
Digne-les-Bains
Avignon
Nice
Marseille
Toulon
Bastia
Ajaccio

- NORTHWEST
- NORTHEAST
- SOUTHEAST
- SOUTHWEST

©éditerra

NORTHWEST

Scale 1: 2,600,000

0 — 50 km
0 — 30 miles

UNITED KINGDOM

Southampton

Plymouth

Cap de
la Hague
**Cherbourg-
en-Cotentin**
Pointe de Barfleur
Barfleur
Valognes

Bayeux

Cae

St-Lô

Coutances

Vire

Flers

Granville
Baie du
Mont

Fougères

Avranches

Mayenne

Ste-Suzann

Laval

Guernsey

Jersey

Golfe de
St-Malo

St-Malo

Dinard

St-Suliac

Dinan

Rennes

Perros-Guirec

Roscoff

Lannion

Baie de
St-Brieuc

St-Brieuc

Morlaix

Brest

Moncontour

Pontivy

Ploërmel

Châteaubriant

Île d'Ouessant

Pointe St-Mathieu

Pointe du Raz

Île de Sein

Locronan

Châteaulin

Quimper

Baie
d'Audierne

Pointe de Penmarch

Lorient

Vannes

Île de Groix

**Rochefort-
en-Terre**

Angers

Belle-Île

Pointe du Croisic

La Baule

St-Nazaire

St-Herblain

Nantes

Rezé

Cholet

Atlantic Ocean

Challans

Île d'Yeu

**La Roche-
s.-Yon**

Bressuire

Parthena

Vouvant

Les Sables-
d'Olonne

Pointe de l'Aiguille

Île de Ré

La Flotte

Ars-en-Ré

La Rochelle

Niort

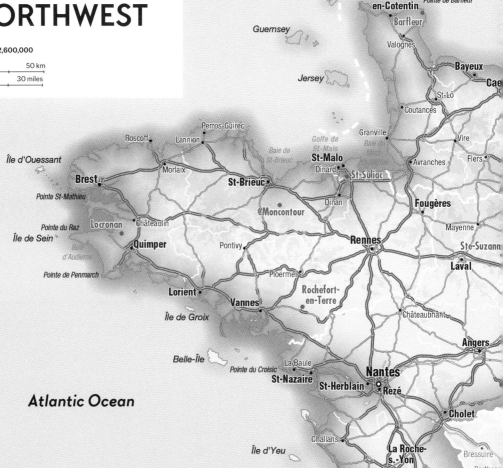

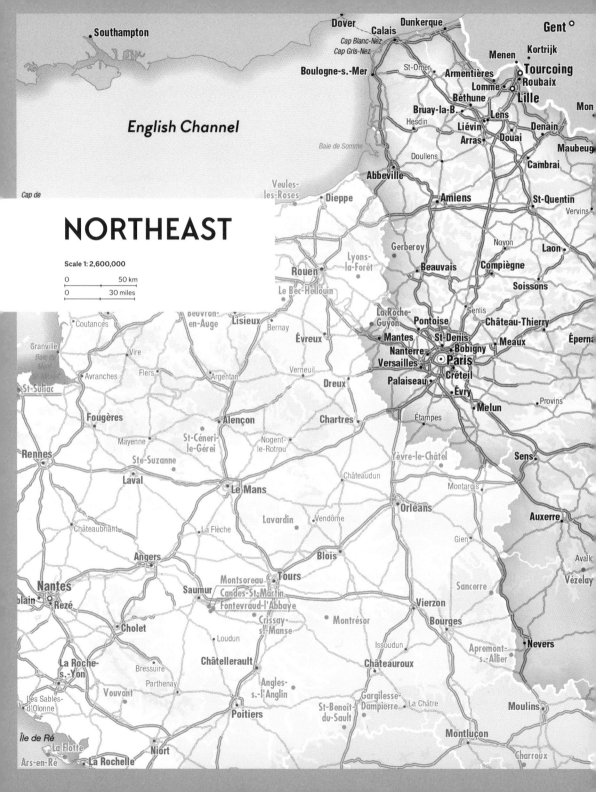

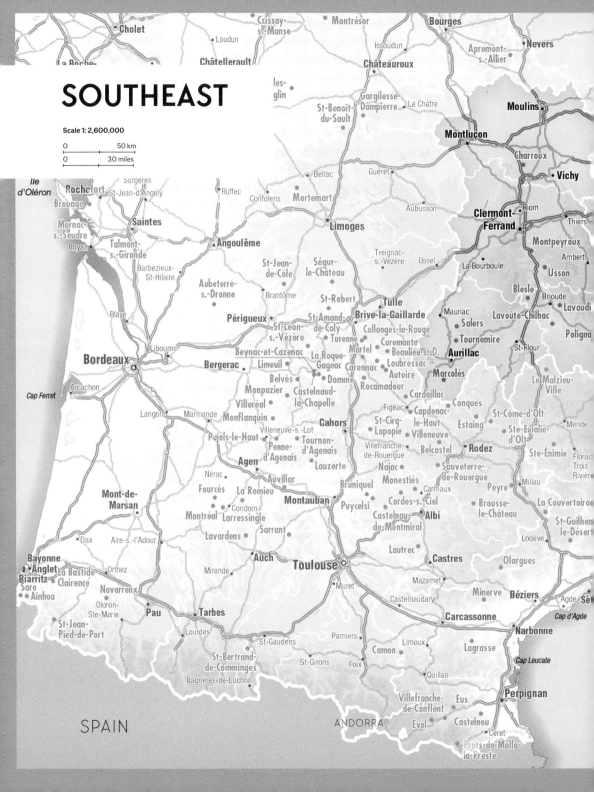

SOUTHEAST

Scale 1: 2,600,000

0   50 km
0   30 miles

Cholet
Crissay-s.-Manse
Montrésor
Bourges
Nevers
Loudun
Châtellerault
La Roche-
Apremont-s.-Allier
Issoudun
Châteauroux
les-glin
Moulins
St-Benoît-du-Sault
Gargilesse-Dampierre
La Châtre
Montluçon
Charroux
Vichy
Surgères
Bellac
Guéret
Clermont-Ferrand
Riom
Thiers
Ile d'Oléron
Rochefort
St-Jean-d'Angély
Ruffec
Confolens
Mortemart
Aubusson
Montpeyroux
Brouage
Limoges
Treignac-s.-Vézère
Ussel
La Bourboule
Ambert
Mornac-s.-Seudre
Saintes
Usson
Royan
Talmont-s.-Gironde
Angoulême
St-Jean-de-Côle
Ségur-le-Château
Blesle
Brioude
Lavaudi
Barbezieux-St-Hilaire
Aubeterre-s.-Dronne
Brantôme
St-Robert
Tulle
Mauriac
Salers
Lavoûte-Chilhac
Blaye
Périgueux
St-Léon-s.-Vézère
St-Amand-de-Coly
Brive-la-Gaillarde
Collonges-la-Rouge
Curemonte
Beaulieu-s.-D.
Tournemire
St-Flour
Poligna
Bordeaux
Libourne
Bergerac
Beynac-et-Cazenac
Limeuil
Turenne
La Roque-Gageac
Martel
Carennac
Autoire
Aurillac
Marcolès
Le Malzieu-Ville
Arcachon
Belvès
Domme
Rocamadour
Cardaillac
Cap Ferret
Monpazier
Castelnaud-la-Chapelle
Figeac
Capdenac-le-Haut
Conques
St-Côme-d'Olt
Mende
Villeréal
Langon
Marmande
Monflanquin
Cahors
St-Cirq-Lapopie
Villeneuve
Estaing
Ste-Eulalie-d'Olt
Pujols-le-Haut
Villeneuve-s.-Lot
Tournon-d'Agenais
Villefranche-de-Rouergue
Belcastel
Rodez
Ste-Énimie
Florac
Trois Rivièr
Penne-d'Agenais
Lauzerte
Najac
Millau
Agen
Auvillar
Bruniquel
Monestiés
Peyre
La Couvertoirad
Nérac
Fourcès
La Romieu
Montauban
Puycelsi
Cordes-s.-Ciel
Carmaux
Brousse-le-Château
St-Guilhem-le-Désert
Mont-de-Marsan
Condom
Larressingle
Sarrant
Castelnau-de-Montmiral
Albi
Lodève
Montréal
Lavardens
Lautrec
Olargues
Dax
Aire-s.-l'Adour
Auch
Toulouse
Castres
Minerve
Béziers
Bayonne
Anglet
La Bastide-Clairence
Mirande
Muret
Mazamet
Agde
Se
Biarritz
Navarrenx
Castelnaudary
Cap d'Agde
Sare
Ainhoa
Oloron-Ste-Marie
Pau
Tarbes
Carcassonne
Narbonne
St-Jean-Pied-de-Port
Lourdes
St-Gaudens
Pamiers
Limoux
Lagrasse
Orthez
Camon
Cap Leucate
St-Bertrand-de-Comminges
St-Girons
Foix
Quillan
Bagnères-de-Luchon
Villefranche-de-Conflent
Eus
Perpignan
SPAIN
ANDORRA
Evol
Castelnou
Céret
Prats-de-Mollo-la-Preste

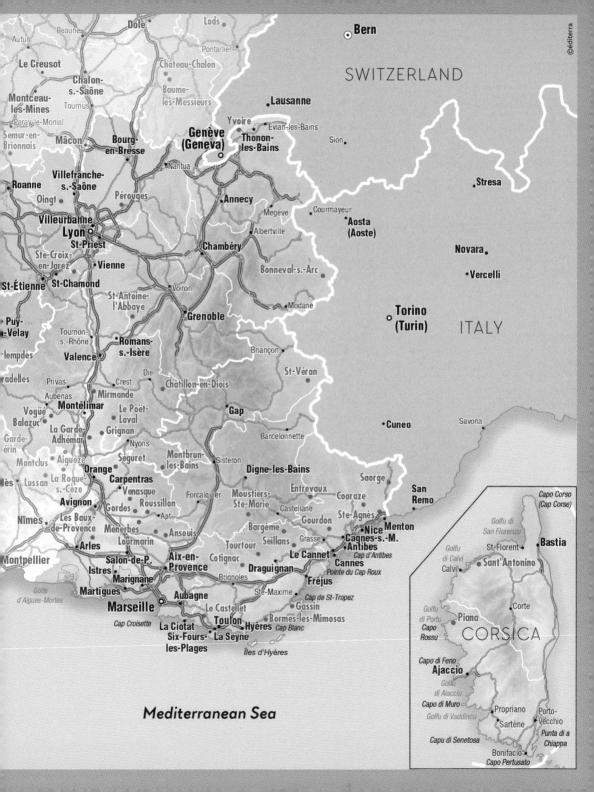

SOUTHWEST

Scale 1: 2,600,000

0 ——————— 50 km
0 ——————— 30 miles

Atlantic Ocean

SPAIN

Cholet
Challans
La Roche-s.-Yon
Bressuire
Parthen
Vouvant
Île d'Yeu
Les Sables-d'Olonne
Pointe de l'Aiguille
Île de Ré
La Flotte
Niort
Ars-en-Ré
La Rochelle
Île d'Oléron
Rochefort
Surgères
St-Jean-d'Angély
Brouage
Mornac-s.-Seudre
Saintes
Royan
Talmont-s.-Gironde
Barbezieux-St-Hilai
Blaye
Libour
Bordeaux
Arcachon
Cap Ferret
Langon
Mont-de-Marsan
Dax
Aire-s.-l'Adour
Anglet
Bayonne
Biarritz
Orthez
La Bastide-Clairence
Navarrenx
Sare
Ainhoa
Oloron-Ste-Marie
Pau
St-Jean-Pied-de-Port
Santander
Bilbao
San Sebastián
Vitoria
(Gasteiz)
Pamplona
Burgos
Logroño

©éditerra

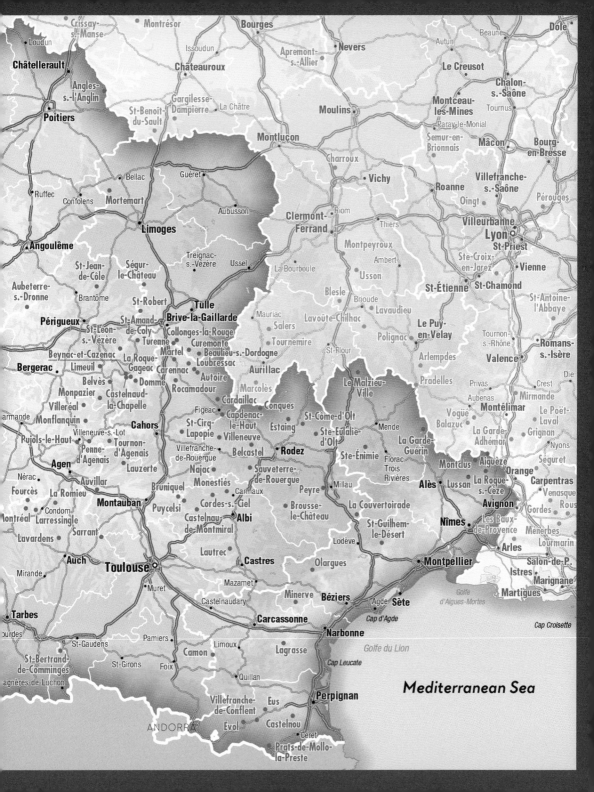

 Apr.: Flower market
(2nd weekend).
Pentecost: Flea market
(weekend).
Aug.: Aiguèze en Couleurs,
street painting festival.
Dec.: Christmas market.

 OUTDOOR ACTIVITIES

Swimming (Ardèche river) •
Canoeing and boating trips
(Gorges de l'Ardèche) •
Walking: Trail from Castelvieil
oppidum (main settlement),
hike through vineyards.

Aiguèze

Between vineyards and the Ardèche river

A fortress perched on a cliff overlooking the Gorges de l'Ardèche, Aiguèze protects its medieval heritage, cultivates vines, and offers a friendly, welcoming atmosphere to visitors. Like any strategic defense site, Aiguèze has had a turbulent past. From 725 to 737 CE, the region was occupied by the Saracens, who gave their name to one of the village's towers. The fortification of the site dates back to the 11th century: it was the work of the count of Toulouse, who wanted to make Aiguèze the outpost for his operations against the region of Vivarais. In the narrow cobbled and vaulted streets, arch-covered balconies, mullioned windows, and arched doorways have pride of place. They lead to the *castelas*, the old ramparts of the castle, which command a splendid view of the Ardèche, garigue (scrubland), and Côtes du Rhône vineyards.

 HIGHLIGHTS

Church (11th century):
Open daily.
Village: Guided tour
in peak season, by appt.
(04 66 39 26 89).

 ACCOMMODATION & EATING OUT

Restaurants
♥ Le Comptoir des Sarrasins
(06 88 08 88 42).

LOCAL SPECIALTIES

Food and Drink
AOC Côtes du Rhône wines •
Honey • Goat cheese
(*pélardons*).
Art and Crafts
Art gallery • Pottery • Craft
studios • Feather creations:
♥ Fizz Feathers
(07 88 05 71 68).

 EVENTS

Market: Thurs. a.m. (Jul. 1st-
Sept. 1st).

 FURTHER AFIELD

•Chartreuse de Valbonne,
monastery (4½ miles/7 km).
•Château de Suze-la-Rousse
(17 miles/27 km).
•Gorges de l'Ardèche:
Vallon-Pont-d'Arc; Grotte
Chauvet 2, cave
reconstruction
(20 miles/32 km).

MBVF NEARBY
•Montclus (9 miles/15 km).
•La Roque-sur-Cèze
(11 miles/18 km).

Gard (30)
Population: 210
Altitude: 292 ft. (89 m)

TOURIST INFO—PROVENCE OCCITANE
04 66 39 26 89
provenceoccitane.com

Art and Crafts

Artisanal cosmetics • Jeweler, artist-creator • Wood and stone carving • Tapestry weaving • Espadrilles • Artisanal carpentry.

 EVENTS

Pentecost: Pilgrimage to Notre-Dame-de-l'Aubépine (Mon.).
Aug.: Patronal festival (15th).

 OUTDOOR ACTIVITIES

Basque pelota • Walking: Route GR 10, and 3 marked trails • Mountain biking: 1 marked trail and Grand Traversée Pays Basque circuit • Horseback riding: Sentier des Contrabandiers.

 FURTHER AFIELD

• Urdax and Zugarramurdi caves (3-5 miles/5-8 km).
• Cambo-les-Bains (7 miles/11.5 km).
• Saint-Jean-de-Luz; Bayonne; Biarritz (14-17 miles/23-27 km).

 MBVF NEARBY

• Sare (5 miles/8 km).
• La Bastide-Clairence (19 miles/31 km).

Ainhoa

All the colors
of the Basque Country

Marrying its green hillsides with the red-and-white façades of its Labourdin and Navarrese houses, Ainhoa displays the colors of the Basque Country along its single street. In the 13th century, the Roman Catholic religious order known as the Premonstratensians set up a vicariate at Ainhoa to provide assistance to pilgrims traveling to Santiago, and a *bastide* (fortified town) emerged from the plain to provide for their welcome. Rebuilt in the 17th century, its finest façades face east. The rings for tying up mules on the *lorios* (doors) of some houses bear witness to their former role as merchant inns on the road to Pamplona. Next to the *fronton* (Basque pelota court), which still hosts a few games in summer, the 13th-century church has been rebuilt, but the cut stones of its lower parts date back to the founding of the *bastide*. Higher up, the Notre-Dame-d'Arantzazu chapel (*arantza* means "hawthorn" in Basque; it is also known as Notre-Dame-de-l'Aubépine in French) stands on the Atsulai mountainside.

 HIGHLIGHTS

Église Notre-Dame-de-l'Assomption: Spanish-style gilded wooden altarpiece.
Maison du Patrimoine: Film on the history of the village and the border area (05 59 29 93 99).
Village: *Bastide, fronton*, church, and open-air washhouse. Guided tour year round, by appt. (05 59 29 93 99).

 ACCOMMODATION & EATING OUT

Hotels
♥ Maison Oppoca**** (05 59 29 90 72).
Restaurants
♥ Oppoca (05 59 29 90 72).

 LOCAL SPECIALTIES

Food and Drink
Pain d'épice (spice cake) • Salted meats and fish • Basque specialties (piment d'Espelette, Kintoa pork, Ossau-Iraty sheep's cheese).

Pyrénées-Atlantiques (64)
Population: 680
Altitude: 394 ft. (120 m)

TOURIST INFO—AINHOA
05 59 29 93 99
ainhoa-tourisme.fr

Angles-sur-l'Anglin

Ancient skills and wall carvings

On the banks of the Anglin, this village boasts a 15,000-year-old history. From the top of the cliff, the ruins of the fortress, built by the counts of Lusignan between the 11th and 15th centuries, overlook the river. At the top of the village, the Église Saint-Martin, with its Romanesque bell tower, stands next to the 12th-century Chapelle Saint-Pierre. The "Huche Corne" offers a magnificent view of the lower part of the village, where the Chapelle Saint-Croix, an old abbey church with a 13th-century doorway, faces the river and its weeping willows. Nearby, the site of the Roc aux Sorciers (Sorcerers' Rock) houses a unique Paleolithic frieze, carved into the limestone 15,000 years ago, which is now protected but has been reconstructed. For 150 years, Angles has been famous for its *jours*: drawn thread embroidery. A tour retraces the history of this traditional craft in the village and many of the houses' windows are adorned with these embroidered works.

 **HIGHLIGHTS**

♥ **Centre d'Interprétation du Roc aux Sorciers**:
Life-size, 65-foot-long (20-m) reconstruction of a prehistoric frieze from the Magdalenian period, to be discovered through innovative re-creations (05 49 83 37 27).
Forteresse d'Angles:
Remains of the fortress built in the 11th–15th centuries. Guided tour Apr.–Sept., by appt. (05 49 83 37 27).
Maison des Jours d'Angles:
Discover the *jours* technique (06 82 00 78 15).
Village: Guided tour Fri. at 3 p.m. for individuals, groups by appt.; Tèrra Aventura outdoor treasure hunt, "Les jours d'Angles sont contés" (tales of the *jours d'Angles*), free year round; video guide available at the tourist info office (05 49 21 05 47).

 ACCOMMODATION & EATING OUT

tourisme-chatellerault.fr

 **LOCAL SPECIALTIES**

Food and Drink
Broyé du Poitou (butter cookies).
Art and Crafts
Antiques • *Jours d'Angles* (openwork embroidery) • Painter • Cross-stitch, lace, decorations, paper, stained glass • Hatmaker, fashion design, and patternmaking workshops.

 EVENTS

Jul.: Crafts days (weekend around 14th).
Aug.: firework display with music (1st Sun.); Des Livres et Vous, book festival (week of 15th).
Nov.: Rouge et Or, art and crafts fair (3rd weekend).

 OUTDOOR ACTIVITIE

Canoeing • Rock climbing • Fishing • Walking: 2 routes, "En passant par Remerle" (3½ miles/6 km) and "Les Certaux" (4½ miles/7 km) • Mountain biking • Horse-drawn carriage rides.

 FURTHER AFIELD

• Parc Naturel Régional de la Brenne (3½ miles/6 km).
• La Roche-Posay (7½ miles/12 km).
• Abbaye de Saint-Savin, UNESCO World Heritage Site (10 miles/16 km).
• Château d'Azay-le-Ferron (16 miles/25 km).
• Chauvigny (16 miles/26 km).

Vienne (86)
Population: 345
Altitude: 331 ft. (101 m)

TOURIST INFO—GRAND CHÂTELLERAULT
05 49 21 05 47
tourisme-chatellerault.fr

Art and Crafts
Bronze sculptures and jewelry • Painter • Ceramics • Organic and handmade soaps.

 EVENTS

Market: Sun. a.m., Place de la Vieille-Fontaine.
May: Les Botanilles, festival and flower market (last fortnight).
Jun.: Ansouis en Musique, music festival.
Sept.: Fête de la Saint-Elzéar (mid-month).

 OUTDOOR ACTIVITIES

Walking: 3 marked trails.

 FURTHER AFIELD

•La Tour-d'Aigues (5 miles/8 km).
•Villages along the Durance river: Cadenet, Pertuis, Mirabeau (6–12 miles/10–20 km).
•Aix-en-Provence (19 miles/30 km).

 MBVF NEARBY
•Lourmarin (7 miles/11 km).
•Ménerbes (21 miles/33 km).
•Roussillon (21 miles/33 km).

Ansouis

A castle in the Pays d'Aigues

Located in the heart of the Pays d'Aigues, with the Grand Luberon mountain range and the Durance river on the horizon, the hilltop village of Ansouis is crowned by a thousand-year-old castle. Spread out in a fan shape, exposed to the sun, the village is crisscrossed by a maze of streets and alleys that offer shade and cool. From the Place Saint-Elzéar, the Rue du Petit-Portail climbs up to a peaceful little square: bordered by the 12th-century perimeter wall, which serves as the façade of the Église Saint-Martin, and by the elegant 13th-century presbytery, it offers a vast panorama of a landscape of vines overlooked by the Grand Luberon. At the top of the village, the castle, which was owned for generations by the Sabran family, condenses a thousand years of castle architecture. The austerity of the medieval fortress on the north side contrasts with the classical southern façade of the 17th-century residence, which overlooks the terraced gardens with their box topiary.

 HIGHLIGHTS

Castle (12th–13th centuries): Remodeled in the 17th century, and now completely restored. Open Apr.–end Oct. (06 84 62 64 34).
Église Saint-Martin (12th-century): Fortified church, formerly the castle's law court; 18th-century statues and altarpieces.
Musée Extraordinaire: Artistic creations as well as a collection of fossils, shells, and furniture (04 90 09 82 64).
Musée de la Vigne et du Vin: More than 2,000 old winemaking tools from the Château Turcan (04 90 09 83 33).

ACCOMMODATION & EATING OUT

luberon-sud-tourisme.fr

 LOCAL SPECIALTIES

Food and Drink
Artisanal ice cream • AOC Luberon wines.

Vaucluse (84)
Population: 1,070
Altitude: 968 ft. (295 m)

TOURIST INFO—LUBERON SUD
04 90 07 50 29
luberon-sud-tourisme.fr

Apremont-sur-Allier

The garden village

Overlooked by a castle and surrounded by landscaped gardens, the village—which was entirely restored in the last century—is reflected in the Allier river. In the Middle Ages, the Château d'Apremont, belonging to the duchy of Burgundy, was a powerful fortress. Four centuries later, in 1894, Eugène Schneider II, the third generation in the dynasty of powerful industrialists from Le Creusot, married Antoinette de Saint-Sauveur, whose family had owned the castle since 1722. Until his death in 1942, Schneider worked tirelessly to restore this castle and, in true Berry style, every house in Apremont. His grandson Gilles de Brissac continued his work, and in 1970 he created a floral park at the foot of the castle, inspired by Vita Sackville-West's garden at Sissinghurst in England. Among the pools, waterfalls, and scent and colors of more than 1,000 tree and flower species, a Chinese covered bridge, a Turkish pavilion, and a belvedere decorated with Nevers faience add a touch of exoticism.

 HIGHLIGHTS

♥ **Parc Floral** (floral gardens, classed as "remarkable" by the Ministry of Culture): 12 acres (5 ha) of English gardens, arboretum, collection of follies (02 48 77 55 06).
♥ **Castle stables**: Immersive tour "Le Voyage d'Eugène Schneider" (Eugène Schneider's journey; 02 48 77 55 06).
Village: Guided tour by appt. (02 48 74 23 93).

 ACCOMMODATION & EATING OUT

Guesthouses and gîtes
♥ Les Maisons d'Apremont ▮▮▮ (02 48 77 55 00).

 LOCAL SPECIALTIES

Food and Drink
Goat and sheep's cheese • Walnut and hazelnut oil • *Brioches aux griaudes/aux escargots* (pork scratching or snail brioches).
Art and Crafts
Pottery studio.

📅 **EVENTS**

Market: organic and local market (1st Sun. of each month).
Easter: Egg hunt in the floral park (Sun.).
May: Fête des Plantes de Printemps (3rd weekend).
Aug.: Candlelit evening in the floral park (last Sat.).
Oct.: Festival of wine, food, and seasonal plants (3rd weekend).

 OUTDOOR ACTIVITIES

Fishing • Walking: Route GR 654; strolling along the banks of the Allier • Cycling: "Loire à Vélo" trail, "Via Allier" trail, cycle routes in the Loire Val d'Aubois region • Canoeing on the Allier and Loire rivers.

📍 **FURTHER AFIELD**

• La Guerche-sur-l'Aubois: "La Tuilerie" tile factory, museum, and visitor center (5 miles/8 km).
• Château de Meauce (6 miles/10 km).
• Espace Métal/Halle de Grossouvre, museum of industry (6 miles/10 km).
• Nevers (9½ miles/15 km).
• Abbaye de Fontmorigny (12 miles/20 km).

Cher (18)
Population: 70
Altitude: 581 ft. (177 m)

TOURIST INFO—PARC FLORAL
02 48 77 55 00
apremont-sur-allier.com/fr
TOWN HALL:
02 48 80 40 17
mairieapremontsurallier.fr

Arlempdes
The first château of the Loire

Arlempdes (pronounced "ar-lond") sits atop a volcanic peak in the Velay, close to the source of the Loire river, and is the location of the Loire's very first castle. The remains of the castle, built by the Montlaur family in the 12th–14th centuries, are at the top of a basalt dike, into which the Loire has cut deep, wild gorges. Crenellated ramparts and curtain walls enclose the ancient courtyard, which is overlooked by the round tower of the keep and the Chapelle Saint-Jacques-le-Majeur; the latter was most likely built in the 11th–12th centuries on the site of a Celtic sanctuary, and stands some 260 ft. (80 m) above the river. At the foot of this imposing castle, behind a 13th-century gateway, the village is laid out around an attractive square, which serves as the forecourt of the Romanesque Église Saint-Pierre—noteworthy for its polylobed door and its four-arched bell gable. From this square, a path leads to the castle, whose entrance is reached via a Renaissance porch.

 EVENTS

Jul.: Open-air rummage sale (around 15th).
Aug.: Fête du Pain, bread festival (1st fortnight).
Nov.: Hot-air balloon flights (1st fortnight).

 OUTDOOR ACTIVITIES

Swimming (no lifeguard) • Fishing • Walking: Route GR 3 and several marked trails • Mountain biking • Quad rides.

 **HIGHLIGHTS**

Castle remains: Guided tour every afternoon Jul.–Aug.; tours by appt. Mar.–Oct. (04 71 57 17 14).
Écomusée de la Ruralité (museum of rural life): Tools and lifestyles of yesteryear, Mar.–Nov. (04 71 57 17 00).
Église Saint-Pierre (11th–12th centuries) **and its belltower** (16th century).

 ACCOMMODATION & EATING OUT

lesgorgesdelallier.fr

 LOCAL SPECIALTIES

Food and Drink
Cheeses • AOP Puy green lentils.

 FURTHER AFIELD

•Lac du Bouchet, lake (11 miles/18 km).
•Le Monastier-sur-Gazeille (14 miles/23 km).
•Lac d'Issarlès, lake (15½ miles/25 km).
•Le Puy (17 miles/28 km).

 MBVF NEARBY

•Pradelles (10½ miles/17 km).

Haute-Loire (43)
Population: 142
Altitude: 2,756 ft. (840 m)

TOURIST INFO—GORGES DE L'ALLIER
04 71 00 82 65
village-arlempdes.fr
lesgorgesdelallier.fr

Ars-en-Ré

Between port and marshes

At the far west of the island, the village's bell tower keeps vigil over the ocean and the Fier d'Ars marshes. Born from the salt marshes created in the 11th century and still exploited by more than sixty salt merchants, Ars is one of the Île de Ré's oldest parishes. The church retains its 12th-century door and its 15th-century bell tower, whose 130-ft. (40-m) black-and-white spire used to serve as a day-mark for seafarers. In the Rue des Tourettes, the two corner towers of the Maison du Sénéchal, built in the 16th century, are a reminder that the village was once under the jurisdiction of a seneschal. Abandoned by ships coming from Northern Europe to load salt, the port now provides shelter for pleasure boats. Enjoyable to explore on foot or by bike, the narrow streets, dotted with hollyhocks, are lined with white houses with green or light blue shutters, typical of the traditional architecture of this region.

 HIGHLIGHTS

Église Saint-Étienne (12th, 15th, and 17th centuries): Romanesque style; arched door, rich furnishings.
Bell tower: Visits Apr.–late Sept. (05 46 09 00 55).
Salt flats: For information on visits, contact Écomusée du Marais Salant in Loix (05 46 29 06 77).

 ACCOMMODATION & EATING OUT

Hotels
♥ Le Sénéchal*** (05 46 29 40 42).

 LOCAL SPECIALTIES

Food and Drink
Strawberries • Shrimp • Oysters • AOP early potatoes • Salt and fleur de sel sea salt • Wine and Pineau.
Art and Crafts
Antique dealers • Painters.

 EVENTS

Market: Tues., Fri., and Sat., 8 a.m.–1 p.m., Place Carnot (Jan.–Apr.).
Summer market: Every day, by the port (Apr.–end Sept.).
Jul.–Aug.: Evening artisanal markets.

 OUTDOOR ACTIVITIES

Bathing: La Grange beach • Cycling: Cycle paths across the marshes to the nature reserve at Fiers d'Ars • Walking: 3 marked trails • Sailing • Horseback riding • Thalassotherapy.

 FURTHER AFIELD

•Saint-Clément-des-Baleines: Lighthouse (3 miles/5 km).
•Les Portes-en-Ré: Maison du Fier et de la Nature, nature reserve (6 miles/10 km).
•Loix: Écomusée du Marais Salant, local heritage museum (7½ miles/12 km).
•La Rochelle (20½ miles/33 km).

 MBVF NEARBY
•La Flotte (11 miles/18 km).

Charente-Maritime (17)
Population: 1,326
Altitude: 10 ft. (3 m)

TOURIST INFO—ILE-DE-RÉ
05 46 09 00 55
iledere.com

Aubeterre-sur-Dronne

The Charente with a southern air

Nestled against a chalky limestone cliff, Aubeterre overlooks the verdant valley of the Dronne river. Around its central square, a labyrinth of roofs and house fronts bedecked with wooden galleries and balconies stretches out. Facing the castle of this old fortress town, which was destroyed by the English and then by the Huguenots, stands the Église Saint-Jacques, with its fine Romanesque façade. At the turn of every street and steep alleyway, the visitor is reminded of Aubeterre's religious past: pilgrims on their way to Santiago de Compostela would stop at the church and three former convents, and the village also features the monolithic Église Saint-Jean, which was carved into the rock near a primitive worship site in the 12th century. For an unforgettable experience, explore the underground building and necropolis beneath its high vaults of light and shade.

 HIGHLIGHTS

Église Saint-Jacques: Built in the 12th century and rebuilt in the 17th century; Romanesque façade with finely carved vaulted archways and Moorish ornamentation.
Monolithic underground Église Saint-Jean: Hewn into the cliff face in the 12th century. A unique construction housing a reliquary, a central relic pit, and a necropolis containing more than 160 stone sarcophagi.
La Maison des Marionnettes et Le Petit Théâtre: Conservation and promotion of puppetry heritage, with an extensive collection of puppets and accessories. Shows in summer (06 14 37 93 47).
Village: Guided group tour all year round, by appt.; individual tours possible in peak season: (06 79 85 81 26).

 ACCOMMODATION & EATING OUT

Campsites
♥ Camping Paradis*** (05 45 98 75 43).

 LOCAL SPECIALTIES

Food and Drink
Foie gras and duck confit • Pineau • Cognac.
Art and Crafts
Antiques • Pottery • Ceramics • Dressmaker • Ironworker • Artisanal leather goods • Hatmaker • Art gallery and workshop • Painters.

 EVENTS

May: Ascension de l'Art, artists' festival (weekend of Ascension)
Jul.: Fête de la Saint-Jacques (last weekend).
Aug.: Evening market (1st Thurs.); musical evenings in Église Saint-Jean.
Sept.: Pottery festival (3rd weekend).

 OUTDOOR ACTIVITIES

Swimming • Canoeing and kayaking • Fishing • Walking • Nature excursions.

 FURTHER AFIELD

• Romanesque churches at Pillac, Rouffiac, and Saint-Aulaye (5 miles/8 km).
• Chalais: "haute ville" and castle (7 miles/11 km).
• Villebois-Lavalette: Castle and covered market (12½ miles/20 km).
• Cognac and Bordeaux vineyards (28 miles/45 km).
• Angoulême (30 miles/48 km).

Charente (16)
Population: 333
Altitude: 295 ft. (90 m)

TOURIST INFO—SUD CHARENTE
05 45 98 57 18
sudchararentetourisme.fr
aubeterresurdronne.com

Autoire

Medieval stone and red tiles amid vines and verdant hills

The village takes its name from the Autoire: the mountain stream that rushes down from the Causse de Gramat limestone plateau in a series of waterfalls before reaching the first ocher manor houses. At the center of a cirque—a deep, high-walled basin—square dovecotes and the corbeled façades of rustic dwellings rub shoulders with the turrets of manor houses. The Laroque-Delprat manor and the Château de Limargue are located downhill from the village. Higher up, the Château de Busqueille, built in the late 16th century, rises above the brown-tiled roofs. Under the successive rule of the baronies of Castelnau and of Gramat, Autoire became one of the vassal towns of the Viscounty of Turenne in the 14th century. One of the village's castles—the Château des Anglais—served as a hide-out for traveling mercenaries during the Hundred Years War. Covered with flat stone *lauzes* (schist tiles) rather than the tiles used on other roofs in the village, the square bell tower stands tall in the square, where four bronze dolphins splash playfully in the fountain.

 HIGHLIGHTS

Église Saint-Pierre (11th–12th centuries): Sole vestige of the ensemble formed with the Château des Peyrusse de Banze.
Château des Anglais: Perched on the cliffside, the castle offers breathtaking views of the Dordogne Valley.
Cascade d'Autoire: Protected waterfall (swimming prohibited), accessible via a hike through the woods from the village.
Village: Guided tour Jul.–Aug. (05 65 33 81 36).

 ACCOMMODATION & EATING OUT

vallee-dordogne.com

 LOCAL SPECIALTIES

Food and Drink
Cabécou cheese • Mushrooms • Honey • Wine • Walnut oil.
Art and Crafts
Weaving workshop • Artisanal leather goods.

 EVENTS

Jul.: Flea market (14th); local saint's day with firework display (last weekend).
Aug.: Gourmet market (1st Sun.).
Oct.: Trail d'Autoire race (1st Sun.).

 OUTDOOR ACTIVITIES

Rock climbing • Fishing • Mountain biking • Walking: Route GR 480 and 8 marked trails.

 FURTHER AFIELD

• Château de Montal, Château de Castelnau, Grottes de Presque, caves (4½ miles/7 km).
• Gouffre de Padirac, chasm (6 miles/10 km).

 MBVF NEARBY
• Loubressac (3 miles/5 km).
• Carennac (8 miles/13 km).
• Rocamadour (12½ miles/20 km).

Lot (46)
Population: 363
Altitude: 738 ft. (225 m)

TOURIST INFO—VALLÉE DE LA DORDOGNE
05 65 33 22 00
vallee-dordogne.com

Auvillar

Between the Garonne river and the Gascony hillsides

Overlooking the luxuriant valley of the Garonne, Auvillar is a perfect example of what a market town in the Occitan region, with its river port, was like. An official stopping place on one of the pilgrimage routes to Santiago de Compostela, the former fiefdom of the kings of Navarre is a subtle blend of brick and stone. The circular grain market—the jewel in the village's crown—fits perfectly within the triangular-shaped plaza lined with arcades and beautiful buildings, some of which date from the 15th century. The imposing clock tower stands at the entrance to the historic center. The Église Saint-Pierre, a former Benedictine priory, has been completely restored today and boasts a rich collection of furniture. The castle's square affords a unique view of the river and the hillsides of Quercy. For a long time, the port was a center for inland waterway transport and for shipping earthenware and goose feathers for quill pens; it has conserved its chapel dedicated to Saint Catherine, the patron saint of mariners, as well as its old slipway.

HIGHLIGHTS

Chapelle Sainte-Catherine (in peak season): Murals and old slipway (05 63 39 89 82).
Église Saint-Pierre (12th-14th centuries): Baroque altarpiece.
Musée du Vieil Auvillar: Collection of 18th- and 19th-century earthenware (more than 600 pieces) and history of navigation on the Garonne (05 63 39 89 82 / 07 82 86 66 15).
Village: Guided group tour, by appt. (05 63 39 89 82).

ACCOMMODATION & EATING OUT

officedetourismedesdeux rives.fr

LOCAL SPECIALTIES

Food and Drink
Jams and honey • Fruit produce • Brulhois wines.
Art and Crafts
Calligrapher • Art galleries • Artists • Soap making • Bric-a-brac store.

EVENTS

Market: Farmers' market Sun. a.m.; organic market Wed. 5 p.m.–7 p.m.
Pentecost: Saint-Noé, Fête des Vignerons et des Félibres, winemakers' and Provençal poets' festival (1st weekend after Pentecost).
Aug.: Port festival and fireworks (15th)
Oct.: Pottery market (2nd weekend).
Dec.: Christmas market (2nd Sat.).

OUTDOOR ACTIVITIES

Fishing • Walking: Route GR 65 and various trails • Greenway cycle paths.

FURTHER AFIELD

• Centrale de Golfech, nuclear site (3½ miles/6 km).
• Merles: Henri IV's oak tree (4 miles/7 km).
• Donzac: Conservatoire des Métiers d'Autrefois, museum of traditional skills (5 miles/8 km).

 MBVF NEARBY

• Lauzerte (21 miles/34 km).

Tarn-et-Garonne (82)
Population: 950
Altitude: 377 ft. (115 m)

TOURIST INFO—DEUX RIVES
05 63 39 89 82
officedetourismedes deuxrives.fr
auvillar.fr

Balazuc

The sentry of the Ardèche

Facing the sunset, Balazuc clings to a steep limestone cliff overlooking the Ardèche river. From the early Middle Ages until the Wars of Religion, the lords of Balazuc—simple knights, crusaders, and troubadours— made this village into an important stronghold. Its historic stature is evident in the 13th-century castle, rebuilt in the 17th and 18th centuries (now privately owned); the 13th-century square tower, whose façade still retains an iron rod on which the public scale for weighing silkworm cocoons used to hang; the fortified Romanesque church, crowned with a Provençal bell gable; and its gates, the Portail d'Été and the Porte de la Sablière. Balazuc has also kept its distinctive layout from the medieval period: a veritable maze of narrow, winding streets, vaulted passageways, and steps carved into the rock. Outside the village, the Chemin Royal leads slowly toward the Ardèche river and, beyond the bridge, to the reemerging hamlet of Le Viel Audon.

 HIGHLIGHTS

Romanesque church (11th century): Stained-glass windows by Jacques Yankel; accessible during exhibitions Jun.–Sept.
♥ **Museum de l'Ardèche**: Exceptional collection of fossils representing 350 million years of local history (04 28 40 00 35).
Le Viel Audon: Center for environmental and sustainable development training.
Village: Guided tour, Wed. a.m., Jul.–Aug. (departure 10 a.m. from Tour Carrée); self-guided visit with information panels.

 **ACCOMMODATION & EATING OUT**

pontdarc-ardeche.fr

LOCAL SPECIALTIES

Food and Drink
Goat cheeses • Herbal produce • AOC Côtes du Vivarais and Coteaux de l'Ardèche wines.
Art and Crafts
Pottery • Jewelry designer • Sculptor.

 EVENTS

Market: Tues., 6.30 p.m., Place de la Croisette (Jul-Aug.).
Jul.-Aug.: Concerts in the church; village festival; folk dance.

 OUTDOOR ACTIVITIES

River swimming (lifeguard Jul.-Aug.) • Canoeing and kayaking • Rock climbing • Fishing • Walking: Marked trails • Mountain biking • "Via Ardèche" greenway cycle trail.

 FURTHER AFIELD

•Ruoms and Largentière (6 miles/10 km).
•Labeaume: Village and gorges (9½ miles/15 km).
•Vallon-Pont-d'Arc and Grotte Chauvet 2, cave (11 miles/17 km).
•Aubenas (12 miles/20 km).

 MBVF NEARBY
•Vogüé (4½ miles/7 km).

Ardèche (07)
Population: 378
Altitude: 600 ft. (183 m)

TOURIST INFO—GORGES DE L'ARDÈCHE - PONT D'ARC
04 28 91 24 10
pontdarc-ardeche.fr

Barfleur

A port facing England

In the Middle Ages, Barfleur was the principal port on the Cotentin Peninsula, and the village's history is tied to that of the dukes of Normandy and England. In 1066, Matilda of Flanders had the flagship *Mora* built here, in which her husband, William, sailed to conquer England. From then on, Barfleur became the principal port of Normandy, where the dukes of Normandy and the kings of England would stay to wait for favorable winds to set sail across the Channel. The village houses are characterized by their flush granite façades and schist roofs topped with terra-cotta finials. The Église Saint-Nicolas, which stands proudly on a rocky headland, seems to watch over the village, while the old Augustinian priory (18th century) encloses a lovely landscaped area. Along the quays, which are packed with trawls, dredges, fish traps, and colorful nets, the rhythm of the tides and the variations in light add to Barfleur's unique charm.

 HIGHLIGHTS

Église Saint-Nicolas (17th–19th centuries): Maritime cemetery; Visitation painting by the 16th-century Flemish school.
Old Augustinian Priory (18th century) **and its garden.**
Chapelle de la Bretonne: Listed stained-glass windows tracing the life of Marie-Madeleine Postel.
Cour Sainte-Catherine: Remains of a former mansion (late 15th–early 16th centuries).
Lifeboat station: First lifeboat station to be built in France, in 1865, modeled on English ones.
Village: Guided tour in peak season (08 05 32 02 00).

 ACCOMMODATION & EATING OUT

barfleur.fr

 **LOCAL SPECIALTIES**

Food and Drink
Scallops, shellfish, and fish.

Art and Crafts
Antiques • Interior decoration • Art gallery • Ceramic artist.

 EVENTS

Market: Tues. and Sat. in peak season, 8 a.m.–1 p.m., Quai Henri-Chardon; Sat. offseason.
Late Jul.–early Aug.: Été Musical de Barfleur, classical music festival.
Aug.: Village des Antiquaires, antiques fair (3rd or 4th weekend); MusikenSaire, rock and pop festival (end of Aug.).

 OUTDOOR ACTIVITIES

Walking: Route GR 223; hiking and mountain biking trails • Water sports: Sailing, kayaking, windsurfing, paddleboarding.

FURTHER AFIELD

•Église de Montfarville; Gatteville lighthouse; Barfleur Point (2–2½ miles/3–4 km).
•La Pernelle (4½ miles/7 km).
•Saint-Vaast-la-Hougue: Vauban towers (9½ miles/15 km).
•Valognes (15½ miles/25 km).
•Cherbourg: Cité de la Mer, science park (18 miles/29 km).

Manche (50)
Population: 550
Altitude: 10 ft. (3 m)

TOURIST INFO—COTENTIN
08 05 32 02 00
encotentin.fr
barfleur.fr

Bargème

A "village perché" in Provence

At 3,599 ft. (1,097 m) altitude, Bargème is the highest village in the Var. Facing the Canjuers and Var mountains, it is still Provençal, yet almost alpine. Sheltered by the ruins of the château, the silhouette of this feudal village stands out on the steep slopes of the Brouis mountain. In 1393, the lordship of the village passed to Foulques d'Agoult de Pontevès. Two centuries later, gripped by religious upheaval, the people of Bargème avenged the neighboring village of Callas, which had been betrayed by Jean-Baptiste de Pontevès, bringing the line of châtelains to an end: after several murders, the inhabitants of Bargème slit Antoine de Pontevès's throat in the middle of Mass in 1595. The parliament of Aix-en-Provence issued a judgment requiring the inhabitants to build an expiatory chapel, Notre-Dames-des-Sept-Douleurs, which is located at the end of the esplanade leading to the castle. The village retains its defensive perimeter wall with two fortified gates that were inserted in the 14th century, as well as the white-stone Romanesque church.

HIGHLIGHTS

Château Sabran-de-Pontevès (12th–13th centuries): Remains of outer defensive elements (free access).
Église Saint-Nicolas (12th century): Restored in 1990–2000, along with its altarpieces.
Chapelle Notre-Dame-des-Sept-Douleurs (1607).
Chapelle Sainte-Pétronille (17th century).
Communal oven (7th century).
Village: Guided tours except Tues. and Wed., mid-Jun.–mid-Sept. (04 94 50 21 94).

ACCOMMODATION & EATING OUT

bargeme.fr

LOCAL SPECIALTIES

Food and Drink
Vegetables • Goat and sheep cheeses • Sheep milk yogurts.
Art and Crafts
Art gallery • Painter • Goat milk soap • Ceramic pottery.

📅 EVENTS

Jun.: Transhumance festival (1st weekend).
Jul.: Concert of ancient music.
Aug.: Saint-Laurent festival (2nd weekend); concert of ancient music.

OUTDOOR ACTIVITIES

Walking and horseback riding: Route GR 49 and 2 marked trails • Hang gliding • Mountain biking.

Q FURTHER AFIELD

• Route Napoléon (6 miles/10 km) and views on the way to Castellane (18 miles/29 km) or Grasse (27½ miles/44 km).
• La Bastide: Summit of Montagne de Lachens (7½ miles/12 km).
• Trigance and its castle (12½ miles/20 km).
• Gorges du Verdon (15½ miles/25 km).

MBVF NEARBY

• Seillans (20½ miles/33 km).

Var (83)
Population: 229
Altitude: 3,599 ft. (1,097 m)

TOURIST INFO—LA DRACÉNIE
04 98 10 51 05
tourisme.dracenie.com
TOWN HALL
04 94 50 21 94
bargeme.fr

La Bastide-Clairence

A stronghold for the arts in the Basque Country

La Bastide-Clairence has a Basque countenance and a Gascon accent. Behind its white façades and its half-timbering painted in red or green, talented artisans and creators are at work. Bastida de Clarenza was founded in 1312 to secure a river port on the Joyeuse, and thus provide the kingdom of Navarre with a new maritime outlet. The town planning typical of the *bastides* (fortified towns) of Aquitaine has been retained here; a grid pattern is observed, with the Place des Arceaux at the center of the village. The church of Notre-Dame-de-l'Assomption, built in 1315, is remarkable for its porch—the only remains of the original 14th-century building—and its lateral cloisters paved with tombstones. The village boasts the world's oldest *trinquet*, or *jeu de paume* court, dating from 1512, and is home to more than a dozen artists and craftspeople, whose creations combine tradition with innovation.

 HIGHLIGHTS

Église Notre-Dame de l'Assomption (14th century): 14th-century porch, courtyard cemetery.
Village: Guided group tour all year round by appt.; guided tours for individuals Jul.-Sept., Tues. 10:30 a.m. (05 59 29 65 05); Tèrra Aventura trail.
Trinquet (1512): The oldest *jeu de paume* court still in use.

 ACCOMMODATION & EATING OUT

Apartment hotels
♥ Les Collines Iduki**** (05 59 70 20 81).
Guesthouses
♥ Maison Perbos 1556 ▮▮▮▮ (07 89 01 83 92).

 LOCAL SPECIALTIES

Food and Drink
Beef and farm produce • Foie gras and duck confit • Sheep, goat, and cow milk cheese • Macarons • *Gâteau basque* • Chocolate.
Art and Crafts
Jewelry designer • Luthier • Picture framer • Wind instrument repair • Artist-designer • Glassmaker • Ceramic artist • Embroidery artist • Artisanal leather goods • Painter • Bladesmith • Artisanal art gallery • Donkey milk cosmetics • Perfumery.

 EVENTS

Market: Farmers' market, Tues. 9 a.m.–12:30 p.m., Jul.–Sept.
Jun. 30-Aug. 30: La Bastide-Clairence festivals.
Jul.: Festi'livre, book festival.
Sept.: Basque Country ceramics market (1st weekend).

 OUTDOOR ACTIVITIES

Jeu de paume • Short educational trail at Pont de Port • Canoeing.

 FURTHER AFIELD

• Isturitz and Oxocelhaya prehistoric caves (8 miles/13 km).
• Bayonne (16 miles/26 km).

MBVF NEARBY
• Ainhoa (19 miles/31 km).
• Sare (24 miles/38 km).
• Saint-Jean-Pied-de-Port (27 miles/43 km).

Pyrénées-Atlantiques (64)
Population: 990
Altitude: 164 ft. (50 m)

TOURIST INFO—PAYS BASQUE
05 59 29 65 05
en-pays-basque.fr

Baume-les-Messieurs

An imperial abbey in the Jura

Baume-les-Messieurs combines the simplicity of a village with the spirituality of the abbey that inspired the founding of the Order of Cluny, which spread throughout the West during the Middle Ages. Nestled in a remote valley formed by the Seille river and typical of the Jura landscape, Baume Abbey experienced remarkable growth throughout the medieval period. From the 9th century, it developed at the instigation of Abbot Berno, later the founder of Cluny, and enjoyed such widespread influence that Frederick Barbarossa made it an imperial abbey. The abbey boasts a rich architecture, with several convent buildings. During the French Revolution, the abbey was divided up into private dwellings. Lulled by the gentle sound of the cloister fountain or by the more intense sound of the Dard tributary, which feeds the Cascade des Tufs—a tuff waterfall—and then flows into the Seille river at the center of the village, the pale-fronted, brown-roofed houses live in harmony with this wild, green valley.

 HIGHLIGHTS

Imperial abbey: Abbey church, 16th-century Flemish altarpiece, 15th-century Burgundian statuary, tomb-chapel. Guided tours, audio guides in English, French, Dutch, German (03 84 44 99 28).
Grottes de Baume: Spectacular caves, ½ mile (1 km) galleries and lighting effects (03 84 48 23 02 / 03 84 44 61 41).
Cascade des Tufs: Tuff waterfalls, landscaped site.

 ACCOMMODATION & EATING OUT

lons-jura.fr

 **LOCAL SPECIALTIES**

Food and Drink
Honey • Abbey products.
Art and Crafts
Artisanal goods in the abbey • Woodwork • Dressmaking • Leather goods • Ironwork • Jewelry • Illustrations • Pottery.

 EVENTS

Jul.-Aug.: Concerts in the abbatial church.
Aug.: Fête des Quilles, pin bowling contest (Sun., early Aug.).
Dec.: Christmas market (1st weekend); Les Fayes, celebration of the winter solstice (25th).

 OUTDOOR ACTIVITIES

Walking, horseback riding, and mountain biking: Route GR 59 • Panoramic viewpoints of the Baume valley: Les Roches (at Crançot), Granges-sur-Baume, and Croix du Suchot.

 FURTHER AFIELD

•Le Pin and Arlay châteaux (10 miles/16 km).
•Lons-le-Saunier (11 miles/18 km).
•Lac de Chalain (15½ miles/25 km).
•Cascades du Hérisson, waterfalls (18½ miles/30 km).

 MBVF NEARBY
•Château-Chalon (7½ miles/12 km).

Jura (39)
Population: 160
Altitude: 1,083 ft. (330 m)

TOURIST INFO—LONS-LE-SAUNIER
03 84 24 65 01
lons-jura.fr

Les Baux-de-Provence

Geological grandeur

Perched on a rocky outcrop in the Alpilles regional nature park, the village of Baux is a beacon in the Provençal countryside. Outlined against the sky, this majestic outcrop dominates the Baux valley, in a landscape that opens onto the Camargue, the Crau plain, and Montagne Sainte-Victoire. The *"baou"* (from the Provençal word baù, meaning rocky escarpment), measuring 3,000 ft. (900 m) in length and 700 ft. (200 m) in width, gave its name to the village. Since the dawn of time, humans have sought refuge in this rocky mass; but the story of Baux really begins in the 10th century, when its lords built a fortress at its very top. The ruins of the medieval citadel still bear witness to the lords' power: from one side to the other, they dominate both the Entreconque valley's olive groves and vineyards, and the La Fontaine valley, where the Mistral wind rushes through the galleries of ancient quarries.

HIGHLIGHTS

Carrières des Lumières: Immersive exhibitions projected in the old stone quarries (04 90 54 34 39).
Château des Baux: Remains of the medieval castle (04 90 49 20 02); free entry to esplanade.
Fondation et Atelier Louis Jou: Works by Louis Jou (master typographer, engraver, printer, publisher), by appt. (04 90 54 34 17).
Musée Yves Brayer: Works by the artist. Exhibitions Apr.–Sept. (04 90 54 36 99).
Musée des Santons: Works by local santon-makers (crib figures). Free entry (04 90 54 34 39).
Village: Themed visits, visits for those with vision or hearing impairment (04 90 54 34 39).

ACCOMMODATION & EATING OUT

Hotels
♥ Le Mas de l'Oulivié**** (04 90 54 35 78).

 LOCAL SPECIALTIES

Food and Drink
AOP Vallée des Baux-de-Provence olives, olive oil • AOC Les Baux-de-Provence organic wines.
Art and Crafts
Lavender spindle workshop • Jewelry designer • Aromatic products • Santon (crib figure) workshops • Soaps • Hatmaker.

EVENTS

Apr.: Salon des Métiers d'Art (early Apr.).
Jun.: Les Baux Pianos festival (late Jun.).
Sept.: Rallye des Vignerons (4th Sat.).

OUTDOOR ACTIVITIES

Golf: 18 holes • Walking: Route GR 6, marked trails • Wine tours • Hiking, cycling, and tours through the Moulin Castelas olive groves and park paths (regulated access to wooded areas Jun.–Sept.; 08 11 20 13 13).

FURTHER AFIELD

• Landscape and villages of the Alpille hills: Eygalières, Fontvieille, Maussane-les-Alpilles, Saint-Rémy-de-Provence (3–22 miles/5–35 km).
• Arles (11 miles/18 km).
• Avignon (18½ miles/30 km).
• Istres (25 miles/40 km).
• Nîmes (28 miles/45 km).

Bouches-du-Rhône (13)
Population: 315
Altitude: 803 ft. (245 m)

TOURIST INFO—LES BAUX-DE-PROVENCE
04 90 54 34 39
lesbauxdeprovence.com

Beaulieu-sur-Dordogne

A "Limousine Riviera" along the Dordogne river

Located on a meander in the Dordogne valley, the medieval village of Beaulieu-sur-Dordogne invites visitors to admire its ancient heritage and enjoy its pleasant lifestyle. This strategic location in the Middle Ages, known in ancient times as Vellinus, was renamed Bellus Locus ("beautiful place" in Latin) when Rodolphe de Turenne, archbishop of Bourges, reached the area and established a Benedictine abbey here. Beaulieu-sur-Dordogne was also situated on a major trade route: barge captains transported their cargo down the river. The façades of old stone houses embellished with sculpted modillions and turrets are evidence of 15th- and 16th-century architecture. The area's temperate climate is ideal for growing strawberries, and in the summer the village celebrates this local specialty, inviting visitors to sample the fruit in all its forms. And it is this gentle way of life that has earned Beaulieu-sur-Dordogne the nickname the "Limousine Riviera."

 **HIGHLIGHTS**

Église Abbatiale Saint-Pierre (9th century): 12th-century sculpted tympanum; several relics including a 12th-century silver-plated Virgin Mary.
Église Notre-Dame or Chapelle des Pénitents Bleus (12th and 14th–15th centuries): Exhibitions.
Embarcadère des Gabares: 45-minute guided river cruise in a flat-bottomed *gabare*, May–Oct.; in summer, festive or gourmet tours Fri. 6 p.m., by appt. (05 65 33 22 00).
Village: Self-guided heritage tour with illustrated booklet; historical tour with Vidéoguide Limousin; guided tour with tourist info center (05 65 33 22 00).

 ACCOMMODATION & EATING OUT

Hotels
♥ Le Beaulieu*** (05 55 91 01 34).
♥ Le Relais de Vellinus** (05 55 91 11 04).
Guesthouses
♥ Le Clos Rodolphe (06 83 38 03 68).

 LOCAL SPECIALTIES

Food and Drink
Strawberries • Strawberry *resquilhète* (cocktail) • *Vin paillé* (straw wine) • Walnuts.
Art and Crafts
Antiques • Mosaic workshop.

 EVENTS

Market: Wed. a.m., Place du Champ de Mars; country farmers' market Jul.–Aug., Mon. 5 p.m.–8 p.m., Place du Monturuc.
Fair: 1st and 3rd Fri. of each month, Place Marbot and Place du Champ de Mars.
May: Fête de la Fraise, strawberry festival (2nd Sun.).
Aug.: Flea market and organic fair (2nd Sun.).
Sept.: Fête Patronale des Corps-Saints, patronal festival (1st weekend).

 OUTDOOR ACTIVITIES

Swimming (no lifeguard) • Canoeing and kayaking • Fishing • Mountain biking • Walking.

 FURTHER AFIELD

• Prudhomat: Château de Castelnau-Bretenoux (6 miles/10 km).
• La Chapelle-aux-Saints: Musée de Néandertal, prehistory museum (8½ miles/14 km).

 MBVF NEARBY
• Carennac (9 miles/15 km).
• Loubressac (10 miles/16 km).
• Curemonte (11 miles/17 km).
• Autoire (11 miles/18 km).

Corrèze (19)
Population: 1,290
Altitude: 482 ft. (147 m)

TOURIST INFO—VALLÉE DE LA DORDOGNE
05 65 33 22 00
vallee-dordogne.com

Le Bec-Hellouin

Spiritual resting place in the Normandy countryside

Between Rouen and Lisieux, this typical Normandy village takes its name from both the stream that flows alongside it and the founder of its famous abbey. The abbey at Bec was founded in 1034, at the time of William the Conqueror, duke of Normandy and England's first Norman king. Its first abbot was Herluin (Hellouin), knight to the count of Brionne. Destroyed and rebuilt several times, it fell into ruin during the French Revolution and Napoleon's Empire. The only vestige of the medieval abbey complex is the tower of Saint-Nicolas (15th century), which still dominates the site. In 1948, the abbey was restored and given new life by a community of Benedictine monks. While Le Bec-Hellouin owes its reputation to the religious prestige of this remarkable building, the village itself is also well worth visiting, with its half-timbered houses with flower-decked balconies in the heart of a verdant landscape of hedgerows and apple orchards.

 HIGHLIGHTS

Abbaye de Notre-Dame-du-Bec: 17th- and 18th-century Maurist (Congregation of Saint Maur) architecture; old abbey church, cloisters (02 32 46 70 70).
Église Paroissiale Saint-André (14th century): 13th–18th-century statuary.
Village: Guided tours Tues. 2.30 p.m. in summer (reservations at tourist info center).

 ACCOMMODATION & EATING OUT

Gîtes
♥ La Maison du Bec*** ▯▯▯ (06 14 20 12 22).

 **LOCAL SPECIALTIES**

Food and Drink
Chocolates • Cookies.
Art and Crafts
Art and antiques • Monastic crafts • Art gallery • Interior decoration • Cabinet of curiosities.

 EVENTS

Jun.: Festival Aquarelle, watercolor festival (2025, and every other year).
Jul.: Rummage sale (closest Sun. to 14th).
Aug.: Les Estivales du Bec, festival of local produce and crafts (1st weekend).

 OUTDOOR ACTIVITIES

Horseback riding • Fishing (Bec stream) • Walking: 3 marked trails and greenway (27½ miles/44 km of multi-trail paths along former railway line: walking, cycling, roller-skating).

FURTHER AFIELD

•Brionne (3½ miles/6 km).
•Sainte-Opportune-du-Bosc: Château de Champ-de-Bataille (7½ miles/12 km).
•Le Neubourg: Musée de l'Ecorché d'Anatomie, museum of anatomy (11 miles/18 km).
•Pont-Audemer, "the Venice of Normandy": Musée A.-Canel (12½ miles/20 km).
•Bernay: Museum, abbey church (13½ miles/22 km).

Population: 402
Altitude: 164 ft. (50 m)

TOURIST INFO—BERNAY TERRES DE NORMANDIE
02 32 44 05 79
bernaynormandie.fr
TOWN HALL
09 62 37 76 63
lebechellouin.fr

Belcastel

Stone and lauze tiles along the banks of the Aveyron

On the old salt route, in the heart of the Rignac region, Belcastel is a *castelnau* (a medieval village situated near a castle) bathed by the Aveyron river. Protected by the valley's wooded slopes, the houses are nestled at the foot of the fortified castle, along the edge of the winding river. From the early days of feudalism, the fortress belonged to the lords of Belcastel, whose influence extended along both sides of the Aveyron, before it changed hands and became the property of the Saunhac family at the end of the 14th century. Left to ruin in the 18th century, the castle was restored in the 1970s by architect Fernand Pouillon; it now looks fondly down on the renovated village with its cobbled streets, communal oven, cattle chutes, and 15th-century stone bridge. A stone's throw from the village, the fortified site of the Roc d'Anglars dates from the 5th century.

 **HIGHLIGHTS**

Castle: Fortress dating from the 9th century; contemporary art galleries inspired by the Animazing Gallery in SoHo, NY (05 65 64 42 16).

Church (15th century): *Way of the Cross* by Casimir Ferrer, recumbent statue on the tomb of Alzias de Saunhac, 15th-century statues (05 65 64 46 11).

Maison de la Forge et des Anciens Métiers (blacksmith and traditional trades): Tours of the village's old smithy and exhibition of tools; permanent exhibition of wood sculptures by artist Pierre Leron-Lesur (05 65 64 46 11).

Village: Guided tour, self-guided tour with audio guide, and treasure hunt for kids 6–12 years; visits for those with vision impairment and reduced mobility (05 65 64 46 11).

 ACCOMMODATION & EATING OUT

tourisme-paysrignacois.com

 LOCAL SPECIALTIES

Food and Drink
Truffade (potato, garlic, and tome fraîche cheese) • Walnuts.
Art and Crafts
Ceramics • Sculptor • Dressmaking • Woodwork.

 EVENTS

Market: Sale and sampling of local products, Fri. evening (Jul.-Aug).
Jun.: Feu de la Saint-Jean, Saint John's Eve bonfire (last Sat.).
Jul.: Local saint's day with village supper and fireworks (penultimate weekend).
Aug.: Belcastel en Scène theater festival (1st weekend).
Sept.: Flea market (1st Sun.).

 OUTDOOR ACTIVITIES

Fishing • Walking: Route GR 62B and 7 marked trails.

FURTHER AFIELD

- Bournazel and its château (9½ miles/15 km).
- Rodez (15½ miles/25 km).

 MBVF NEARBY

- Sauveterre-de-Rouergue (17 miles/27 km).
- Conques (23 miles/37 km).
- Capdenac-le-Haut (24 miles/39 km).

Aveyron (12)
Population: 200
Altitude 1,335 ft. (407 m)

TOURIST INFO—PAYS RIGNACOIS
05 65 64 46 11
tourisme-pays-rignacois.com

Belvès

(Commune of Pays de Belvès)

The village of seven bell towers

Dominating the verdant valley of the Nauze river from its hilltop position, Belvès provides a sweeping panorama across the landscape of Périgord Noir. Owing to its strategic position, the village has had a turbulent past, despite the protection it received from both its rampart walls and from Pope Clement V, who granted Belvès the status of papal town when he was archbishop of Bordeaux (1297-1305). Besieged and invaded several times during the Hundred Years War and, later, the Wars of Religion, Belvès has nevertheless miraculously conserved numerous vestiges from its tumultuous past: troglodyte cave dwellings; towers and bell towers from the Middle Ages; and residences and mansions displaying Gothic flamboyance blended with Renaissance artistry. In the heart of the village, a historic covered market comes to life once a week, where visitors can sample the many tasty products of Périgord.

 HIGHLIGHTS

Troglodyte cave dwellings: Discover how peasants lived here in the 13th–18th centuries; games book for kids aged 6-13 (05 53 31 71 00).
Castrum: Guided tour in peak season, self-guided tours all year round (05 53 31 71 00).
Église de Notre-Dame-de-l'Assomption (13th–15th centuries): Renaissance paintings.
Castle and wall paintings (14th–16th centuries): Furnished rooms and the sole wall paintings in Aquitaine representing the Nine Valiant Knights of legend, as well as a historical scene of Belvès in 1470 (06 35 29 13 71).
La Filature de Belvès: Spinning mill and vast machine room. Self-guided tours and activities for kids (05 53 31 83 05).
Village: Guided group tour by appt. (05 53 31 71 00); self-guided family tour with educational booklet for kids.

 ACCOMMODATION & EATING OUT

perigordnoir-valleedordogne.com

 LOCAL SPECIALTIES

Food and Drink
Foie gras • Honey • Organic farm produce.
Art and Crafts
Antiques • Bladesmith • Cabinetmaker • Painters • Metalworker • Wool spinner • Sculptor • Stained-glass artist • Mosaic artist.

 EVENTS

Market: Sat. a.m., Place de la Halle.
Jul.-Aug.: Bach festival (late Jul.-early Aug.); gourmet market (Wed. evening).
Aug.: Medieval festival (1st or 2nd Sun.).
Oct.: Relay trail, the crusades in Périgord Noir (around 20th).

 OUTDOOR ACTIVITIES

Swimming • Horseback riding • Fishing • Walking: 75 miles (120 km) of marked trails, Route GR 36 and other routes along the Saint James's Way to Santiago de Compostela • Aerial sports.

 FURTHER AFIELD

• Abbaye de Cadouin (8½ miles/14 km).
• Sarlat (22 miles/35 km).

 MBVF NEARBY
• Monpazier (10 miles/16 km).
• Castelnaud-la-Chapelle (11 miles/18 km).
• Limeuil (12 miles/19 km).
• Beynac-et-Cazenac (14 miles/23 km).
• La Roque-Gageac (14 miles/23 km).
• Domme (15 miles/24 km).

Dordogne (24)
Population: 1,337
Altitude: 591 ft. (180 m)

TOURIST INFO—PÉRIGORD NOIR - VALLÉE DORDOGNE
05 53 31 71 00
perigordnoir-valleedordogne.com

Bergheim
The land of Gewurztraminer

Surrounded by Alsace's *grands crus*, Bergheim is known as the village with nine towers. Germanic and Celtic in origin, the village's name means "the mountain house," in reference to Bergheim's hilltop position that affords a spectacular view. In the Middle Ages, the village endured wars of succession that culminated in a fire in 1287. The event proved decisive and led Henri de Ribeaupierre, lord at the time, to fortify the citadel in 1312 by constructing ramparts to protect it from further attacks. Today, with its double walls flanked by eight round towers topped with pointed roofs, and a single square tower, Bergheim is one of the rare French villages to have preserved most of its original fortifications. The surrounding vineyards produce some of Alsace's *grands crus* and have earned Bergheim a reputation as the "Gewurztraminer capital": the village hosts an annual festival in celebration of the renowned grape variety.

 HIGHLIGHTS

Église Notre-Dame de l'Assomption (14th–19th centuries): Paintings and sculptures.
La Maison des Sorcières: History of witch trials held in Bergheim in the 16th and 17th centuries; gardens (03 89 73 18 64).
Bergheim wine trail: Self-guided tour (information panels); guided tour with a winemaker, Jul.–Aug., Wed. 9:30 a.m.–12 p.m. (03 89 73 23 23).
Old synagogue (16th–17th centuries): Exhibitions, conferences, concerts.
Rampart tour: Hour-long walk around the village ramparts (03 89 73 23 23).
Jardin d'Aneth (ramparts): Medieval garden with heirloom plants and small fruit-bearing bushes.
Village: Guided tours Jul.–Aug., Mon. 11 a.m.; treasure hunt for kids aged 4–12 (03 89 73 23 23).

 **ACCOMMODATION & EATING OUT**

Gîtes and vacation rentals
♥ Manoir des Sens (03 89 22 50 05).
♥ S'Harzala ▮▮▮▮ (03 89 73 74 27).

 **LOCAL SPECIALTIES**

Food and Drink
AOC Alsace wines, and Altenberg and Kanzlerberg *grands crus* • Alsatian cookies • ♥ Staehly artisanal distillery (03 89 73 74 27).

Art and Crafts
Jewelry

 EVENTS

Market: Mon. 7 a.m.–12 p.m., Place du Dr Walter.
Jul.: Fête du Gewurztraminer (late Jul.).
Oct.: Fête de la nature (2nd weekend).

 **OUTDOOR ACTIVITIES**

Fishing • Walking: 2 marked trails • Mountain biking.

 **FURTHER AFIELD**

• Orschwiller: Château du Haut-Koenigsbourg (7 miles/11 km).
• Colmar (10½ miles/17 km).
• Gertwiller: Musée du Pain d'Épice et de l'Art Populaire Alsacien (Gingerbread and Alsatian folk art museum; 20 ½ miles/33 km).

 **MBVF NEARBY**
• Route des Vins d'Alsace: Hunawihr (4 miles/6 km), Ribeauvillé (2½ miles/4 km), Riquewihr (5 miles/8 km).
• Eguishem (15 miles/24 km).

Haut-Rhin (68)
Population: 2,070
Altitude: 705 ft. (215 m)

TOURIST INFO—PAYS DE RIBEAUVILLÉ ET RIQUEWIHR
03 89 73 23 23
ribeauville-riquewihr.com

Beuvron-en-Auge

The flavors of Normandy

Nestled between valleys dotted with apple trees and half-timbered farmhouses, and centered around its covered market, Beuvron is a showcase for the Pays d'Auge. In the 12th century, Beuvron consisted of only a small medieval castle and a church. By the end of the 14th century, however, the town was in its heyday, thanks to the renowned resident Harcourt family, who had royal connections. They helped establish the town's commercial activities up until the French Revolution, and built the present church and chapel of Saint-Michel de Clermont overlooking the Auge valley. Bedecked with geraniums and decorated in rendered plaster or pink brick, the façades of the wooden-frame houses recall the village's four centuries of glory, while the steep roofs are covered with slates or tiles. Beuvron-en-Auge perpetuates the region's traditions and specialties, with its restaurants and boutiques surrounding the covered market, its local producers, and its stud farms dotted throughout the countryside.

 HIGHLIGHTS

Church (17th century): 18th-century main altar, stained-glass windows by Louis Barillet, pulpit in Louis XVI style.
Chapelle de Saint-Michel-de-Clermont (12th–17th centuries): Statues of Saints Michael and John the Baptist. Viewpoint over the Pays d'Auge.
Haras de Sens: Stud farm that breeds, raises, and trains trotters; group tours by appt. (02 31 79 23 05).
Espace des Métiers d'Art: Six art studios, in the former school (02 31 39 59 14 / 06 83 15 32 28).
Village: Guided tours for individuals in peak season, and for groups by appt. (02 31 39 59 14).

 ACCOMMODATION & EATING OUT

Guesthouses
♥ Le Pavé d'Hôtes (02 31 39 39 10).
Gîtes
♥ La Maison Harmony**** (06 63 11 26 98).
Restaurants
♥ Le Pavé d'Auge (02 31 79 26 71).

 LOCAL SPECIALTIES

Food and Drink
AOC-AOP cider and the Cider Route • Calvados.
Art and Crafts
Antiques • Fashion designer • Ceramic artist • Illustrator • Cabinetmaker • Chocolatier • Bladesmith • Photographer • Porcelain decorator.

 EVENTS

May: Geranium fair (early May); Pierres en Lumières, local historic building festival (1st fortnight).
Jul.: Antiques fair (2nd week).
Aug.: Puces Beuvronnaises, flea market (early Aug.).
Oct.: Traditional cider festival, boogie-woogie at Haras de Sens stud farm (around 20th).

 OUTDOOR ACTIVITIES

Fishing • Walking (1 marked trail) • Cycle path (route 1401).

 FURTHER AFIELD

•Pays d'Auge region: Churches, manor houses, and castles (½–16 miles/1-25 km).
•Cambremer (6 miles/10 km).
•Côte Fleurie, Cabourg (9½ miles/15 km).
•Deauville (17 miles/28 km).
•Caen (19 miles/30 km).

Calvados (14)
Population: 200
Altitude: 33 ft. (10 m)

TOURIST INFO—NORMANDIE CABOURG PAYS D'AUGE
02 31 39 59 14
normandie-cabourg-paysdauge-tourisme.fr

Beynac-et-Cazenac

Two villages, a castle, and a river

At the foot of an imposing castle that surveys the Dordogne, Beynac-et-Cazenac is a beautiful spot enhanced by the river and the gastronomic specialties of the region. Occupied since the Bronze Age (c. 2000 BCE), the naturally defensive site of Beynac became the seat of one of the four baronies of Périgord during the Middle Ages. Besieged by Richard the Lionheart, then demolished by Simon de Montfort, the castle was rebuilt before being captured and recaptured during the Hundred Years War by the armies of both the English and French kings. It was then abandoned during the French Revolution. The castle towers over the *lauze* (schist-tiled) rooftops and golden façades of the quaint village. Nestling between river and cliff, and protected by a wall in which only the Veuve gateway remains, Beynac long made its living from passing trade on the Dordogne thanks to the *gabarres* (sailing barges), used today for river trips.

 HIGHLIGHTS

Château de Beynac: 12th–17th-century buildings, restored in the 20th century. Self-guided tour with audio guide; guided group tour on appt. (05 53 29 50 40).
Village: Information desks and multilingual QR codes; art trail along the river; guided tour Jul.–Sept., Mon. 10:30 a.m. (booking and departure from tourist info office); guided tour by appt. rest of year (05 53 31 45 42).
♥ **Gabarres de Beynac**: Boat trips along the Dordogne river (05 53 28 51 15).

ACCOMMODATION & EATING OUT

beynac-et-cazenac.fr

LOCAL SPECIALTIES

Food and Drink
Duck, goose • Traditional preserves.
Art and Crafts
Painter • Painter-enamelists • Metal artist.

EVENTS

Market: Mid-Jun.–mid-Sept., Mon. a.m., by the river.
Aug.: Nuit des Étoiles, astronomy festival (early Aug.); summer festival and fireworks (15th).
Dec.: Christmas market (1st weekend).

OUTDOOR ACTIVITIES

Canoeing and kayaking • Fishing • Walking: 2 marked trails • Balloon flights: ♥ Montgolfières et Châteaux (06 71 14 34 96) • Mountain biking: 5 marked trails.

FURTHER AFIELD

• Parc de Marqueyssac (1 mile/2 km)
• Sarlat (7 miles/11 km)

MBVF NEARBY

• Castelnaud-la-Chapelle: Châteaux de Castelnaud and des Milandes; Ecomusée de la Noix, walnut museum (2½ miles/4 km).
• La Roque-Gageac (3 miles/5 km).
• Domme (7 miles/11 km).
• Belvès (14 miles/23 km).
• Limeuil (18 miles/29 km).
• Saint-Léon-sur-Vézère (21 miles/33 km).
• Saint-Amand-de-Coly (22 miles/36 km).
• Monpazier (24 miles/38 km).

Dordogne (24)
Population: 550
Altitude: 427 ft. (130 m)

TOURIST INFO—SARLAT PÉRIGORD NOIR
05 53 31 45 45
sarlat-tourisme.com
beynac-et-cazenac.fr

Blangy-le-Château

In the heart of the Norman hills

Nicknamed the "Little Rome of Calvados" for the seven hills that surround it, Blangy-le-Château is an ode to the Norman countryside. Located in the Chaussey valley, between Pont-l'Évêque and Lisieux, it owes its name to its medieval origins and 11th-century château, of which only a few stones remain. The houses lining the Grande Rue are typical of the Pays d'Auge, with timber frames and cob walls (16th and 18th centuries) or embellished with brick and crowned with ceramic ornamentation (19th century). They follow *le fil de l'eau*, a narrow channel running down the street—a reminder that two rivers flow through the village and that the château was once encircled by a moat. Constructed in the 16th century, the ancient inn Coq Hardi is one of the village's oldest and most remarkable residences. The events program at the Chaussey valley's open-air theater, situated at the foot of the motte-and-bailey fortifications, caters to fans of nature and culture.

 HIGHLIGHTS

Village: Tourist trail through village along the *fil de l'eau* water feature (incl. former girls' school and its belfry, former wash house, Coq Hardi inn, medieval manor house, 17th-century manor, 15th-century Église Notre-Dame, vestiges of the château and motte-and-bailey fortifications, the Grande Rue) and guided tours (02 31 64 12 77).

 ACCOMMODATION & EATING OUT

terredauge-tourisme.fr

 LOCAL SPECIALTIES

Food and Drink
Honey • Cider • Calvados • Apple juice • Normandy cheeses.

Art and Crafts
Ceramic artist-potter • Wood sculptor • Tapestry artist • Photographer.

 EVENTS

Market: Thurs. a.m., outside the Salle Multi-Activités.
May: Flea market; Livres à Vous, book festival.
Jul.-Aug.: Festival du Solo, live solo performances.
Sept.: Blangy en Folie, concerts and performances (1st Friday); Fête de la Saint Gorgon, patron saint of village.
Nov.-Dec.: Christmas market.

 OUTDOOR ACTIVITIES

Walking • Horseback riding • Fishing on the Touques (France's top river for sea trout fishing).

 FURTHER AFIELD

• Lac Terre d'Auge leisure park (5½ miles/9 km).
• Pont-l'Evêque (6 miles/10 km).
• Beaumont-en-Auge (9 miles/15 km).
• Lisieux: Basilica, Carmelite convent, cathedral (10 miles/16 km).
• La Côte Fleurie: Deauville, Trouville-sur-Mer (12½–14 miles/ 20–22 km).
• Honfleur (16 miles/26 km).

 MBVF NEARBY
• Beuvron-en-Auge (20 miles/32 km).

Calvados (14)
Population: 856
Altitude: 98 ft. (38 m)

TOURIST INFO—TERRE-D'AUGE
02 31 64 12 77
terredauge-tourisme.fr

Blesle

Benedictine memories at the gateway to the Haute-Loire

At the end of a narrow, isolated valley conducive to meditation, the echoes of Benedictine monks' prayers have for centuries blended with the murmurs of the rivers that bring life to the village of Blesle. At the end of the 9th century, Ermengarde, countess of Auvergne, founded an abbey dedicated to Saint Peter here; two centuries later, the barons de Mercoeur built a mighty fortress. The village grew up under the protection of these two powers: one spiritual, the other secular. It became one of the *bonnes villes* (which received privileges and protection from the king in exchange for providing a contingent of armed men) of Auvergne, and welcomed lawyers and merchants alongside its tanners, weavers, and winegrowers. Sheltered within its medieval wall, Blesle invites visitors to discover its exceptional heritage spanning more than ten centuries, including the keep and watchtower—the only remnants of the fortress—the Église Saint-Pierre, and almost fifty houses, many of which are half-timbered.

 **HIGHLIGHTS**

Église Abbatiale Saint-Pierre (12th–13th centuries): Church; collection of liturgical vestments, silver plate, statues from the abbey; tours of collection by appt. (04 71 74 97 49).
Musée de la Coiffe: Headdresses, bonnets, ribbons, hats from the region (late 18th century–early 20th century; 04 71 76 27 08).
Village: Guided tours by appt. in peak season for individuals, all year round for groups; large-print and Braille guidebooks for those with vision impairment (04 71 74 97 49).

 **ACCOMMODATION & EATING OUT**

tourisme-brioudesud
auvergne.fr

 LOCAL SPECIALTIES

Food and Drink
Charcuterie, salted meats •
Local cheeses • Local craft beer, liqueurs, and wines.
Art and Crafts
Antiques • Pottery.

 EVENTS

Market: Fri. from 5 p.m., Place du Vallat (Jul.–Aug.)
Jul.: Painting and sketching competition in the streets (2nd Sat.).
Aug.: Les Apéros Musique festival (weekend around 15th); summer fair (weekend before 15th).
Nov.: Foire Saint-Martin, fair (11th).

 OUTDOOR ACTIVITIES

Fishing • Walking: 17 trails • Mountain biking: 2 trails.

 FURTHER AFIELD

•Cézallier: Valleys and plateau (4½–12½ miles/7–20 km).
•Brioude (13½ miles/22 km).
•Ardes-sur-Couze: Safari park (15½ miles/25 km).

 MBVF NEARBY
•Lavaudieu (19 miles/31 km).

Haute-Loire (43)
Population: 602
Altitude: 1,706 ft. (520 m)

TOURIST INFO—BRIOUDE SUD-AUVERGNE
04 71 74 02 76
tourisme-brioudesudauvergne.fr

Bonneval-sur-Arc

A village of open spaces

Lying between the Vanoise national park and the Grand Paradis national park in Italy, Bonneval's backdrop is nature writ large. Ringed by mountains at the bottom of the Haute Maurienne valley, it was long considered the end of the earth. But now each winter, when the road to the Col de l'Iseran closes, the inhabitants of Bonneval turn their isolation to their advantage by developing tourism that respects both this remarkable environment and its ancient traditions of shepherds and artisans. Down the road from Tralenta, whose residences lining the Arc river lead straight to ski slopes, the huge stone houses topped with *lauzes* (schist tiles) and tall chimneys still encircle the cheese dairy, the Grande Maison, and the old village church. Above the rooftops, the Albaron, Levanna, and Ciamarella mountains, rising to nearly 13,000 ft. (4,000 m), tower over an exquisite amphitheater of glaciers: 42 square miles (11,000 hectares) twinkle in the winter silence, or gurgle in summer with the sound of streams and waterfalls.

 HIGHLIGHTS

Espace Neige et Montagne (snow and mountain museum): Daily life and local crafts, winter sports and historic mountaineering at Bonneval (04 79 05 95 95).
Village: Guided group and individual tours (04 79 05 95 95).

 ACCOMMODATION & EATING OUT

haute-maurienne-vanoise.com

 LOCAL SPECIALTIES

Food and Drink
Charcuterie, salted meats • Cheeses (Beaufort and Bleu de Bonneval).
Art and Crafts
Scroll saw portraits • Pottery • Drap de Bonneval fabric.

EVENTS

Market: Sun. 9 a.m.–6 p.m. (Dec.-Apr. and Jul.-Aug.).

Jan.: La Grande Odyssée, international dog-sled race (13th–14th).
Mar.: Rencontres d'Escalade sur Glace, ice climbing event (around 15th).
Jun.: L'Iserane Cyclo Challenge (around 25th).
Jul.: Fête du Rocher, artisanal market, via ferrata, traditional haymaking, etc. (13th–14th).

 OUTDOOR ACTIVITIES

Summer: Mountaineering, canyoning, climbing, walking, via ferrata, skiiing • Paragliding • Fishing in lake and mountain streams. Winter: Alpine skiing, cross-country skiing, snowshoe outings, glacier walks, ice climbing, ice skating on natural ice.

 FURTHER AFIELD

• Col de l'Iseran (8½ miles/14 km).
• Vanoise national park (12½ miles/20 km).
• Val-d'Isère (19 miles/30 km). Col du Mont Cenis and lake (22 miles/35 km).

Savoie (73)
Population: 264
Altitude: 5,906 ft. (1,800 m)

TOURIST INFO—HAUTE-MAURIENNE VANOISE
04 79 05 95 95
haute-maurienne-vanoise.com

Bormes-les-Mimosas

Impressions of Provence

Tucked into the Massif Maures, the houses of Bormes-les-Mimosas are enveloped by the colors and scents of Provence. In the 9th century, the Italian Bormani tribe found refuge from Saracens and pirates on this lush hill overlooking the Mediterranean Sea, and this fishing community was at the origin of the village. Ramparts were added in the 12th century, and the village grew on the hillside at the foot of its feudal castle. After withstanding the centuries, it now offers visitors a labyrinth of narrow medieval streets and colorful façades to discover. In this exceptional environment, where more than 700 plant species flower throughout the year, the mimosa benefits from the particularly clement winters and has been an official part of the village's identity since 1968. The wealth and variety of plant life in the village has earned it many distinctions. From its position at the top of the hill, the Chapelle Notre-Dame-de-Constance offers a stunning view of one of the world's most beautiful bays.

 **HIGHLIGHTS**

Musée d'Histoire et d'Art: Historical tour in augmented reality; temporary exhibitions; collection of 19th- and 20th-century paintings (04 94 71 56 60).
Église Saint-Trophyme (18th century): Frescoes.
Chapelle Saint-François-de-Paule (16th century): 18th-century altarpiece.
Chapelle Notre-Dame-de-Constance (12th century): Perched above the village (at 1,062 ft./324 m), accessible via the Circuit des Oratoires.
Maison des Artistes: Typical Provençal house hosting exhibitions (04 94 71 56 60).
Parc Gonzales: Terraced garden classed as "remarkable" by the Ministry of Culture.
Fort de Brégançon (14th century): Presidential residence. Guided tours by appt. (04 94 01 38 38).
Village: Self-guided tour along the Chemin des Sages; guided botanical or historical tours Sat. and Sun., all year round (04 94 01 38 38).

 ACCOMMODATION & EATING OUT

bormeslesmimosas.com

 LOCAL SPECIALTIES

Food and Drink
AOP Côtes de Provence and Côtes de Provence La Londe wines • Honey • Craft beers • Teas and herbal teas.
Art and Crafts
Milliner • Painters • Potters • Soap maker • Photographers • Sculptors • Glassmaker.

 EVENTS

Market: Wed. 7 a.m.–1 p.m., Place Saint-François.
Jan.: Mimosalia, plant show (4th weekend).
Feb.: Corso Fleuri, flower parade (3rd weekend).
Jul.–Aug.: FIESTA, Argentinian tango festival (early Jul.); Nuit du Livre, literary festival (1st week Aug.).
Sept.: Festival du Moulin, contemporary music (early Sept.); Escapade Gourmande, food festival (last weekend).
Dec.: Santon market (early Dec.); Noël à Bormes (late Dec.).

 OUTDOOR ACTIVITIES

Walking • Cycling • Water sports.

 FURTHER AFIELD

• Port de Bormes-les-Mimosas: departures for Îles d'Or and Port-Cros nature park (3½ miles/6 km).
• Cap Nègre; Domaine du Rayol – Jardin des Méditerranées; Saint-Tropez; La Rade de Toulon (8–22 miles/13–35 km).

 MBVF NEARBY
• Gassin (19 miles/31 km).

Var (83)
Population: 411
Altitude: 505 ft. (154 m)

TOURIST INFO—BORMES-LES-MIMOSAS
04 94 01 38 38
bormeslesmimosas.com

Brouage (Commune of Marennes-Hiers-Brouage)

Fortified town in the marshes

Between the Île d'Oléron and Rochefort, the fortified town of Brouage looks down over the gulf of Saintonge and its marshland. Seen from above, Brouage reveals its multiple facets, from the singular landscape of the marshland, which in the Middle Ages was turned into the salt cellar for the whole of Northern Europe, to its 12th-century fortifications, built by order of Cardinal Richelieu, then governor of Brouage. The village was created by Samuel de Champlain, founder of the city of Quebec and father of New France, and still bears witness to its rich history with its Halle aux Vivres—originally a granary—foundries, underground ports, gunpowder magazine, and church. Beyond the ramparts, the manufacture of salt has given way to oyster farming, mussel farming, and animal husbandry, while inside the village, shops and artists' workshops have taken the place of market stalls and bring to life the simple, bright façades typical of Charentes architecture.

 HIGHLIGHTS

Église Saint-Pierre (17th century): Memorial to the religious origins of New France, tombs of rich 17th-century salt merchants, soldiers, and former governors; stained-glass windows celebrating France-Quebec relations.
Halle aux Vivres (17th–20th centuries): Permanent exhibition on the history of Brouage and the salt trade; information center on military architecture (06 48 85 80 60).
Ramparts: 1 mile (2 km) long and 26 ft. (8 m) high, reinforced with 7 bastions and 19 watchtowers; panoramic views over the marshland from the rampart walk.
Village: Geocaching trail (Tèrra Aventura app.); guided tour for individuals during French school vacations and Apr.–Sept., by appt. for groups (05 46 85 19 16).

 ACCOMMODATION & EATING OUT

brouage-tourisme.fr

 LOCAL SPECIALTIES

Food and Drink
Salt • Oysters • Artisanal confectionery • Local and Quebec products.
Art and Crafts
Pottery • Artisanal jewelry designer • Painter • Designer of leather objects • Lacemaker • Glassmaker.

 EVENTS

May: Foire des Remparts, sale of local and artisanal products in streets around church (8th).
Jun.: Costumed historical festival (late Jun.).
Jul.–Aug.: Nuits Buissonnières, tales by torchlight, Thurs.; Mardis Famille and Jeudis de Brouage (shows, games, activities), Tues. and Thurs.; designers' markets.
Nov.: Rummage sale in village streets (1st).

 OUTDOOR ACTIVITIES

Walking • Cycle path in Marais de Brouage.

 FURTHER AFIELD

•Saint-Just-Luzac and Moulin des Loges (6 miles/10 km).
•Bourcefranc-le-Chapus and Fort Louvois (7 miles/11 km).
•Île d'Oléron (9 miles/15 km).
•Rochefort-sur-Mer, Saint-Sornin, and Tour de Broue (11 miles/18 km).

 MBVF NEARBY
•Mornac-sur-Seudre (19 miles/30 km).

Charente-Maritime (17)
Population: 170
Altitude: 10 ft. (3 m)

TOURIST INFO—ÎLE D'OLÉRON ET DU BASSIN DE MARENNES
05 46 85 19 16
brouage-tourisme.fr

Brousse-le-Château

Medieval stopover where the Tarn and Alrance rivers meet

Brousse-le-Château stands on the banks of the Alrance river, overlooked by the imposing silhouette of its medieval castle that gives the village its name. Between the 10th and 17th centuries, the fort grew steadily until it filled the whole rock dominating the village, while also strengthening the position of the counts du Rouergue, and then, from 1204 onward, the d'Arpajon family, one of whom became a duke and French dignitary in the 17th century. Restoration work started in 1963, funded by the Vallée de l'Amitié charity, after which the castle opened to the public. Between the Middle Ages and the Renaissance, Brousse was a typical fortress: its keep, towers, ramparts, arrow-slits, crenellations, and machicolations indicate its military function, while the lord's apartments and the gardens reveal the level of comfort that was to be found there. Crossing the 14th-century stone bridge over the Alrance brings visitors to the road at the bottom of the village.

 EVENTS

Market: Tues. a.m. (Jul.–Aug.).
Jul.: Bonfire and fireworks at the castle (13th).
Aug.: Local saint's day with traditional stuffed chicken (3rd weekend).

OUTDOOR ACTIVITIES

Swimming • Fishing • Canoeing and kayaking • Boating • Walks • Mountain biking.

HIGHLIGHTS

Castle: Typical of the medieval Rouergue military style. Interior includes lord's apartments, well and water tank, bread oven (05 65 99 45 40).
Church (15th century): Dedicated to Saint James the Greater (05 65 99 41 14).

ACCOMMODATION & EATING OUT

tourisme-muse-raspes.com

LOCAL SPECIALTIES

Food and Drink
Spit cake • Goat cheese and dairy products • Local wines.
Art and Crafts
Artists' studio: jewelry, soaps, essential oils, leather, silk scarves, pottery, and paintings • Artists' association: mandalas, dreamcatchers, candles.

FURTHER AFIELD

• Châteaux de Coupiac, de Saint-Izaire, and de Montaigut (9½–12½ miles/15–20 km).
• Peyrebrune tower, Saint-Louis dolmen, Ayssènes, Saint-Victor, and Melvieu (12½ miles/20 km).
• Lévezou lakes and Villefranche-de-Panat (12½ miles/20 km).
• Saint-Affrique (22 miles/35 km).

Aveyron (12)
Population: 170
Altitude: 787 ft. (240 m)

TOURIST INFO—PAYS DE LA MUSE ET DES RASPES DU TARN
05 65 62 50 89
tourisme-muse-raspes.com
brousselechateau.net

Bruniquel

Defying the enemy from the cliff top

Bruniquel and its medieval castles sit atop a high rocky promontory, towering over the village and surveying the confluence of the Aveyron and Vère rivers. Bruniquel certainly shows its defensive side to approaching visitors: the massive façades of its 600-year-old castles perched on the escarpment are truly impressive. The village itself feels completely different, however, showcasing medieval houses that are beautifully conserved. It is wonderful to wander down the flower-bedecked streets, with their ornate façades of mullioned windows and twin bay windows, bearing witness to the village's rich mercantile past—a heritage that many artisans are reviving today. Although indelibly touched by its medieval history, this ancient stronghold of the counts of Toulouse in fact has much older roots: inside an extraordinary cave, a mass of stalagmites—the only one of its kind in the world—dates from 176,000 years ago.

HIGHLIGHTS

Chateaux: Vaulted chambers, chapel, state room, Renaissance gallery; exhibitions on prehistory (05 63 67 27 67).
Le Bec de Corbin medieval park: Equestrian shows and recreational workshops (06 10 74 61 69).
Maison Poisson – Musée Jean-Gabriel Goulinat: Exhibition dedicated to the painter (1883-1972), temporary exhibitions.
Village: Self-guided tour with audio guide all year round (05 63 67 29 84).

ACCOMMODATION & EATING OUT

gorges-aveyron-tourisme.com

LOCAL SPECIALTIES

Art and Crafts
Jewelry designer • Ceramic artist • Potter• Glass artist • Woodturner • Spinning • Textiles.

EVENTS

Market: Sat. 8 a.m.–1 p.m., (Jun.–Sept.)
Jul.: Festival d'Autan, chamber music festival (last fortnight).
Jul.-Aug.: Festival des Châteaux de Bruniquel (late Jul.–early Aug.).
Sept.: Les Nuits Frappées de Bruniquel, drumming festival (1st Sat.).

OUTDOOR ACTIVITIES

Walking: Route GR 46 and 5 marked trails • Cycling: 5 circuits • Canoeing and kayaking.

FURTHER AFIELD

•Penne: Castle (6 miles/10 km).
•Montricoux, Bioule, and Montauban (3–18½ miles/5–30 km).
•Gorges de l'Aveyron and Caylus (4½–22 miles/7–35 km).

MBVF NEARBY
•Puycelsi (8 miles/13 km).
•Castelnau-de-Montmiral (13½ miles/22 km).

Tarn-et-Garonne (82)
Population: 614
Altitude: 541 ft. (165 m)

TOURIST INFO—MIDI-QUERCY GORGES DE L'AVEYRON
05 63 67 29 84
gorges-aveyron-tourisme.com
bruniquel.fr

Camon

An abbey and 400 roses

Nestling at the bottom of a valley in Ariège, Camon encloses within its ramparts a historic fortress-abbey and lanes lined with roses. Situated on a bend in the Hers river, on the boundary between Ariège and Aude, the village grew out of an abbey that was founded in the 10th century by Benedictine monks. After becoming a priory belonging to the abbey of Lagrasse, the monastery was destroyed and rebuilt several times during the Middle Ages, and was eventually encircled with ramparts in the 16th century. The village that visitors can discover today is typical of the fortified villages of the Ariège *département*, whose houses made from local materials hunch together cheek by jowl and are topped with curved Roman roof tiles. Camon is also dubbed "the village of 400 roses" and celebrates this delicate flower every May.

HIGHLIGHTS

Village: Abbey, church, ramparts. Guided tours in Jul.–Aug. (05 61 68 83 76).
Cabanes (stone huts) **of Camon**: Themed walk around the historic drystone winegrowers' huts; wild orchids in springtime. To visit, contact town hall (05 61 68 12 07).
Roseraie: Fragrant rose garden (free entry).

ACCOMMODATION & EATING OUT

Guesthouses
♥ L'Abbaye-Château de Camon (05 61 60 31 23).

LOCAL SPECIALTIES

Food and Drink
Charcuterie • *Croustades* (flaky fruit pastries) • Beef.

EVENTS

May: Fête des Roses and classical music festival (3rd Sun.).
Jun.–Sept.: Evening gourmet and festive markets. Wed. 5 p.m.–11 p.m.

OUTDOOR ACTIVITIES

Canoeing • Fishing (accessible fishing facilities) • Walking • Voie Verte: greenway suitable for walking, mountain biking, and horseback riding.

FURTHER AFIELD

•Chalabre: Fortified town; Lac de Montbel; Puivert: Castle, museum; Nébias: Natural maze (6– 12½ miles/9.5–20 km).
•Mirepoix and Vals (7½–15½ miles/12–25 km).
•Lavelanet and Château de Montségur (10–22 miles/16–35 km).

Ariège (09)
Population: 140
Altitude: 1,148 ft. (350 m)

TOURIST INFO—PYRÉNÉES CATHARES
05 61 68 83 76
pyreneescathares.com
camon09.org

Candes-Saint-Martin

Bright reflections where rivers meet

Built on a hillside, Candes gazes at its own reflection in the waters of the Vienne and Loire. Springing up where two rivers merge, Candes was for centuries a village of barge people, who contributed to the busy traffic on the Loire and the Vienne by selling local wines, plum brandies, and tufa stone from their *toues* (traditional fishing boats) and barges on the Loire. Indeed, the striking whiteness of tufa stone beneath the dark slate or tiled roofs still brightens the houses and the imposing collegiate church in the village. Built between 1175 and 1225 on the very site of a primitive church founded by Saint Martin, the church, which was fortified in the 15th century, is dedicated to this bishop of Tours, who brought Christianity to Gaul. One of its stained-glass windows recreates the nocturnal removal of his body by monks from Tours. More than sixteen centuries after his death, Saint Martin is still revered through legends of his many miracles.

 HIGHLIGHTS

Collégiale Saint-Martin (12th–13th centuries): Collegiate church in Plantagenet Gothic style, fortified in the 15th century.
Centre Permanent d'Initiative à l'Environnement du Patrimoine Fluvial: Center devoted to area's river heritage; boat trips in Jul. and Aug. (02 47 95 93 57).
 Musée d'Art Urbain – Street Art Parc: Tour dedicated to street art in the gardens of the Château de Môh (07 55 85 25 04).
Village: Guided tours of village and/or church by the Association des Amis de Candes (02 47 95 90 71).

 **ACCOMMODATION & EATING OUT**

Hotels
♥ Le Château de Candes – Art & Spa (07 55 85 25 04).
Gîtes
♥ Logis La Renaissance ❚❚❚ (02 47 27 56 10).

LOCAL SPECIALTIES

Food and Drink
AOC wines from Touraine, Chinon-Touraine, and Saumur-Touraine.
Art and Crafts
Creative workshop-boutique (fashion, tapestry, herbalism) • Bladesmith • Ceramics • Goldsmith • Perfumer • Painters • Lighting artist • Inuit art gallery.

 EVENTS

Market: Sat. a.m., 9 a.m.–1 p.m., east car park.
Jul.–Aug.: Les Flâneries Piétonnes, cultural activities, Sun. p.m.
Nov.: Fête de la Saint Martin (around 11th).

 OUTDOOR ACTIVITIES

Bathing: Confluence beach (no lifeguard) • Fishing • Boat trips • Walking: riverside path, Via Sancti Martini • Cycling: "Loire à Vélo" trail.

 FURTHER AFIELD

• Abbaye de Fontevraud (4½ miles/7 km).
• Seuilly: Maison La Devinière, Rabelais's house and museum (9½ miles/15 km).
• Chinon (10½ miles/17km).
• Châteaux of the Loire and Indre (12–23 miles/19–37 km).

MBVF NEARBY
• Montsoreau (½ mile/1 km).

Indre-et-Loire (37)
Population: 185
Altitude: 131 ft. (40 m)

TOURIST INFO—AZAY-CHINON VAL DE LOIRE
02 47 93 17 85
azay-chinon-valdeloire.com

Capdenac-le-Haut

From Roman emperor to count of Toulouse

Perched on a protruding rock, more than 360 ft. (110 m) above a meander in the Lot river, Capdenac "on high" suffered attacks by Julius Caesar and Simon de Montfort. Shaped like the figurehead at the prow of a ship, Capdenac allegedly got its Occitan name from the configuration of the site. It was coveted for its strategic position, and the medieval fortress, for which it is best known today, was conquered in the 13th century by the count of Toulouse. However, much earlier it was the location of one of the most important Roman towns in Quercy: Uxellodunum, the site of Roman emperor Julius Caesar's last battle against the Gauls. The Gaulish spring and Caesar's spring, fed by magnificent underground cisterns, are reminders of these ancient times. The monumental gates to the citadel, the keep, and several handsome 18th-century residences reveal Capdenac's second face—one that shows signs of having lived through the vicissitudes of the Middle Ages.

 **HIGHLIGHTS**

Jardin des 1001 Pattes: Ecological garden featuring an enormous insect hotel.
Jardin Médiéval des Cinq Sens: Plants arranged according to the 5 senses—smell, sight, touch, taste, and a fountain to stimulate hearing; medicinal plants (05 65 38 32 26).
Église Saint-Jean-Baptiste (18th century): Statues, altarpiece decorated with sculpted motifs.
Fontaine des Anglais: Troglodyte spring with two underground pools.
Donjon, or La Tour de Modon (13th–14th centuries): Historic and prehistoric museum (05 65 38 32 26).
Musée Uxellodunum: Exhibition on prehistory, the Gallo-Roman era and the Middle Ages; terrace with panorama (05 65 38 32 26).
Village: Self-guided tour with Les Clefs de Capdenac-Le-Haut, available free of charge at tourist info office (05 65 38 32 26).

 ACCOMMODATION & EATING OUT

tourisme-figeac.com

 LOCAL SPECIALTIES

Food and Drink
Goat cheese • *Fouaces* (brioche/cake).
Art and Crafts
Organic soapmaker • Mosaic artist.

 EVENTS

Summer market: Wed. a.m., Place de la Mairie (Jul.-Aug.)
Aug.: Evening market (2nd Thurs.).
Sept.: Local saint's day (3rd weekend).

 OUTDOOR ACTIVITIES

Walking: 2 marked trails.

 FURTHER AFIELD

• Figeac: Musée Champollion, museum on the history of writing and Jean-François Champollion (3½ miles/6 km).
• Peyrusse-le-Roc (10½ miles/17 km).
• Villefranche-de-Rouergue (20½ miles/33 km).

 MBVF NEARBY
• Cardaillac (10 miles/16 km).
• Belcastel (24 miles/39 km).

Lot (46)
Population: 1,112
Altitude: 853 ft. (260 m)

TOURIST INFO—GRAND FIGEAC-VALLÉES DU LOT ET DU CÉLÉ
05 65 38 32 26 /
05 65 34 06 25
tourisme-figeac.com

Cardaillac

The powerhouse of Quercy

The powerful feudal Cardaillac family founded this village on the fringes of Quercy and Ségala, and gave it its name. When Pépin the Younger (714-768) granted Cardaillac lands to his knight Bertrand and descendants, he guaranteed a bright future for the village. The fort, completed in the 12th century, sits on a triangular spur, with two cliffs providing natural fortifications. Three towers are all that survive of the ramparts: the round tower, the clock tower (which served as the prison), and the tower of Sagnes, which affords a panoramic view of the village. Cardaillac was attacked during both the Hundred Years War and the Wars of Religion; these events drove the local people to become the most fervent Protestant community in Haut Quercy, and they participated in the destruction of Saint Julian's Church. The church was restored to Catholicism by the Edict of Nantes, then rebuilt in the 17th century, when the fort passed into the hands of Protestant reformers. At the Revocation of the Edict of Nantes, the ramparts and towers were razed to the ground.

 HIGHLIGHTS

Fort: Ruins of 11th-century medieval fort (Sagnes and clock towers); guided visits in summer (05 65 34 06 25).
Medieval kitchen garden: Medicinal and dye plants; self-guided tour with information panels (05 65 40 14 32).
Musée Éclaté: Multisite museum on the history of the village since the Middle Ages (05 65 40 10 63).
Village: Signposted route with information panels; guided tours by appt. (05 65 34 06 25).

 ACCOMMODATION & EATING OUT

tourisme-figeac.com

 LOCAL SPECIALTIES

Art and Crafts
Soap making.

 EVENTS

Market: Sun. 8.30 a.m.–1 p.m., Place du Boulodrome.
May: Foire du Renouveau, flea market, rummage sale, and artisanal products; potters' market (Whit Monday).
Jun.: National gardens day (1st Sun.).
Nov.: Foire Saint-Martin, fair (1st Sun.).

 OUTDOOR ACTIVITIES

Fishing (lake; Murat 1st category permit) • Walking: Route GR 6 and marked trails • Mountain biking.

 FURTHER AFIELD

•Figeac (6 miles/10 km).
•Lacapelle-Marival (9½ miles/15 km).
•Vallée du Célé (15½ miles/25 km).

 MBVF NEARBY
•Capdenac-le-Haut (10½ miles/17 km).
•Rocamadour (25 miles/40 km).

Lot (46)
Population: 622
Altitude: 1,175 ft. (358 m)

TOURIST INFO—GRAND FIGEAC-VALLÉES DU LOT ET DU CÉLÉ
05 65 34 06 25
tourisme-figeac.com
cardaillac.fr

Carennac

Renaissance elegance and Quercy charm

Carennac sits on the banks of the Dordogne, facing the Île de Calypso, where it shelters medieval houses huddled together around an ancient monastery. In the days when it was called Carendenacus, the village was centered around a church that was dedicated to Saint Sernin and annexed to Beaulieu Abbey. On the orders of Cluny Abbey, the parish became a priory, and in the 11th century it built the existing Église Saint-Pierre; the 12th-century portal with its magnificent carved tympanum and one of the cloister's galleries still remain from the original Romanesque building. The village houses in stone that are typical of Quercy surround the church, some boasting ornate mullioned windows or watchtowers, and reveal all the appeal of a monastic village beside the Dordogne.

 **HIGHLIGHTS**

Église Saint-Pierre and cloister (11th–12th centuries): Chapter house with late 15th-century sculpture of the Entombment, 16th-century bas-reliefs depicting the Life and Passion of Christ.
Espace Patrimoine, Château des Doyens heritage center (16th-century building): Permanent exhibition on the area's natural, architectural, and patrimonial wealth (05 65 33 81 36).
Priory and village: Guided tours by appt. (05 65 33 81 36 / 05 65 33 22 00).

 ACCOMMODATION & EATING OUT

vallee-dordogne.com

 **LOCAL SPECIALTIES**

Food and Drink
Walnuts and walnut oil.

Art and Crafts
Ceramic artist • Marquetry • Leather goods • Sculptor.

 EVENTS

Market: Tues. 5–8 p.m. (Jul.–Aug.).
Aug.: Festive market (mid-Aug.).

 OUTDOOR ACTIVITIES

Canoeing and kayaking • Fishing • Walking: Route GR 52 • Mountain biking.

 FURTHER AFIELD

• Châteaux de Castelnau and Montal, Saint-Céré (6–10 miles/10–16 km).
• Gouffre de Padirac, chasm (5½ miles/9 km)

 MBVF NEARBY

• Loubressac (6 miles/10 km).
• Rocamadour (6–12½ miles/10–20 km).
• Vallée de la Dordogne: Beaulieu-sur-Dordogne (7 miles/11 km); Autoire (8 miles/13 km); Curemonte (9½ miles/15 km); Martel (11 miles/18 km); Collonges-la-Rouge (14 miles/23 km); Turenne (15 miles/24 km).

Lot (46)
Population: 413
Altitude: 387 ft. (118 m)

TOURIST INFO—VALLÉE DE LA DORDOGNE
05 65 33 22 00
vallee-dordogne.com

 LOCAL SPECIALTIES

Food and Drink
AOC Bandol and Côte-de-Provence wines • Olive oil.
Art and Crafts
Art galleries • Soap making • Antiques • Painters • Jewelry • Engraver • Candlemakers.

EVENTS

Market: Sat. 8 a.m.–1 p.m., Place Herrischried, Plan du Castellet.
Jan. 2: Fête de la Saint Clair.
Jul.: Les Nuits du Conte, storytelling festival (20th–25th); Virtuoses Sous les Étoiles, classical music festival (last fortnight).
Sept.: Les Médiévales, medieval fair (1st weekend).

Le Castellet

The art of living in the backlands of the Var

Near the shores of the Mediterranean, at the foot of the Massif de la Sainte-Baume, Le Castellet stands watch over the great winemaking estates of the Bandol region. Due to its strategic position on a wooded bluff overlooking the Sainte-Baume ridge, in the 15th century Le Castellet was chosen for the construction of a seignorial castle and fortifications, of which two gates remain. Today, this advantageous and peaceful location affords a wonderful view of lavender fields, olive groves, and vineyards. Le Castellet has maintained a tradition of artisan pottery, and many workshops fill the steep, narrow streets leading to the castle. Several small squares scattered around the village invite visitors to relax while admiring the stone façades, and pastel-colored doors and windows. Known for its motorsport racetrack, the Circuit Paul Ricard, built in 1970 and located several miles from the medieval town, Le Castellet now promotes its heritage and lifestyle.

 HIGHLIGHTS

Église de la Transfiguration-du-Sauveur (11th–12th and 18th centuries): Triple-arched bell gable.
Église de la Nativité de la Vierge (18th century).
Chapelle Sainte-Anne du Castellet (17th century).
Castle (15th century): Town hall and exhibition space.
Musée de la Vigne et du Vin du Domaine de Ray-Jane: Wine cellar and museum with 30,000 coopering and winemaking tools (04 94 98 64 08).
Trou de Madame viewpoint: View over the Massif de la Sainte-Baume.
Circuit Paul Ricard: Guided tour (04 94 98 36 66).
Village: Arts trail (self-guided tour with booklet); guided tour (04 94 32 79 13).

 ACCOMMODATION & EATING OUT

Restaurants
♥ La Farigoule (06 75 51 43 30).

OUTDOOR ACTIVITIES

Walking: "Le Font de Mars" trail • Mountain biking • Flightseeing tours.

 FURTHER AFIELD

•Le Beausset; Saint-Cyr-sur-Mer; Bandol; Sanary-sur-Mer (3–9 miles/5–15 km).
•Toulon (16 miles/25 km).

Var (83)
Population: 473
Altitude: 984 ft. (300 m)

TOURIST INFO—GABRIEL TAMBON
04 94 32 79 13
lecastellet.fr

Castelnau-de-Montmiral

The treasure of the counts of Armagnac

The *bastide* (fortified town) of Castelnau-de-Montmiral boasts a rich heritage bequeathed by the counts of Toulouse and Armagnac. Proudly perched on its rocky outcrop, the village is ideally situated as a lookout and, in the Middle Ages, saw remarkable growth and the building of a seignorial castle coupled with an impregnable fortress. The castle was destroyed in the 19th century, but part of the fortifications have been preserved, along with the Porte des Garrics, dating from the 13th century. At the center of the *bastide*, founded in 1222 by the Count of Toulouse Raymond VII, 16th- and 17th-century houses surround the covered square and old well. The Église Notre-Dame-de-l'Assomption contains a superb Baroque altarpiece, a Pietà, and a 16th-century Pensive Christ, as well as the reliquary cross of the consuls from the late 14th century: a masterpiece of southern religious goldsmithery, which was originally decorated with 354 precious stones.

 HIGHLIGHTS

Église Notre-Dame-de-l'Assomption (15th–16th centuries): 14th-century cross, altarpiece, Pensive Christ, Pietà, frescoes.
Castelnau, Pages d'Histoire: Permanent exhibition at tourist info center (08 05 40 08 28).
Village: Guided tour mid-Jul.–late Aug. (08 05 40 08 28).

 ACCOMMODATION & EATING OUT

Gîtes
♥ Les Gîtes de Crabet***
🛏🛏🛏 (06 87 42 06 73).

 LOCAL SPECIALTIES

Food and Drink
Foie gras, duck confit, duck breast (*magret*) • AOC Gaillac wines.
Art and Crafts
Perfumery • Painter • Art gallery • Leather goods • Woodwork • Sculptor.

 EVENTS

Market: Tues. a.m., Place des Arcades.
Pentecost: Village festival (weekend).
Jul.-Aug.: Les Musicales, rock, blues, and pop festival (mid-Jul.).
Aug.: Castelroc rock festival (mid-Aug.); Honey and local produce fair (15th).

 OUTDOOR ACTIVITIES

Vère-Grésigne leisure park: Swimming, fishing, paddleboats, miniature golf, tennis, mountain-bike trail • Walking: Routes GR 36 and 46 and several marked trails.

FURTHER AFIELD

•Penne (16 miles/26 km).

 MBVF NEARBY
•Puycelsi (8 miles/13 km).
•Bruniquel (13½ miles/22 km).
•Cordes-sur-Ciel (14 miles/23 km).
•Monestiés (20 miles/32 km).

Tarn (81)
Population: 1,060
Altitude: 951 ft. (290 m)

TOURIST INFO—LA TOSCANE OCCITANE
08 05 40 08 28
la-toscane-occitane.com
castelnaudemontmiral.com

Castelnaud-la-Chapelle

A tale of two châteaux

Clinging to the cliffside overlooking the confluence of the Dordogne and Céou rivers, the Château de Castelnaud and its houses, which are typical of the Périgord region, are arranged in tiers along the steep, narrow streets. Built in the 12th century on a strategic site for controlling the region's main river and land transportation routes, the Château de Castelnaud was much coveted during the many wars that marked the Middle Ages. Abandoned during the French Revolution, it was even used as a stone quarry in the 19th century, until it was listed as a historic monument in 1966, and thus prevented from falling into total ruin. Today, after extensive restoration, it once again casts its shadow over the valley, offering an exceptional view over the neighboring villages of Beynac-et-Cazenac and La Roque-Gageac, and it houses the medieval warfare museum. Not far from the river, the Château des Milandes preserves the memory of jazz entertainer Josephine Baker, who owned the property from 1947 to 1968.

 LOCAL SPECIALTIES

Food and Drink
Walnuts and walnut oil • Truffles.
Art and Crafts
Miniature models • Textiles • Wooden toys and games.

 EVENTS

Jul.: Fête de la Plage, beach festival (weekend after 14th).

 HIGHLIGHTS

Château de Castelnaud (12th century, restored): Musée de la Guerre au Moyen Âge (medieval warfare museum), with a collection of 200 items of weaponry and armor, furniture, scenography (05 53 31 30 00).
Château des Milandes (15th century): Château and gardens classed as "remarkable" by the Ministry of Culture; exhibition on the life of Josephine Baker (05 53 59 31 21).
Domaine de Vielcroze: Traditions of walnut and truffle cultivation; tours of the walnut grove, museum, oil press; discovery tour (05 53 59 69 63).
Gardens of the Château de Lacoste: Boxwood and rose garden, vegetable garden, park (05 53 29 89 37).

 ACCOMMODATION & EATING OUT

perigordnoir-valleedordogne.com

 OUTDOOR ACTIVITIES

Canoeing and kayaking • Walking: Route GR 64 and marked trails • Mountain biking • Horseback riding.

 FURTHER AFIELD

•Sarlat (8 miles/13 km).

 MBVF NEARBY
•La Roque-Gageac (2 miles/3 km).
•Beynac-et-Cazenac (2½ miles/4 km).
•Domme (6 miles/10 km).
•Belvès (11 miles/18 km).
•Limeuil (20½ miles/33 km).
•Monpazier (21 miles/34 km).

Dordogne (24)
Population: 447
Altitude: 459 ft. (140 m)

TOURIST INFO—PÉRIGORD NOIR-VALLÉE DORDOGNE
05 53 31 71 00
perigordnoir-valleedordogne.com

Castelnou

In the foothills of the Pyrenees

Nestled in the Aspres, at the foot of the Canigou mountain, Castelnou is a medieval village that typifies Catalan rural architecture. Founded in the 10th century, the village seems to have been forgotten by time, after having been the capital of the viscountcy of Vallespir for more than three centuries. It is surrounded by two limestone plateaus—the Causse de Thuir and the Roc de Majorque (1,453 ft./443 m altitude)—and the ruggedness of this steep, tiered, stone-built site contrasts pleasantly with the intimacy of the flower-filled lanes that are brought to life by the many artisans. The village has preserved its medieval appearance, with its fortified walls punctuated by eight towers and four gates at the four cardinal points, its watchtower, and its 10th-century viscount's castle.

 HIGHLIGHTS

Château de Castelnou (10th century): Guided tour of the castle and garden; self-guided tour with audio guide available in French/English/Catalan; booklet in braille and notebooks "Les Faciles à Lire" and "Le Patrimoine en Images," May–Sept. (04 68 84 69 20).

Église Santa Maria del Mercadal (12th century): Catalan Romanesque style.

Village: Guided tour by appt. (04 68 28 32 38).

 ACCOMMODATION & EATING OUT

Gîtes
♥ La Font (06 87 12 73 72).

 LOCAL SPECIALTIES

Food and Drink
Organic and biodynamic Côtes du Roussillon wines • Sheep cheese • Honey and bee products • Olive oil • Fruits and vegetables • Fruit juices • Preserves.

Art and Crafts
Painters • Sculptors • Wirework workshop • Mosaic artist • Potter • Wood turner • Eggshell artworks • Lampshades • Jewelry designer • Creative card making.

EVENTS

Market: Tues. 9 a.m.–7 p.m. (mid-Jun.–mid-Sept.); Les Créateurs en Fête, creatives fair (1st Sun. Jun.-Sept.) and Le Dimanche des Peintres, artists fair (3rd Sun. Jun.-Sept.), Marché Pittoresque area.

May: Spring agricultural fair (late May).

Jun.: Les Lucioles de Castelnou, 11-mile/18-km night trek (3rd Sat.).

Jul.: Les Médiévales, medieval festival (last weekend).

Aug.: Pintura, international painting contest (last weekend).

 OUTDOOR ACTIVITIES

Walking • Mountain biking.

 FURTHER AFIELD

• Camélas; Fontcouverte; Monastir-del-Camp; Sainte-Colombe; Serrabonne (2½–9½ miles/4–15 km).
• Thuir: Byrrh wine cellars; Perpignan (13 miles/21 km).
• Elne (19 miles/31 km).

 MBVF NEARBY

• Eus (18 miles/29 km).
• Villefranche-de-Conflent (23 miles/37 km).

Pyrénées-Orientales (66)
Population: 295
Altitude: 804 ft. (245 m)

TOURIST INFO— ASPRES-THUIR
04 68 28 32 38 /
04 68 53 45 86
aspres-thuir.com
castelnou.fr

Soap making • Upholsterer/ decorator • Art galleries • Enameled lava • Wirework: ♥ L'Atelier Fil de Fer (06 67 10 65 80).

EVENTS

Aug.: Fête des Artistes et Artisans, art and craft fair (1st Sun.).
Nov.: Fête de la Soupe, soup festival (1st Sat., unless 1 Nov.).
Dec.: Christmas market (3rd weekend).

Charroux

A trading town in Bourbonnais

At the crossroads of Roman roads, Charroux became a tax-free stronghold at the time of the dukes of Bourbon. This fortified city flourished in the Renaissance owing to its tannery and winemaking, as well as the fairs and markets that it held regularly, and thus attracted merchants, notaries, doctors, and clergymen. The Halle (covered market), built in the early 19th century, has retained its old wooden pillars, which are protected from horse-and-cart collisions by large stone blocks. Despite the church being burned down twice during the Wars of Religion, Charroux has retained its Église Saint-Jean-Baptiste with its distinctive truncated bell tower. From the Cour des Dames—a magical place in the village center—the narrow streets pass by the house of the Prince of Condé and end at the gates of the ramparts, one of which—the Porte d'Occident— was bestowed with the village clock in the 16th century. During recent years, Charroux has reclaimed its identity as a place of trade, and draws many artists and craftspeople.

HIGHLIGHTS

Musée de Charroux: Museum of popular arts (04 70 58 39 93/04 70 56 87 71).
Église Saint-Jean-Baptiste (12th century).
Village: Guided tour, by appt., all year round for groups and Wed. 11 a.m. Jul.–Aug. for individuals (04 70 56 87 71).

ACCOMMODATION & EATING OUT

valdesioule.com

LOCAL SPECIALTIES

Food and Drink
Chocolates • Jams • Confectionery • Foie gras • Walnut and hazelnut oil • Mustards • Saffron• AOC St-Pourçain-sur-Sioule wines • Teas and coffees.
Art and Crafts
Mother-of-pearl creations: ♥ La Boutique du Nacrier (06 73 35 98 97). • Candles • Minerals • Potter-ceramist • Bead artist and glass maker •

OUTDOOR ACTIVITIES

Walking: Routes GRP du Val de Sioule, Grande Traversée du Massif Central, Saint James's Way, and Via Sancti Martini, marked trails • Mountain biking.

♀ FURTHER AFIELD

• Bellenaves: Musée de l'Automobile; Chantelle: Abbey; Jenzat: Maison du Luthier/Museum; Fleuriel: Historial du Paysan Soldat; Gannat: Paléopolis, dinosaur park; Gorges de la Sioule (3–8 miles/5–13 km).
• Saint-Pourçain-sur-Sioule: Musée du Vin; vineyards (12½ miles/20 km).
• Vichy (18½ miles/30 km).

Allier (03)
Population: 363
Altitude: 1,355 ft. (413 m)

TOURIST INFO—VAL DE SIOULE
04 70 56 87 71
valdesioule.com

Château-Chalon

Flagship of the Jura vineyards

Overlooking the valley of the Seille river and the Bresse plain, Château-Chalon watches over its vineyards, the birthplace of *vin jaune*—a white wine that resembles dry sherry. Between the grasslands and forests of the Jura plateau and the vineyards huddled beneath the cliff, the village emerged around a Benedictine abbey. The Église Saint-Pierre, covered with *lave* limestone roof tiles, is still visible today, as are the remains of a medieval watchtower. Lined with sturdy winemakers' houses, which are often flanked by a flight of steps and feature large arched openings, nearly every street in Château-Chalon leads to one of the four viewpoints overlooking the vineyards, where Savagnin reigns supreme. In the heart of the village, the old cheese dairy has been reopened to share the secrets to making Comté. L'École d'Autrefois, reconstructed as it was in 1928, harks back to the schools of yesteryear, while the Maison de la Haute Seille houses the tourist information center and an interactive museum on wine and terroir.

 HIGHLIGHTS

Maison de la Haute Seille: Interactive museum and introduction to the Jura vineyards (03 84 24 76 05).
Église Saint-Pierre (12th century): Romanesque and Gothic art; murals; furniture; reliquaries, goldsmithery, and statues from the abbey.
École d'Autrefois: School furniture and teaching materials from 1880–1930; activities Apr.–Oct. (03 84 24 76 05).
Vigne-Conservatoire: Plot of 53 old Jura grape varieties from the 19th century (03 84 44 62 47).

 ACCOMMODATION & EATING OUT

jurabsolu.fr

 LOCAL SPECIALTIES

Food and Drink
Cheeses • AOC wines (Château-Chalon; Côtes du Jura, Crémant du Jura, Macvin du Jura, Vin de Paille) • Bresse chicken in *vin jaune*.
Art and Crafts
Gallery of local crafts.

 EVENTS

Apr.: Fête de la Saint-Vernier (3rd Sun.).
Jul.: Local history show (6th–23rd).
Dec.: Les Fayes, winter solstice festival (25th).

 OUTDOOR ACTIVITIES

Walking: Routes GR 59 and 5 marked trails for the vineyards • Mountain biking: 5 certified circuits • Electric bike excursions.

 FURTHER AFIELD

•Château de Frontenay (4 miles/6 km).
•Château d'Arlay (7 miles/11 km).
•Poligny and Arbois (7½–9½ miles/12–15 km).
•Lons-le-Saunier (11 miles/18 km).

 MBVF NEARBY
•Baume-les-Messieurs (7½ miles/12 km).

Jura (39)
Population: 145
Altitude: 1,529 ft. (466 m)

TOURIST INFO—JURABSOLU, DESTINATION BRESSE ET VIGNOBLES
03 84 44 62 47
jurabsolu.fr

Châteauneuf

A castle in Auxois

Situated at the fore of the village, the castle with its medieval military architecture is reflected in the waters of the Burgundy Canal. The fortress was built in the late 12th century by Jean de Chaudenay to control the old road from Dijon to Autun. It owes its austere bearing to its polygonal curtain wall flanked by massive towers and wide moats, which are crossed via one of the old drawbridges transformed into a fixed bridge. In the inner courtyard, the original keep is surrounded by two 15th-century *corps de logis* (central buildings). Below the castle, the church contains a Renaissance-style pulpit and a 14th-century Virgin and Child. Opposite the building is the Maison Blondeau, one of many old merchant houses from the 14th, 15th, and 16th centuries, recognizable by their turrets, ornamented cartouches, mullioned windows, and ogee lintels. From there, the view takes in the wooded hillsides of Auxois, with the mountains of the Morvan and the Autunois region in the background.

 HIGHLIGHTS

Castle: 12th-century keep, 15th-century *grand logis* (Flemish tapestries), residence of Philippe Pot (15th century), chapel (15th-century paintings, copy of recumbent statue of Philippe Pot at the Louvre), 14th-century south tower; multimedia visitor interpretive center; medieval garden; activities for kids (03 80 49 21 89).
Église Saint-Jacques-et-Saint-Philippe (16th century): Statues, 14th-century Virgin and Child (03 80 49 21 64).
Village: Guided tour by appt. (03 80 49 21 59).

 ACCOMMODATION & EATING OUT

Restaurants
♥ Bistrot des Prés Verts (03 62 02 21 21).

LOCAL SPECIALTIES

Art and Crafts
Antiques • Ceramics •

Sculptors • Painters • Wood sculptors.

 EVENTS

Jul. (even years): Medieval market (last weekend).
Oct.: Mass of Saint Hubert and gourmet and local produce market (1st Sun.).
Dec.: Christmas Mass with living Nativity scene (24th).

 OUTDOOR ACTIVITIES

Horseback riding • Fishing • Mountain biking • Cycle route • Walking: Tour around Auxois lakes, Romanesque chapels trail.

 FURTHER AFIELD

• Castles in Auxois: Chailly-sur-Armançon, Commarin, Mont-Saint-Jean (5–18½ miles/8–30 km).
• Burgundy Canal: Boat trip; Pouilly-en-Auxois (6 miles/10 km).
• Abbaye de la Bussière; Vallée de l'Ouche (7½ miles/12 km).
• Beaune; Burgundy vineyards (22 miles/35 km).
• Dijon (27 miles/43 km).

Côte-d'Or (21)
Population: 80
Altitude: 1,558 ft. (475 m)

TOURIST INFO—POUILLY-BLIGNY
03 80 90 77 36
tourismepouillybligny.fr
chateauneuf-cotedor.fr

Châtillon-en-Diois

Between vineyards and mountains

"Nestled between two mountainsides, this is a peaceful, quiet village. The word most often pronounced here is 'sun.'" Taken from his novel *Les âmes fortes*, these words by Jean Giono bear witness to the writer's love of this village nestled at the foot of the Glandasse mountain and surrounded by one of the highest vineyards in France. Initially, there was a simple feudal castle, of which little now remains, built on a rocky outcrop, but over the centuries a village gradually coalesced around its first landmark: the Église Saint-Nicolas, built around 1200. Following attacks by the troops of Olivier du Guesclin, new ramparts were built, then the Pont de Baïn bridge, to facilitate access to the village by cart, and, finally, several houses, which formed the *viols* (from the Latin *via*)—the region's traditional narrow streets. Renowned for its wines, the village also appeals to plant lovers, with more than 150 species planted throughout the village.

 HIGHLIGHTS

Village: Heritage tour (dep. Champ de Foire, near the washhouse); botanical tour (dep. Place Dévoluy); guided tours (04 75 21 10 07).
Église Saint-Julien (17th century)**.**
Circuit des Cabanons: Discover the vineyards and their 70 huts (dep. Cave du Maupas).

 **ACCOMMODATION & EATING OUT**

diois-tourisme.com

 **LOCAL SPECIALTIES**

Food and Drink
Diois wines (AOC Châtillon-en-Diois) and Clairette de Die.
Art and Crafts
Pottery• Artisanal candles.

 EVENTS

Market: Fri. 8 a.m.–1 p.m., Place du Champ de Foire.
Jul.: Local saint's day (2nd weekend); rummage sale (3rd Sun.).
Aug.: Festival Arts et Vigne, art and wine festival (1st–2nd Sun.).

OUTDOOR ACTIVITIES

"La Roche et l'Eau" geological discovery circuit • Forêt Giono, forest • Walking: Cirque d'Archiane and Sentier des Vautours (vulture trail) • Mountain biking • Canyoning.

FURTHER AFIELD

•Claps de Luc and Saut de la Drôme: Spectacular rockslide into the Drôme river (8½ miles/14 km).
•Die: Roman remains; archaeological museum; Cave Jaillance and Muséo'bulles (cellar, wine tasting) (9 miles/15 km).
•Vassieux-en-Vercors (16 miles/26 km).

Drôme (26)
Population: 546
Altitude: 1,847 ft. (563 m)

TOURIST INFO—PAYS DIOIS
04 75 21 10 07
diois-tourisme.com

 EVENTS

Market: Sun. a.m., Place Alexandre Mari.
May: Voix du Basilic, book festival (around 20th).
Jun.: Fête de la Saint-Jean, *Joïa* (bonfire) and dance (4th weekend); Ultra-Trail Côte d'Azur Mercantour (around 20th).
Jul.: Pilo (traditional sport from Nice) world championship (1st Sat.)
Aug.: Fête de l'Olivier, olive tree festival (mid-Aug.).

Coaraze

The sunshine village

A short distance from the Mercantour national park, Coaraze is a medieval village bathed in sunlight. In the middle of olive trees, the cobblestone lanes of Coaraze lead to the 14th-century church, whose interiors were embellished in the 18th century with 118 cherubs in a polychrome décor, in the Baroque style from Nice. The Chapelle Bleue (blue chapel)—decorated with frescoes in different shades of blue by Angel Ponce de Léon in 1962—is an oratory dedicated to the Virgin Mary. The Chapelle Saint-Sébastien, which is decorated with 16th-century frescoes, stands alongside the old mule track that linked the village to Nice. With its steep, narrow streets, its houses with pink-tiled roofs, pale roughcast walls, and pastel shutters, and its fountains and squares, Coaraze is evocative of nearby Italy. One distinctive feature of the village is its sundials designed by numerous artists, including Jean Cocteau, Henri Goetz, Mona Christie, Angel Ponce de Léon, Gilbert Valentin, Georges Douking, and Patrick Moya, among others.

 HIGHLIGHTS

Chapelle Saint-Sébastien: 16th-century frescoes, by appt. (04 93 79 37 47 / 04 93 79 34 80).
Église Saint-Jean-Baptiste (14th century): Baroque interior.
Chapelle Bleue: Old oratory dedicated to the Virgin Mary; frescoes by Angel Ponce de Léon.
Olive groves: Tour from Route des Olivaies (04 93 37 78 78).
Village: Guided tour by appt (04 93 79 37 47 / 04 93 79 34 80).

 ACCOMMODATION & EATING OUT

coaraze.fr

 LOCAL SPECIALTIES

Food and Drink
Organic olive oil • Honey, jams.
Art and Crafts
Ceramics • Jewelry designer • Soap making • Artistic wood turning.

 OUTDOOR ACTIVITIES

Walking: 30 marked trails.

 FURTHER AFIELD

• Rocca Sparvièra: Medieval village ruins (3½ miles/5.5 km).
• Hilltop villages of Lucéram, Contes, Berre-les-Alpes, Peillon (5½–12 miles/ 9–20 km).
• Nice and the Côte d'Azur (16 miles/25 km).
• Peira-Cava; Forêt de Turini; Col de Turini (17 miles/27 km).

 MBVF NEARBY
• Sainte-Agnès (24 miles/39 km).

Alpes-Maritimes (06)
Population: 825
Altitude: 2,188 ft. (667 m)

TOURIST INFO—MAISON DU PATRIMOINE
04 93 79 37 47
TOWN HALL
04 93 79 34 80
coaraze.fr

Collonges-la-Rouge

Russet-colored Corrèze

Between hills and valleys, surrounded by greenery, Collonges-la-Rouge is renowned for its architectural heritage built in red sandstone. Constructed around a Benedictine priory founded in the 8th century, the village became the seat of the viscounts of Turenne in the 13th century; it is adorned with noble houses, castles, and religious buildings with imposing proportions, slate or *lauze* (schist stone) roofs, turrets and watchtowers. The Église Saint-Pierre, built in the 11th and 12th centuries, bears witness to the time when Collonges was one of the stopping places on the Saint James's Way pilgrim route via Rocamadour. The Priory gate, which is vaulted and ogival, and the Flat gate (it has no tower) are the only remains of the village's ramparts. Remarkably well preserved, Collonges-la-Rouge displays a rare homogeneity, setting itself apart through its harmonious colors, its architecture, and its medieval ambience.

 **HIGHLIGHTS**

Chapelle des Pénitents (15th century): Contemporary stained-glass windows.
Église Saint-Pierre (11th-12th centuries): Carved tympanum, double nave.
Maison de la Sirène (16th century): Typical furnished Collonges house, history of the village (07 82 27 41 39).
Château de Vassinhac (16th century): Château and park (05 55 84 06 20).
Grain and wine market (16th century) **and communal oven.**
Faille de Meyssac: 1 road route and 1 walking route to discover the geologic fault and geology of the region.
Village: Guided evening tour by torchlight; treasure hunt; themed guided tour, Jul.-Aug. (05 65 33 22 00).

 ACCOMMODATION & EATING OUT

Hotel-restaurants
♥ Le Relais Saint-Jacques (05 55 25 41 02).
Campsites
♥ Camping de Collonges-la-Rouge*** (05 55 25 41 59).

 LOCAL SPECIALTIES

Food and Drink
Duck (and specialties) • Walnuts • Cabécou cheese • Clafoutis and *flaugnarde* (fruit desserts) • Fruit liqueurs • Ratafia• Honey.
Art and Crafts
Leather and wood artisans • Hats • Bladesmith • Painters • Pottery • Glass • Artisanal perfumes and soaps • Precious stones and jewelry.

 EVENTS

Jun.: La Nuit Romantique, romantic festival (Sat. after summer solstice).
Mid-Jul.-mid-Aug.: Theater (Tues. evening).
Aug.: Fête du Pain, bread festival (1st weekend).

 OUTDOOR ACTIVITIES

Walking and mountain biking: Route GR 480 and several marked trails.

 FURTHER AFIELD

•Noailhac: Espace de Découverte de la Faille de Meyssac et de la Pierre, geological center (1 mile/2 km).
•Saillac: Musée de la Noix, walnut museum; church (2 miles/3 km).
•Brive-la-Gaillarde; Aubazine: Abbey and irrigation canal (12½ miles/20 km).

 MBVF NEARBY
•Vallée de la Dordogne: Turenne (6 miles/10 km), Curemonte (7½ miles/12 km), Beaulieu-sur-Dordogne (12½ miles/20 km), Carennac (15 miles/24 km).

Corrèze (19)
Population: 492
Altitude: 755 ft. (230 m)

TOURIST INFO—VALLÉE DE LA DORDOGNE
05 65 33 22 00
vallee-dordogne.com

Conques
(Commune of Conques-en-Rouergue)

Muse of Romanesque artists

A center for Romanesque art, Conques is a treasure trove of works born of the faith of medieval artists. Conques was established on the slope of a valley shaped like a shell (*concha* in Latin, hence its name), at the heart of a rich forested massif situated at the confluence of two rivers: the Ouche and the Dourdou. Its heyday, in the 11th and 12th centuries, coincided with the building of the abbey church—a true masterpiece of Romanesque architecture. Beneath its vaults, 250 capitals are enhanced by contemporary stained-glass windows designed by Pierre Soulages (1919-2022), and on the tympanum of its western portal 124 figures in stone illustrate the Last Judgment. The Barry and Vinzelle gates—remnants of the ramparts built during the same period—flank a village where stone reigns supreme; the houses display façades that combine half-timbering, yellow limestone, and red sandstone, and are topped with splendid silver shale roofs.

 HIGHLIGHTS

Abbatiale Sainte-Foy: Carved tympanum, Romanesque capitals, stained-glass windows by Soulages. Guided tour (05 65 72 85 00); evening guided tour of the tribunes May–Sept., 9:30 p.m.; illuminations on the tympanum 10:15 p.m.; self-guided tour with rental of digital tablets; guided group tour all year round, by appt. (05 65 72 85 00).
Trésor de Sainte-Foy: Open daily (05 65 72 85 00); guided group tour all year round, by appt. (05 65 72 85 00).
Village: Guided tour suitable for those with vision impairment: guidance, models, tour books (05 65 72 85 00).

 ACCOMMODATION & EATING OUT

tourisme-conques.fr

 **LOCAL SPECIALTIES**

Food and Drink
Conquaises (walnut shortbread) • Badines de Conques cookies • Conques wine.
Art and Crafts
Antiques • Bead artist • Intaglio engraver • Leather goods • Painter • Saddler • Wood carver • Stone carver • Low-warp weaving • Ceramics • Illuminator • Art jewelry • Stained glass.

 EVENTS

Jul.–Aug.: Les Rencontres Musicales (late Jul.–early Aug.); Soirées Métiers d'Art en Lumière, artisan festival by candlelight.
Oct.: Procession de la Sainte-Foy (6th or 1st Sun. after 6th).

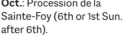

 OUTDOOR ACTIVITIES

Canoeing and kayaking • Walking: Routes GR 62, 65, 465, and 7 marked trails. • Cycling circuits: Vallée du Lot (V86), Voie de Conques • Trail running route • Fishing • Paddleboarding.

 FURTHER AFIELD

• Vallée du Dourdou: Gorges; viewpoint at Le Bancarel (1 mile/2 km).
• Vallon de Marcillac: AOP vineyards and wine route (11 miles/18 km).
• Salles-la-Source: Waterfall (15½ miles/25 km).

MBVF NEARBY
• Estaing (23½ miles/38 km).
• Belcastel (24 miles/39 km).

Aveyron (12)
Population: 1640
Altitude: 820 ft. (250 m)

TOURIST INFO—CONQUES-MARCILLAC
05 65 72 85 00
tourisme-conques.fr

Cordes-sur-Ciel

Living above the clouds

Perched on high and overlooking the valley, Cordes-sur-Ciel is a charming medieval village and one of the main *bastides* (fortified towns) in the Occitan region. Following the Albigensian Crusade, when fighting left many places in ruins, a policy of reconstruction was established in southwest France. It was during this period that Cordes-sur-Ciel was created and officially inaugurated, in 1222, by Raymond VII, Count of Toulouse. Initially made up of local limestone walls, the *bastide* grew as it flourished economically, welcoming merchants and craftsmen in its imposing covered market, which is now listed as a historic monument. Today, its heritage, its narrow, cobblestone streets, its fortified gates, its magnificent houses with Gothic façades, and its panoramic view over the Cérou valley continue to be a source of inspiration.

 **HIGHLIGHTS**

La Halle (covered market): 24 octagonal pillars, 16th-century cast-iron cross, well.
Musée des Arts du Sucre et du Chocolat – Yves Thuriès: Sugarwork and chocolate creations by national and world champions. Tours suitable for those with hearing impairment (05 63 56 02 40).
Musée Charles Portal: Museum devoted to local history, art, and heritage (09 72 87 07 95).
Jardin des Paradis: Gardens classed as "remarkable" by the Ministry of Culture, on the village's fortified terraces (07 67 83 09 67).
Église Saint-Michel (12th, 14th, and 15th centuries): Altarpieces, artworks from the 16th–19th centuries, Renaissance-style painted vaults and pillars by Gayral. Guided tour by appt. (05 63 56 00 15).
Musée d'Art Moderne et Contemporain: Permanent and temporary exhibitions housed in the Maison du Grand Fauconnier (05 63 56 14 79).
Village: Guided tour mid-Jul.–mid-Aug. (08 05 40 08 28).

 **ACCOMMODATION & EATING OUT**

la-toscane-occitane.com

 **LOCAL SPECIALTIES**

Food and Drink
Croquants de Cordes cookies • Foie gras.
Art and Crafts
Jewelry designer • Ceramics • Bladesmith • Artisanal wood and leather goods • Painters • Photographers • Soapmaker • Sculptor • Illuminator • Glassblower.

 EVENTS

Market: Sat. 7.30 a.m.–1 p.m, Place de la Bouteillerie.
Jul.: Fêtes du Grand Fauconnier, medieval festival (14th); classical music festival (21st-27th).
Aug.: Fête Occitane de Cordes (15th).

 OUTDOOR ACTIVITIES

Walking: Routes GR 46, GRP Penne–Cordes-sur-Ciel, circular walks around the village • Hot-air balloon flights • Donkey rides.

 FURTHER AFIELD

• Albi (15½ miles/25 km).
• Gorges de l'Aveyron (17 miles/27 km).

 MBVF NEARBY
• Castelnau-de-Montmiral (14 miles/23 km).
• Najac (16 miles/26 km).
• Puycelsi (18½ miles/30 km).

Tarn (81)
Population: 850
Altitude: 919 ft. (280 m)

TOURIST INFO—LA TOSCANE OCCITANE
08 05 40 08 28
la-toscane-occitane.com
mairie.cordessurciel.fr

Cotignac
The "Rock" of Provence Verte

At the foot of its famous tuff cliff, Cotignac is rooted in a landscape that celebrates art and terroir, in the heart of Provence Verte. Cotignac was once dominated by a feudal castle of which only the two watchtowers built into the cliff remain, offering a stunning view to the horizon. On the hilltop stands a sanctuary where the Virgin Mary is said to have appeared in 1519 and where Louis XIV stopped in 1660 while on a pilgrimage. The village is nestled at the foot of a huge cliff measuring 262 feet (80 m) in height and 1,312 feet (400 m) in length, formed by an ancient waterfall originating from the Cassole river. The torrent also left behind petrified waterfalls and hollow cavities that once provided shelter for the inhabitants. Cotignac's charm comes through in its colorful houses, its Provençal vegetation, its terroir, and the many art galleries that bring a creative spirit to the village.

 HIGHLIGHTS

Le Rocher (rock) **and its troglodyte cave dwellings**: Accessible walking tour; view of the village.
Sanctuaire Notre-Dame des Grâces (16th century): Self-guided tour daily, 7 a.m.–7 p.m. (8 p.m. in summer).
Monastère Saint-Joseph du Bessillon (17th–20th century): Spring water accessible to pilgrims; chapel open to visitors during the day and services (04 94 04 63 44).
Église Notre-Dame de l'Annonciation (13th century): 16th-century bell, 19th-century organ, 18th-century polychrome marble high altar.
Chapelle Saint-Martin (12th century): First religious building in the village.
Église Saint-Pierre (13th century): 19th-century organ and listed furnishings.
Centre d'Art La Falaise: Exhibitions, concerts, and conferences (04 94 59 28 76).
Carré et Cercle des Arts: Exhibition spaces and artist talks (04 94 72 60 20).
Village: Self-guided tour with printed guide and information panels; guided tours from tourist info center (04 94 04 61 87).

 ACCOMMODATION & EATING OUT

Guesthouses
♥ Chez Lucie: Maison Troglodyte (06 83 96 90 23).
Hotels
♥ Lou Calen (04 98 14 15 29).
Restaurants
♥ Le Jardin Secret (04 98 14 15 29).

 LOCAL SPECIALTIES

Food and Drink
Quince • Olive oil • AOP Côte-de-Provence wines.
Art and Crafts
Ceramics • Glassmaking • Leather goods • Woodwork.

 EVENTS

Market: Tues. 8 a.m.–1 p.m., Cours Gambetta and Place Joseph Sigaud.
Jul.: Foulée de Cotignac, festive running race (14th).
Mid-Jul.–mid Aug.: Les Toiles du Sud, open-air film festival.
Oct.: Quince festival (last weekend).

 OUTDOOR ACTIVITIES

Rock climbing • Walking: 3 marked trails • Cycling.

 FURTHER AFIELD

• Sillans la Cascade (4½ miles/7 km)
• Draguignan; Lac de Sainte-Croix (22½–23 miles/36–37 km).

 MBVF NEARBY
• Tourtour (17 miles/28 km).

Var (83)
Population: 2,200
Altitude: 755 ft. (230 m)

TOURIST INFO—PROVENCE VERTE ET VERDON TOURISME
04 94 04 61 87
la-provence-verte.net /ot_cotignac

La Couvertoirade

In the footsteps of the Templars

At the heart of the wide-open spaces of the Causse du Larzac, La Couvertoirade is the handiwork of the Templars and Hospitallers. Built in the 12th century, the Château de La Couvertoirade formed part of the command network developed by the Templars throughout the West and in the Holy Land. After they were declared heretics in the early 14th century by Philippe le Bel, the Templars—whose grand master was condemned to death at the stake—were superseded by the Hospitallers, who inherited all their assets. The latter, too, were soldier-monks and encircled the citadel with ramparts in the 15th century to protect it from attack and from epidemics. From the top of the ramparts, the view stretches over Larzac and the whole of the village: at the foot of the 12th-15th-century church, a labyrinth of narrow streets lined with "Caussenard"-style houses (built of thick stone for protection) and 16th- and 17th-century mansions provides an enticing place to stroll.

 HIGHLIGHTS

Village: 15th-century ramparts, 12th-century castle, Hospitallers' church, 14th-century oven. Self-guided tour with or without audio guide, or guided tour; evening tours in summer (05 65 58 55 59).

ACCOMMODATION & EATING OUT

Restaurants
♥ Auberge du Chat Perché (05 65 42 14 61).

LOCAL SPECIALTIES

Food and Drink
Sheep cheese • Local charcuterie • Spit cake.
Art and Crafts
Art galleries • Workshops in summer (pottery, weaving, sculpting) • Jewelry designer • Artisanal leather goods.

 EVENTS

Evening farmers' market: Thurs. 7– 9 p.m., La Placette (Jul. 1st-Aug. 31st).

 OUTDOOR ACTIVITIES

Trail through the rocks • Walking: Routes GR 71 C and GR 71 D and circular walks around the village • Mountain biking.

 FURTHER AFIELD

• Gorges of the Dourbie; Nant: Romanesque churches (8½ miles/14 km).
• Larzac Templar and Hospitaller sites: La Cavalerie; Sainte-Eulalie-de-Cernon (reptilarium, rail bike); Viala-du-Pas-de-Jaux; Saint-Jean-d'Alcas (12½–18½ miles/20–30 km).
• Lodève (15 miles/24 km).
• Cirque de Navacelles (21 miles/34 km).
• Millau Viaduct (22 miles/35 km).

Aveyron (12)
Population: 189
Altitude: 2,546 ft. (776 m)

TOURIST INFO—LARZAC ET VALLÉES
05 65 62 23 64
tourisme-larzac.com
TOURIST INFO—LA COUVERTOIRADE
05 65 58 55 59
lacouvertoirade.com

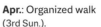 **EVENTS**

Apr.: Organized walk (3rd Sun.).
Jul.: Artistes au Village (early Jul.); Théâtre de l'Ante, open-air theater tour.
Aug.: Classical and modern theater; American Indian festival (2nd weekend).

 OUTDOOR ACTIVITIES

Walking: 2 marked trails • Communal garden • Park • Fishing.

Crissay-sur-Manse

A backdrop of tufa stone in the Touraine

Known as "Cryseio" in the 9th century (meaning "place where a fortress stands"), Crissay has preserved its castle, its houses, its gardens, and two washhouses bordering the Manse river, which meanders beneath the poplars. Originally a castellany belonging to L'Île-Bouchard and the Archdiocese of Tours, Crissay became the fiefdom of the Turpin de Crissé family for almost five centuries. In the 15th century, the Château de Crissay was built on the foundations of the old fortress. This seigneurial residence was never completed, nor lived in, and today only the main building, the 11th- and 12th-century keep, and underground shelters remain. Commissioned by the Turpins and finished in 1527, the church contains two 16th-century wooden statues representing Saint John and the Virgin, a piscina with floral *rinceaux* in the chancel, and the tomb of Catherine du Bellay, a cousin of the poet Joachin du Bellay (c. 1522-1560).

 HIGHLIGHTS

Château de Crissay (15th century): Owned by an association; paid access to grounds, chapel, old tufa quarry, 13th-century ruins, and vegetable garden, Jun.–Sept.; cultural events all summer (06 22 63 44 93).
Église Saint-Maurice (16th century): 16th-century statues.

 ACCOMMODATION & EATING OUT

azay-chinon-valdeloire.com

 LOCAL SPECIALTIES

Food and Drink
Goat cheeses • Honey • Chardonnay, vin de pays, and AOC Chinon wine.
Art and Crafts
Art galleries • Historic bookshop.

 FURTHER AFIELD

•Les Roches-Tranchelion: Ruins of castle and collegiate church (1 mile/2 km).
•Vallée de la Vienne: From L'Île-Bouchard to Chinon (4½–13½ miles/7-22 km).
•Panzoult: Cave des Vignerons, sculpted wine cellars (4½ miles/7 km).
•Tavant: Church frescoes (7 miles/11 km).
•Azay-le-Rideau: Castle (12 miles/19 km).

Indre-et-Loire (37)
Population: 110
Altitude: 197 ft. (60 m)

TOURIST INFO—AZAY-CHINON VAL DE LOIRE
02 47 45 44 40
azay-chinon-valdeloire.com
crissaysurmanse.fr

Curemonte

A village of lords and winegrowers

Punctuated by the towers of its three castles, the profile of Curemonte stands out above the Sourdoire and Maumont valleys. The village is built on a long sandstone spur. Standing near the three castles—the square-towered Saint-Hilaire, the round-towered Plas, and La Johannie—the Romanesque Église Saint-Barthélemy contains an altarpiece from 1672, and altars of Saint John the Baptist and the Virgin Mary from the 17th and 18th centuries. The late 18th-century covered market houses a Gothic cross shaft. In an enduringly simple, rural atmosphere, elegant Renaissance residences stand side by side with old winegrowers' houses in a harmony of pale sandstone and brown roof tiles. Outside the village, the Romanesque Église Saint-Genest, decorated with 15th-century paintings, houses a museum of religious artifacts, while the recently restored Église de La Combe is a masterpiece of late 11th-century architecture and one of the oldest religious buildings in Corrèze.

LOCAL SPECIALTIES

Food and Drink
Garlic and shallots • Dandelion jam and aperitifs (Lou Pé Dé Gril) • Craft beers.

 OUTDOOR ACTIVITIES

Fishing • Walking: Route GR 480 and the "Boucle Verte" circular route linking Curemonte to Collonges-la-Rouge.

 **HIGHLIGHTS**

Châteaux de Saint-Hilaire and des Plas: Guided tours Jul.–Sept. (05 55 25 47 57 / 05 55 25 34 76).
Église Saint-Barthélemy (12th century): 17th-century wooden altarpiece.
Église de La Combe (11th century): Exhibitions in summer.
Église Saint-Genest (14th century): Museum of religious artifacts.
Village: Guided tour by Les Amis de Curemonte association all year round, by appt. (06 80 40 98 63 / 06 59 26 73 04); "Le Village des Trois" route on the Tèrra Aventura app.

 ACCOMMODATION & EATING OUT

vallee-dordogne.com

 FURTHER AFIELD

• La Chapelle-aux-Saints: Prehistoric site; Musée de l'Homme de Néandertal, museum (2 miles/3 km).
• Brive-la-Gaillarde: Market; Jardins de Colette, gardens (25 miles/40 km).

MBVF NEARBY
• Vallée de la Dordogne: Collonges-la-Rouge (7½ miles/12 km), Beaulieu-sur-Dordogne (8 miles/13 km), Carennac (8½ miles/14 km), Turenne (11 miles/18 km).
• Loubressac (14 miles/23 km).
• Autoire (16 miles/26 km).

Corrèze (19)
Population: 208
Altitude: 689 ft. (210 m)

TOURIST INFO—VALLÉE DE LA DORDOGNE
05 65 33 22 00
vallee-dordogne.com

Art and Crafts
Jewelry • Painter • Antiques • Natural cosmetics • Ceramics.

 EVENTS

Market: Thurs. a.m., Place de la Halle.
Jun.: Amateur theater festival (2nd weekend).
Jul.: Dance, fireworks (14th).

 OUTDOOR ACTIVITIES

Canoeing and kayaking • Walking: Route GR 64 and marked trails, Chemin d'Amadour, Chemins de Harrison Barker • Air sports: Light and ultralight aircraft • Mountain biking.

 FURTHER AFIELD

• Sarlat (7½ miles/12 km).

 MBVF NEARBY
• La Roque-Gageac (3 miles/5 km).
• Castelnaud-la-Chapelle (5½ miles/9 km).
• Beynac-et-Cazenac (6 miles/10 km).
• Belvès (15½ miles/25km).
• Les Eyzies (21 miles/34 km).
• Saint-Amand-de-Coly (23 miles/37 km).

Domme

A panoramic viewpoint over the Dordogne

On the edge of a breathtakingly high cliff, Domme offers a remarkable view over the Dordogne valley. Towering 492 ft. (150 m) over the meandering river, Domme's exceptional site accounts for it being one of the most beautiful *bastides* (fortified towns) in the southwest of France. It is also a coveted place marked by a long and turbulent history. Its ramparts, fortified gates, and towers, which served as prisons in the early 14th century, stand as imposing witnesses of its past. From the Place de la Rode, randomly dotted along flower-decked streets, are fine houses with golden façades and irregular roofs covered with brown tiles, such as the Maison du Batteur de Monnaie, embellished with a triple mullioned window, and the former courthouse of the seneschal, both built in the 13th century. Continuing on from the Place de la Halle, Domme offers a sweeping vista of the valley and its landscapes, marked by cultivated land and forests.

 HIGHLIGHTS

Église Notre-Dame-de-l'Assomption (17th century): Open daily.
Les Mystérieux Graffiti: Guided or self-guided tours of the graffiti carved in the prison walls (05 53 31 71 00).
Cave with concretions: Largest accessible cave in the Périgord Noir. Ascent by panoramic elevator with a view over the Dordogne valley (05 53 31 71 00).
Village: Tour in Jul. and Aug., by appt. offseason (05 53 31 71 00); tour of the village by tourist train.

 ACCOMMODATION & EATING OUT

perigordnoir-valleedordogne.com

 LOCAL SPECIALTIES

Food and Drink
Geese • Walnuts • Domme wine.

Dordogne (24)
Population: 907
Altitude: 689 ft. (210 m)

TOURIST INFO—PÉRIGORD NOIR - VALLÉE DORDOGNE
05 53 31 71 00
perigordnoir-valleedordogne.com

Eguisheim

Into the round

A stone's throw from Colmar, Eguisheim—the birthplace of wine-growing in Alsace—winds in concentric circles around its castle. The future Pope Leo IX (1002-1054) was born in the heart of this village. With every step, from courtyard to fountain, or from lane to square, the ever-present curve changes one's perspective of the colorful houses arrayed with flowers, half-timbering, and oriel windows. Rebuilt in the Gothic style, the Église Saint-Pierre-et-Saint-Paul is distinguished by its high square tower of yellow sandstone, and a magnificent tympanum depicting Christ in Majesty flanked by the two patron saints, Peter and Paul. The winegrowers' and coopers' houses, with their large courtyards, are a reminder that, as well as being a feast for the eyes, Eguisheim also delights the palate with its *grand cru* wines, which are celebrated with festivals throughout the year.

 HIGHLIGHTS

Chapel of the Château Saint-Léon (19th century): Relics of Pope Leo IX.
Église Saint-Pierre-et-Saint-Paul (11th-14th centuries): Polychromed wooden statue known as "the Opening Virgin" (13th century).
Parc des Cigognes (stork garden): Free entry to the enclosure; guided tour Tues. mid-Jun.–mid-Sept.
Vineyards: Guided tour of the wine route and guided tasting session, by appt. with winegrowers or Sat. mid-Jun.–mid-Sept. and Tues. in Aug. (03 89 23 40 33).
Village: Discovery tour (information panels with QR codes) and guided tour (03 89 23 40 33).

 ACCOMMODATION & EATING OUT

Hotels
♥ Hostellerie du Château*** (03 89 23 72 00).

 LOCAL SPECIALTIES

Food and Drink
Pretzels • *Pain d'épice* (spice cake) • Mushrooms • Alsatian charcuterie • AOC Alsace wines and Eichberg and Pfersigberg *grands crus*.
Art and Crafts
Painting • Upholstery.

 EVENTS

Market: Tues., 5–7:30 p.m., Parc du Millénaire (May–Oct.).
Jul.: Eguisheim wine festival and Nuit des Grands Crus (2nd fortnight).
Sept.: Fête du Vin Nouveau, new wine festival (last weekend).
Oct.: Fête du Champignon, mushroom festival (last weekend).

 OUTDOOR ACTIVITIES

Ultralight aircraft • Cycling • Walking: 12 marked trails • Segway rides.

 FURTHER AFIELD

•Hautes Vosges: Vallée de Munster; Col de la Schlucht (3–18½ miles/5–30 km).
•Colmar (3½ miles/6 km).
•Château du Hohlandsbourg and Five Castles route (5 miles/8 km).

 MBVF NEARBY
•Riquewihr (10½ miles/17 km).
•Hunawihr (12 miles/19 km).

Haut-Rhin (68)
Population: 1,763
Altitude: 689 ft. (210 m)

TOURIST INFO—PAYS D'EGUISHEIM ET ROUFFACH
03 89 23 40 33
tourisme-eguisheim-rouffach .com

Entrevaux
Citadel of the Alps

Seated at the foot of a rocky ridge sloping down to the clear waters of a bend in the Var river, this fortified village embodies a perfect blend of landscapes and architecture typical of the southern Alps. A former Roman town, Entrevaux developed around a rocky overhang, dominated by its imposing citadel perched 512 ft. (156 m) above the village. Confined within its ramparts, the town began gradually migrating toward the left bank of the Var in the 10th century. In 1693, Vauban strengthened Entrevaux's fortifications on the orders of Louis XIV. The village still bears traces of its agricultural past, including its aqueduct, washhouse, and flour and oil mills, one of which is still in operation. Entrevaux is characterized by its medieval architecture, as seen in its royal gate and drawbridge, as well as its many tall houses and shops. The 17th-century cathedral blends into the landscape, its Gothic architecture mingling with the surrounding mountains and olive trees.

 HIGHLIGHTS

Citadel: Gunpowder museum, old dungeons, keep, underground passages, 360° panoramic view of the village; open daily (04 93 05 46 73).
Cathédrale Notre-Dame de l'Assomption d'Entrevaux (17th century): Painting of the Assumption of Mary (17th century), organ (18th century).
Musée de la Moto: Collection of 100 European motorcycle models; open weekends and public holidays Apr.–Jun. and Sept.; open daily Jul.–Aug. (06 62 16 12 70).
Oil and flour mills: Self-guided tour with videos and games via the mobile app; free loan of tablets from tourist info center (04 93 05 46 73).
Parcours Chemin de Ronde: Exhibitions on the history, traditions, and customs of Entrevaux; Apr.–Nov., admission fee.
Village: Self-guided heritage tour, map available at tourist info center; guided group tour (04 93 05 46 73).

 ACCOMMODATION & EATING OUT

Campsites
♥ Camping du Brec*** (04 93 05 42 45).

 LOCAL SPECIALTIES

Food and Drink
Secca de boeuf (dried and salted beef) • Olive oil • Honey • Apples and fruit juices • *Pain d'épice* (spice cake).

Art and Crafts
Jewelry • Art gallery • Fresco artist.

 EVENTS

Market: Fri. 7 a.m.–1 p.m., Place Moreau (Apr.–Oct.).
Apr.: Plant fair (last Sat.).
Jun.: Pilgrimage of Saint John the Baptist (weekend following summer solstice).
Sept.: Fall fair (last Sat.).
Oct.: Jean Rolland criterium (2nd or 3rd weekend).

 OUTDOOR ACTIVITIES

Walking: Routes GR 4, GRP Vallée de la Vaïre, and several circuits and hiking paths • Fishing • Canoeing • Rafting.

FURTHER AFIELD

•Puget-Théniers (5 miles/8 km).
•Annot (8½ miles/14 km).
•Gorges de Daluis and du Cians (11 miles/18 km).
•Lac de Castillon (19 miles/30 km).

Alpes-de-Haute-Provence (04)
Population: 810
Altitude: 1,362–5,056 ft. (414–1,541 m)

TOURIST INFO—VERDON TOURISME
04 93 05 46 73
verdontourisme.com

Estaing

One family, one castle

A short distance from the Gorges du Lot, set against a backdrop of greenery, Estaing is distinguished by an imposing castle that overlooks the *lauze* (schist tile) roofs of the houses. The illustrious Estaing family left its mark on the history of the former province of Rouergue, but also on that of France. The Château des Comtes d'Estaing (11th century to present) mixes Romanesque, Gothic, Flamboyant, and Renaissance styles. On the Place François Annat, the 15th-century church, which has some remarkable altarpieces and stained-glass windows, houses the relics of Saint Fleuret. The fine Renaissance houses at the heart of the village continue to attract tourists. Providing a magnificent entrance point to the village from the Saint James's Way is the 16th-century Gothic bridge, which is on the UNESCO World Heritage list and offers unique views of the castle, the village's crowning feature.

 HIGHLIGHTS

❤ **Castle** (11th century to present): Open in tourist season. Self-guided visit of the restored rooms; paid guided tour by appt. (05 65 44 72 24).

Église Saint-Fleuret (15th century): Gilded wooden altarpieces (17th and 18th centuries); relics of Saint Fleuret; contemporary stained-glass windows by Claude Baillon.

Chapelle de l'Ouradou (16th century): Gothic chapel with four-eyed bell gable (05 65 44 10 63).

Village: Guided group tour by appt. at the tourist info center; tour by torchlight Jul.–Aug. (05 65 44 10 63).

 **ACCOMMODATION & EATING OUT**

terresdaveyron.fr

 LOCAL SPECIALTIES

Food and Drink
White, red, and rosé wines, AOC and IGP Aveyron wines.
Art and Crafts
Bag and accessory designer • Jewelry designer • Bladesmith • Illuminator.

📅 **EVENTS**

Market: Wed. 6 p.m., on the quay (Jul.–Aug.).
Jun. 15–Sept. 15: Son et Lumière d'Estaing, 1,500 Ans d'Histoire, sound and light show (Wed. evening).
Jul.: Fête de la Saint-Fleuret, traditional parade (1st Sun.).

Aug.: Nuit Lumière, illumination of the village by candlelight, fireworks (15th).
Sept.: Les Médiévales d'Estaing, medieval festival (2nd weekend).

 OUTDOOR ACTIVITIES

Trout fishing • Walking: Routes GR 65 and 6; topographic guide (23 circular walks), and walking tour of the village • Trail circuit.

 FURTHER AFIELD

•Maison de la Vigne, du Vin, et des Paysages d'Estaing (3 miles/5 km).
•Villecomtal (9½ miles/15 km).
•Gorges de la Truyère (15½ miles/25 km).
•Laguiole; Aubrac (16 miles/26 km).

 MBVF NEARBY
•Saint-Côme-d'Olt (8½ miles/14 km).

Aveyron (12)
Population: 492
Altitude: 1,050 ft. (320 m)

TOURIST INFO—TERRES D'AVEYRON
05 65 44 10 63
terresdaveyron.fr

Jan.: Fête de la Saint-Vincent (22nd).
Easter Monday: Goig Dels Ous, Catalan Easter songs presented by the Cant'Eus choir.
Jun.: Croisée d'Arts, contemporary art festival (1st weekend).
Jul.: Mès De Jazz, jazz festival (1st weekend).
Aug.: Les Nits d'Eus, music and theater festival; Course des Lézards, trail racing (last Sun.).

Eus

A feel of the South

Eus is filled with the fragrance of orchards, old olive groves, and the garigue (scrubland). The village, which takes its name from the surrounding *yeuses* (holm oaks), is built on terraces sheltered from the wind. Designed for defense, it drove off the French in 1598 and the Spanish army, which at that time dominated the region, in 1793. The 18th-century Église Saint-Vincent stands on the site of the Roman camp that kept watch over the road from Terrenera to Cerdagne, and of the former castle chapel, Notre-Dame-de-la-Volta, built in the 13th century. At the entrance to Eus, a Romanesque chapel is dedicated to the patron saint of wine-growers and to Saint Gaudérique. It opens onto a 13th-century porch made from pink marble from Villefranche-de-Conflent. Clinging to the steep, cobblestone streets, the old restored shale-stone houses give the village a harmonious feel.

 HIGHLIGHTS

Romanesque chapel (11th–13th centuries).
Église Saint-Vincent (18th century): 17th- and 18th-century altarpieces and statues.
Musée La Solana: Popular traditions, 19th- and 20th-century tools, agricultural machinery, and everyday objects (04 68 96 50 21).

 ACCOMMODATION & EATING OUT

tourisme-canigou.com

 LOCAL SPECIALTIES

Food and Drink
Regional fruit and vegetables • Fruit juices • Cider • Honey.
Art and Crafts
Wrought ironwork • Paintings • Photographs • Sculptures • Stained glass • Art gallery.

 OUTDOOR ACTIVITIES

Walking: 9 marked trails • Adventure and leisure park (Kap'oupa Kap).

 FURTHER AFIELD

• Prades; Abbaye Saint-Michel-de-Cuxa (3½ miles/6 km).
• Marcevol: Priory (6 miles/10 km).
• Vernet-les-Bains; Abbaye Saint-Martin-du-Canigou (11 miles/18 km).

 MBVF NEARBY

• Villefranche-de-Conflent (7½ miles/12 km).
• Évol (15 miles/24 km).

Pyrénées-Orientales (66)
Population: 377
Altitude: 1,270 ft. (387 m)

TOURIST INFO—CONFLENT-CANIGÓ
04 68 05 41 02
tourisme-canigou.com

Évol (Commune of Olette)

"A piece of sky on the mountain"

In the foothills of the Massif du Madrès, on the side of a valley, the hamlet of Évol springs forth from the mountain. According to Catalan bard Ludovic Massé, who was born here in 1900, Évol, "far from everything," is "a piece of the sky on the mountain whose only shade is from clouds." Invisible from the road that leads from the plain to Cerdagne, the village emerges like a jewel in its verdant setting. Overlooked by the old fortress of the viscounts of So and the bell tower of the Romanesque church, Évol remains in perfect harmony with the mountain, which provides a livelihood for its shepherds and can be seen in the shale of its walls and the blue *lauzes* (schist tiles) of its roofs. Along the winding, flower-filled streets, bread ovens, a fig-drying kiln, barns, and interior courtyards bear witness to the daily life of a bygone era.

HIGHLIGHTS

Église Saint-André (11th century): Conjuratory (small religious building), 15th- and 16th-century altarpieces, Romanesque statue of the Virgin (13th century).
Viscounts' castle ruins (13th century): Preserved tower, viewpoint.
Chapelle Saint-Étienne (13th century, rebuilt in 18th century).
Musée des Arts et Traditions Populaires: Museum of popular arts and traditions housed in a former school. Reconstruction of a classroom, old tools, library of Ludovic Massé (Catalan writer). Guided tour by appt., Évol la Médiévale association (04 68 97 09 72 / 06 13 04 19 86).
Village: Guided tour (04 68 97 09 72 / 06 13 04 19 86).
Église Saint-André d'Olette (11th–17th centuries).

ACCOMMODATION & EATING OUT

tourisme-canigo.com

LOCAL SPECIALTIES

Art and Crafts
Jewelry.

EVENTS

Market: Fri. 8 a.m.–1 p.m, Place du Village, Olette.
Late Apr.–early May: Transhumance des Mérens (horses).

OUTDOOR ACTIVITIES

Trout fishing (Évol river) • La Bastide lakes • Walking • Mountain biking: "Madres-Coronat" trails.

FURTHER AFIELD

• Saint-Thomas-les-Bains (6 miles/10 km).
• Prades (11 miles/18 km).
• Vernet-les-Bains: Abbaye Saint-Martin-du-Canigou (12 miles/19 km).

MBVF NEARBY

• Villefranche-de-Conflent (8 miles/13 km).
• Eus (15 miles/24 km).

Pyrénées-Orientales (66)
Population: 347
Altitude: 2,625 ft. (800 m)

TOURIST INFO—CONFLENT-CANIGÓ
04 68 05 41 02
tourisme-canigo.com

Flavigny-sur-Ozerain

A sweet-smelling site

First established at the time of Julius Caesar and Vercingetorix, Flavigny owes its reputation to a religious activity that is still very much alive and an aniseed candy that is enjoyed the world over. The Romans chose this location during the siege of Alesia in 52 BCE, and it grew into a Gallo-Roman settlement named "Flaviniacum," after Flavinius, a Roman officer. The town expanded with the founding of the Benedictine abbey of Saint-Pierre, which is where the famous candies are now produced. The parish church of Saint-Genest, with nave and aisles partially surmounted by a 13th-century gallery, contains stalls made by the brotherhood in the 15th century. Remnants of the medieval fortifications include the Portes du Val, de la Poterne, and du Bourg, as well as the *chemin de ronde* (wall-walk), from where the view stretches out over the green hills of Auxois.

HIGHLIGHTS

Crypt of the Abbaye Saint-Pierre (8th century).
Église Saint-Genest (13th–16th centuries): Gothic style, 15th-century stalls and rood screen (07 57 40 75 87 / 03 80 96 21 73).
♥ **Aniseed factory**: In the former Abbaye Saint-Pierre; free entry and tastings, museum (03 80 96 20 88).
Hélixine: Organic snail farmer, tours in peak season (07 83 38 96 33).
Maison des Arts Textiles et du Design: Algranate museum-collection, exhibitions, traditional Auxois weaving workshop (03 80 96 20 40).
Domaine de Flavigny-Alésia vineyards: Self-guided tour of the winery and free tasting (03 80 96 25 63).
Brasserie de Flavigny: Tour of the fermenting room (06 16 26 51 22).
Village: Guided group tour by appt. (07 57 40 75 87).

ACCOMMODATION & EATING OUT

Guesthouses
♥ La Flavignienne (06 31 28 41 51).

LOCAL SPECIALTIES

Food and Drink
Abbaye de Flavigny aniseed confectionery • Vins de pays des Coteaux de l'Auxois • Organic snails • Flavigny beer.
Art and Crafts
Art galleries • Pottery • Essential oils.

EVENTS

Jun.: Livres au Jardin, book festival (early Jun.); La Nuit Romantique (first Sat. after summer solstice).
Aug.: PontiCelli cello workshops (early Aug.).
Oct.: Marché de la Saint-Simon, regional market (penultimate Sun.).
Dec.–Jan.: Christmas market, nativity scenes in streets.

OUTDOOR ACTIVITIES

Fishing • Mountain biking • Walking and horseback riding: 5 marked trails • Mountain trail course.

FURTHER AFIELD

• Archaeological site of Alésia; Château de Bussy-Rabutin; Venarey-les-Laumes: Burgundy Canal (3–6 miles/5–10 km).
• Semur-en-Auxois; Buffon: Foundry; Montbard; Abbaye de Fontenay (10½–15½ miles/17–25 km).

MBVF NEARBY
• Châteauneuf (25 miles/40 km).

Côte-d'Or (21)
Population: 300
Altitude: 1,398 ft. (426 m)

TOURIST INFO—PAYS D'ALÉSIA ET DE LA SEINE
03 80 96 89 13
alesia-tourisme.net
TOWN HALL
03 80 96 21 73
flavigny-sur-ozerain.fr

La Flotte

Port on the Île de Ré

Facing the Pertuis Breton tidal estuary and the mainland, the village of La Flotte encircles the harbor, bathed in the ocean's light. Although now effectively a peninsula, since it was joined to the mainland by a long bridge, the island of Ré has lost none of its magical light, which changes with the tides. The gentle landscapes of this "sandy, windswept island," as Cardinal Richelieu called it, combine coastal flowers, vines, and salt marshes with fields of fruit and vegetables and oyster beds, and its green-shuttered houses are dazzlingly white. In a natural environment that has been impeccably preserved, La Flotte contributes the soulful remains of the Abbaye des Châteliers; the imposing Fort La Prée, built in the 17th century in the face of English invasions; and, if the visitor winds their way through the maze of restored and flower-decked lanes around the Église Sainte-Catherine, a picturesque harbor bustling with pleasure craft all year round. On the other side of its double pier, the ocean still separates (disregarding the bridge) the "white island" from the mainland.

 **HIGHLIGHTS**

Fort La Prée (17th century): A Vauban construction. Apr.–Sept. and last fortnight of Oct.; guided tour by appt. (05 46 09 73 33).

La Maison du Platin: Museum dedicated to life on Île de Ré, with collections on the island's traditional occupations (05 46 09 61 39).

Ruins of the Cistercian Abbaye des Châteliers (12th century): Self-guided tour or guided tour by appt. (05 46 09 61 39).

Église Sainte-Catherine (15th–19th centuries): Paintings and votive offerings, bell donated by Cardinal Richelieu in 1632 (05 46 09 60 13).

Village: Guided tour by appt. (05 46 09 61 39).

 ACCOMMODATION & EATING OUT

iledere.com

 **LOCAL SPECIALTIES**

Food and Drink
Ré oysters • Spring vegetables • Pineau, wines • *Sel de Ré* (salt).

Art and Crafts
Art galleries • Painters.

 EVENTS

Market: Daily, 8 a.m.–1 p.m., Rue du Marché.
May: Fête du Port (around 20th).
Jul.–Aug.: Musical events at the harbor; evening market (daily).

Aug.: La Flotte Met les Voiles, gathering of old sailing vessels and firework display (mid-Aug.).

 OUTDOOR ACTIVITIES

Swimming (lifeguard) in Jul. and Aug. (Plage de l'Arnérault) • Horseback riding • Pleasure boating • Shellfish gathering • Bike rides (rental) • Water sports: Swimming, sailing, windsurfing.

 FURTHER AFIELD

•La Rochelle (9½ miles/15 km).
•Îles d'Aix, Madame, and d'Oléron (18½– 28 miles/30–45 km).
•Rochefort (25 miles/40 km).
•Marais Poitevin, region (25 miles/40 km).

 MBVF NEARBY
•Ars-en-Ré (10½ miles/17 km).

Charente-Maritime (17)
Population: 2,903
Altitude: 56 ft. (17 m)

TOURIST INFO— DESTINATION ÎLE DE RÉ
05 46 09 00 55
iledere.com

Fontevraud-l'Abbaye

A royal stopover in the Saumur region

The narrow, flower-lined streets of Fontevraud, situated on the borders of the Anjou, Poitou, and Touraine regions, are home to the last residence of the Plantagenets, located in the village's royal abbey. No fewer than four women's priories and one men's priory were founded in the 12th century in this remote area surrounding the "fount of Évraud." With the support of several popes and the counts of Anjou, who would later sit on the throne of England, the priories grew to become a royal abbey that is now the largest preserved Romanesque monastic ensemble in France. For fifty years, the Centre Culturel de l'Ouest (western cultural center) has been promoting all forms of contemporary artistic creation on the site. The pleasures of visiting this bustling village include strolling along narrow streets lined with tuffeau stone façades embellished with hollyhocks, meeting master craftspeople, and exploring the Loire-Anjou-Touraine regional nature park.

 HIGHLIGHTS

Abbey: Abbey church (12th century) with recumbent statues of Henry II, Eleanor of Aquitaine, Richard the Lionheart, and Isabella of Angouleme; cloister; Romanesque kitchens (12th century); archaeological crypt; refectory known as the *salle capitulaire* (16th century) and treasury; museum of modern art (02 41 51 73 52).
Église Paroissiale Saint-Michel (12th, 15th, and 17th centuries): 17th-century gilded wood altar.
Village: Heritage trail (includes Fontaine Saint-Mainbœuf, Pont-Boucherie, Église Saint-Michel, dovecotes, Rue Robert d'Arbrissel, and Chapelle Notre-Dame-de-Pitié) with informative leaflet (available at tourist info center or town hall, 02 41 51 79 45).

 ACCOMMODATION & EATING OUT

ot-saumur.fr

 **LOCAL SPECIALTIES**

Art and Crafts
Ceramics • Illuminator • Painter • Soapmaker • Stained-glass artist.

 EVENTS

Market: Wed. 8:30 a.m.–12 p.m., Place des Plantagenêts.
Dec.: Holiday light display; Noël à Fontevraud, Christmas cultural festival.

 **OUTDOOR ACTIVITIES**

Walking: Routes GR 3 and GR de Pays—Loire à Vélo, Chemin d'Aliénor, Circuit d'Abbaye en Châteaux • Horseback riding: Route d'Artagnan.

 FURTHER AFIELD

• Turquant: Village Métiers d'Art en troglo, artisan studios in troglodyte caves (4 miles/6.5 km).
• Saumur: Château; Cadre Noir interpretive center (9 miles/15 km).
• Doué-la-Fontaine: Zoo, troglodyte caves (10 miles/16 km).
• Montreuil-Bellay: Château (11 miles/18 km).

 MBVF NEARBY
• Montsoreau (2½ miles/4 km).
• Candes-Saint-Martin (3 miles/4.5 km).

Maine-et-Loire (49)
Population: 1,522
Altitude: 262 ft. (80 m)

TOURIST INFO—FONTEVRAUD-L'ABBAYE
02 41 51 79 45
TOURIST INFO—SAUMUR - VAL DE LOIRE
02 41 40 20 60
ot-saumur.fr

Art and Crafts

Antiques • Jewelry and accessories designer • Craft boutique.

EVENTS

Apr.: Flower market (last weekend).
May: Pottery and ceramics market (4th weekend).
Jul.: Antiquarian book fair (3rd Sun.).
Aug.: Jazz in Fourcès (mid-Aug.); village fair (3rd weekend).

Fourcès

A medieval ring in Gascony

On the banks of the Auzoue river, Fourcès opens up like a living history book. The village's round plaza occupies the site where the motte-and-bailey castle, built in the 11th century and destroyed in the 15th century, once stood. At the western entrance to the village, the Tour de l'Horloge (clock tower), built in the 12th century, opens onto a pretty square lined with plane trees, where medieval oak timber framed houses are arranged in a ring, alongside more recent residences from the 17th and 18th centuries. Set against a theatrical backdrop of arcades and half-timbered façades, the square hosts an exceptional flower market each year. The church, dedicated to Saint-Laurent, was built on the remains of a former Romanesque church dating from the 13th century. It was rebuilt around 1870 in a neo-Gothic style and features outstanding stained-glass windows. On the banks of the river, the 15th-century Renaissance-style château has been converted into a charming guesthouse.

HIGHLIGHTS

Arboretum: Free entry.
Église Saint-Laurent (13th century) **and Église Sainte-Quitterie** (pre-Romanesque).
La Galerie de Mémoire (memory gallery): Old tools in a contemporary atmosphere. By appt., in the village.
Village: Guided group tours by appt. (05 62 28 00 80). Visitor information and treasure hunt available to download on tourismecondom.com or at tourist info center; Geocaching trail "La Clé des Champs, Les Portes d'Orée" (Tèrra Aventura app.).

ACCOMMODATION & EATING OUT

tourisme-condom.com

LOCAL SPECIALTIES

Food and Drink
Armagnac • Foie gras, duck fillet and confit • AOC Côtes de Gascogne wines.

OUTDOOR ACTIVITIES

Fishing • Leisure park • Open air escape game ("Le Mystère de la Croix Occitane," Mon. and Thur., Jul.–Aug., at tourist info center,) • Walking: GR 654 and several marked trails.

FURTHER AFIELD

• Bastide de Mézin (5½ miles/9 km).
• Condom (8 miles/13 km).
• Château de Cassaigne (9½ miles/15 km).

 MBVF NEARBY
• Larressingle (6 miles/10 km).
• Montréal (3½ miles/6 km).

Gers (32)
Population: 260
Altitude: 213 ft. (65 m)

TOURIST INFO—
LA TÉNARÈZE
05 62 28 00 80
tourisme-condom.com

La Garde-Adhémar

A jewel of nature and heritage in the Tricastin

La Garde-Adhémar exudes a mellow ease. Its medieval charm invites visitors to stroll the steep, cobblestoned streets and wander the fortifications, with their gates and elements of the château and fortified town. Vestiges of the Renaissance castle, built by Antoine Escalin, lie at the far end of the village. The Romanesque Église Saint-Michel and the Chapelle des Pénitents-Blancs are testimony to 12th-century Provençal architecture. The Jardin des Herbes stretches out below the church; the garden's French design, flowerbeds, and aromatic and medicinal plants make it a slice of paradise that willingly unveils all of its secrets. A number of hiking paths shaded by holm oaks and rosemary guide visitors towards the *lavoir* (washhouse) at the edge of the village. The Val des Nymphes, located less than 1½ miles (2 km) away, was once a Gallo-Roman, then later Christian, place of worship. Today, all that remains is the 12th-century Chapelle Notre-Dame.

HIGHLIGHTS

Église Saint-Michel (12th century): Western apse, statue of Notre-Dame-du-Bon-Secours (12th century), votive altar to nymph goddesses.
Jardin des Herbes: Botanical and medicinal gardens classed as "remarkable" by the Ministry of Culture, with 170 species cultivated on ¾ acre (3,000 m²) of terraces.
Village: Guided tour by appt. (04 75 04 40 10).
Val des Nymphes and Chapelle Notre-Dame (12th century; 1 mile/2 km from the village): Mysterious stone vats with lapidary markings, hiking trails.

ACCOMMODATION & EATING OUT

Gîtes
♥ La Closerie d'Escalin ♙♙♙ (04 75 04 98 48).

LOCAL SPECIALTIES

Food and Drink
Goat cheeses • Fruits • Olive oil • Truffles • Lavender • Wines.
Art and Crafts
Ceramist and enameler • Art galleries and studios • Paintings • Pottery • Sculptures.

OUTDOOR ACTIVITIES

Walking: 2 marked trails and Sentier des Arts • Mountain biking: Marked trails • Horseback riding trail.

⚲ FURTHER AFIELD

• Tricastin villages: Clansayes, Saint-Paul-Trois-Châteaux, Saint-Restitut (4½–9½ miles/7-15 km).
• Pierrelatte: Crocodile farm (4½ miles/7 km).
• Châteaux de Grignan and de Suze-la-Rousse, Valréas (10½-17 miles/17-27 km).

MBVF NEARBY

• Séguret (25½ miles/41 km).

Drôme (26)
Population: 1,149
Altitude: 558 ft. (170 m)

TOURIST INFO—DRÔME SUD PROVENCE
04 75 04 40 10
drome-sud-provence.com

La Garde-Guérin

(Commune of Prévenchères)

In the knights' shadow

The archetype of a fortified village, La Garde-Guérin has retained its 12th-century structure. The fortified village can be seen from afar, as it is built at an altitude of nearly 3,000 ft. (900 m), and is remarkably situated 1,300 ft. (400 m) above the nearby Chassezac Gorge. The site is crossed by the Régordane Way, a natural communication route linking the Mediterranean to the Auvergne through Nîmes and Le Puy. In the Middle Ages, a community of knights, known as the *chevaliers pariers* (knights with equal rights), settled in the village to provide protection to travelers using this route and safeguard their animals and goods. Inside the ramparts stand the tall watchtower and the former Chapelle Saint-Michel, as well as the walls of the castle that the Molette de Morangiès family built in the 16th century. Today, the site's history and its rugged natural landscape lend a wild and mysterious beauty to La Garde-Guérin.

HIGHLIGHTS

Village: Guided group tour (04 66 46 87 12 / 06 74 97 22 32).
Église Saint-Michel (12th century): Romanesque former chapel of the village; gilded wooden statue of Saint Michael (18th century), painting of the Crucifixion.
Castle remains: 12th-century tower, 72 ft. (22 m) high on five levels.

ACCOMMODATION & EATING OUT

lagardeguerin.fr

LOCAL SPECIALTIES

Food and Drink
Comptoir de la Regordane: Beef, Lozère lamb and pork • Organic lake trout • Pâtés • Honey • Chestnut products • Craft beers • Fruit juices • Jams.
Art and Crafts
La Parérie (artisans collective): Creations in wood, metal, leather, glass, textiles, wicker.

EVENTS

Jun.: Transhumance (1st Sun. after 15th).
Aug.: Prévenchères festival (1st weekend); Fête du Pain, bread festival (2nd weekend); Festival des Pastorels, shepherds' festival (mid-Aug.).

OUTDOOR ACTIVITIES

Canyoning • Rock climbing and Via Corda • Walking and mountain biking: Routes GR 700 (Chemin de Régordane) and GR 70 (Chemin de Stevenson), numerous marked trails • Caving • Golf: 9 holes • Trout fishing (in the Chassezac).

FURTHER AFIELD

• Lac de Villefort and Lac de Rachas, lakes (3 miles/5 km).
• Prévenchères: Château de Castanet, 12th-century church and its *tilleul de Sully*, a historic linden tree (3½ miles/6 km).
• Mas de La Barque and Mont Lozère (15½ miles/25 km).
• Langogne (23 miles/37 km).

MBVF NEARBY
• Pradelles (28 miles/45 km).

Lozère (48)
Population: 257
Altitude: 2,953 ft. (900 m)

TOURIST INFO—MONT-LOZÈRE
04 66 46 87 30
destination-montlozere.fr
lagardeguerin.fr

Gargilesse-Dampierre

George Sand's refuge

This romantic village, with its harmonious houses overlooked by the château and church, stretches out over a sloping headland rich in vegetation. In 1857, novelist George Sand discovered this village, whose "houses are grouped around the church, planted on a central rock, and slope down along narrow streets toward the bed of a delightful stream, which, a little further on and lower down, loses itself in the Creuse." Only a postern and two round towers survive of the medieval castle, the rest of which was destroyed in 1650 during the Fronde (civil wars, 1648–53) and the extant château was built on its ruins in the 18th century. The 11th–12th-century Romanesque church, with its fine white limestone stonework, adjoins it. Following in the footsteps of Léon Detroy (1859-1955), many artists have found their inspiration here, perpetuating the artistic tradition of the village and exhibiting their works.

 **HIGHLIGHTS**

Castle (12th-18th century): Art gallery (02 54 47 76 16 / 06 81 19 65 53).

Romanesque church (12th century): Capitals with narrative carvings, including the 24 elders in the Book of Revelation and biblical scenes; crypt with 13th–16th-century frescoes depicting the Instruments of the Passion and scenes from Mary and Jesus's lives; painted wooden Virgin (12th century). Guided tour daily in peak season (02 54 47 85 06).

Villa Algira, Maison de George Sand: Collection of the author's personal effects in her former vacation home (06 07 04 44 80 / 06 81 19 65 53).

Musée Serge Delaveau: Collection of works by the painter, who lived in Gargilesse: 02 54 47 85 06 / 06 31 86 47 94).

 ACCOMMODATION & EATING OUT

gargilesse.fr

 LOCAL SPECIALTIES

Food and Drink
Goat cheese (*Gargilesse*).
Art and Crafts
Picture framer • Metalworker • Art galleries • Pottery • Jewelry • Sculptor • Ceramics • Terrarium • Puppeteer.

 EVENTS

Mar.-Apr.: European Artistic Craft Days (late Mar.- early Apr.); Easter in Gargilesse (Easter weekend)
May: Flower and farm produce market (2nd Sun.).
Jul.: Gourmet market (3rd Wed.).
Aug.: Art exhibition in the street (Sun. before 15th); harp and chamber music festival (3rd week).
Sept.: Journées du Livre, book fair (2nd weekend).

 OUTDOOR ACTIVITIES

Swimming • Fishing • Walking: Routes GR Pays Val de Creuse and 654, Chemin de Compostelle (Saint James's Way), and 3 marked trails.

 FURTHER AFIELD

• Gorges de la Creuse (1 mile/2 km).
• Lac d'Éguzon, lake (7 miles/11 km).
• Argenton-sur-Creuse (8½ miles/14 km).
• Crozant (11 miles/18 km).

 MBVF NEARBY
• Saint-Benoît-du-Sault (15 miles/24 km).

Indre (36)
Population: 270
Altitude: 476 ft. (145 m)

TOURIST INFO—VALLÉE DE LA CREUSE
02 54 47 85 06
lavalleedelacreuse.fr
gargilesse.fr

Gassin

A peaceful haven on the Côte d'Azur

From its ridge encircled by vineyards and forests, Gassin has a unique view of the peninsula and Gulf of Saint-Tropez. Alongside the protection of its surrounding landscape, the development of the new village next door has also been sensitively handled—a feat that has earned Gassin several international awards. In addition to exploring the new village, visitors can enjoy a stroll through the maze of winding lanes in the old village, with its façades weathered by time, accompanied by the fragrance of oleanders, bougainvilleas, and jasmine. From the Deï Barri terrace, the view stretches from the Îles d'Hyères to the Massif des Maures and, when the Mistral has blown the clouds away, to the snow-capped summits of the Alps.

 HIGHLIGHTS

Église Notre Dame de l'Assomption (16th century): Historic font, 17th century reliquary of Saint Lawrence.
Vineyards: 10 estates offering tours and tastings; tourist train in peak season (04 98 11 56 51).
Jardin Botanique L'Hardy-Denonain: Botanical garden classed as "remarkable" by the Ministry of Culture, with Provençal and Mediterranean species. Tours Apr.–Oct. (04 94 56 18 72 / 04 98 11 56 51).
Jardin de Gassin: Rose garden with more than 300 varieties (06 78 48 03 00).
Medieval village: Free guided tour Mon. 4 p.m. Apr.–Oct., 5:30 p.m. Jul.–Aug.; temporary themed routes (certain school vacations; 04 98 11 56 51).

 **ACCOMMODATION & EATING OUT**

gassin.eu

 LOCAL SPECIALTIES

Food and Drink
Jams • Olive oil • AOC Côtes de Provence wines.
Art and Crafts
Interior decoration • Painters • Pottery • Soap making.

 EVENTS

Feb.: La Gassinoise, cross-country run and Nordic walking (2nd weekend).
Jun.: Montée Historique de Gassin, automobile race (2nd weekend); Polo Rider Cup, international tournament.
Aug.: Fête de la Saint-Laurent (1st weekend).

 **OUTDOOR ACTIVITIES**

Swimming (no lifeguard) • Horseback riding • Walking: Chemin de la Chapelle • Mountain biking • Golf: 18 holes • Sailing.

 FURTHER AFIELD

•Ramatuelle; Saint-Tropez; Pampelonne coastal path; Grimaud (3–6 miles/5–10 km).
•Massif des Maures; La Garde-Freinet; Jardins du Rayol, botanical gardens (8½–12½ miles/14–20 km).

Var (83)
Population: 2,642
Altitude: 656 ft. (200 m)

TOURIST INFO—GASSIN
04 98 11 56 51 | gassin.eu

Gerberoy

The roses of Picardy

On the border between two villages that were once rivals, the houses of Gerberoy combine Normandy and Picardy traditions, with wattle-and-daub half-timbering and brick slabs. The village, on the edge of the Pays de Bray, had a castle built in 922 at the instigation of the viscount of Fulco, lord and first vidame of Gerberoy. His son and successor completed the structure with a keep, a hospital, and a collegiate church in 1015. The square tower that controlled the curtain wall is the only remnant of the castle that once adjoined the collegiate church of Saint-Pierre. Rebuilt in the 15th century after being burned by the English, the latter still houses riches in its chapter house. Captivated by "the silent Gerberoy," the postimpressionist painter Henri Le Sidaner (1862–1939) created beautiful Italian-style gardens here that are visible from the ramparts, and helped to make Gerberoy a village of roses, which have been celebrated every year since 1928. The village's new museum takes visitors on a journey through time, bringing this enchanting setting to life.

 HIGHLIGHTS

Collégiale Saint-Pierre (11th and 15th centuries): 15th-century stalls, 18th-century sacristy credens.
Jardins Henri Le Sidaner: Terraces of the old fortress transformed by artist Le Sidaner into gardens (1 acre/4,000 m²), classed as "remarkable" by the Ministry of Culture; artist's studio/museum (03 44 46 32 20).
Jardin des Ifs: Garden unique in France for the age and size of its yew trees, awarded the "Jardin Remarquable" and "Arbre Remarquable" labels (07 66 20 51 41).
Musée Municipal: New museum experience showcasing Gerberoy's history and heritage (03 44 46 32 20).
Village: Guided group tour all year round by appt. (03 44 46 32 20).

 ACCOMMODATION & EATING OUT

gerberoy.net

 LOCAL SPECIALTIES

Art and Crafts
Rose products (soaps, preserves, candles) • Potter.

 EVENTS

Jun.: Fête des Roses, rose festival (1st Sun.); Moments Musicaux de Gerberoy, music festival.
Nov.: Country market (last Sun.).

 OUTDOOR ACTIVITIES

Walking: Route GR 125 and 3 marked trails.

 FURTHER AFIELD

•Picardie Verte and its valleys: Songeons; Hétomesnil; Saint-Arnoult (6–25 miles/10–40 km).
•Pays de Bray: Saint-Germer-de-Fly (8 miles/13 km).
•Forges-les-Eaux (22 miles/35 km).

 MBVF NEARBY

•Lyons-la-Forêt (22½ miles/36 km).

Oise (60)
Population: 83
Altitude: 617 ft. (188 m)

TOURIST INFO—LA PICARDIE VERTE ET SES VALLÉES
03 44 46 32 20
gerberoy-picardieverte.com
gerberoy.net

Gordes

Jewel of the Luberon

Like an eagle's nest perched on the foothills of the Monts de Vaucluse, facing the famous Luberon mountain, Gordes is the archetypal Provençal village. Surrounded by a mosaic of holm oaks, wheat fields, and vines, the village seems to form a cascade with its dry-stone houses clinging steadfastly to the rock. Numerous artists—including André Lhote (1885-1962), Pol Mara (1920-1998), and Victor Vasarely (1906-1997)—have been drawn by Gordes's rich history, architecture, and heritage, as well as its marvelous views, cobbled winding lanes, and fountain shaded by a plane tree on the Place du Château. A short distance from the village stands the Abbaye de Sénanque, at the edge of a lavender field that enhances the pale stone of its façade in springtime; this perfect example of Cistercian architecture is still inhabited by monks today.

 **HIGHLIGHTS**

Abbaye de Sénanque (12th century): Guided tour of church, dormitory, cloister, and chapter house (04 90 72 02 75).

Cellars of the Palais Saint-Firmin: Troglodytic rooms, cisterns, and old seigneurial oil press. Documentary and tour with MP3 audio guide (04 90 72 02 75).

Moulin des Bouillons / Musée du Vitrail: One of the oldest preserved oil mills, presses from the 1st to the 14th centuries; stained-glass museum at the same site (04 90 72 22 11).

Castle (16th century): Exhibitions by artists who have lived in Gordes or that relate to the history of the village, and temporary exhibitions (04 90 72 02 75).

Village des Bories: Museum of rural dry-stone dwellings (*bories*) (04 90 72 03 48).

Village: Guided tour by appt.; themed and evening tours Jul.-Aug. (04 90 72 02 75).

 ACCOMMODATION & EATING OUT

Hotels
♥ Le Mas de la Sénancole*** (04 90 76 76 55).

 LOCAL SPECIALTIES

Food and Drink
Honey • AOC Côtes du Ventoux wine • Olive oil.
Art and Crafts
Jewelry • Art galleries • Pottery • Sculptor.

 EVENTS

Market: Tues. a.m., Place du Château.
Aug.: Les Soirées d'Été festival (1st fortnight).
Dec.: Veillée Calendale, Christmas songs and tasting of the thirteen desserts, representative of Jesus and his apostles (1st fortnight); Christmas market.

 OUTDOOR ACTIVITIES

Walking: Route GR 6 and 2 marked trails • Cycling: "Gordes à Vélo" route • Mountain biking and electric mountain bike rentals.

 FURTHER AFIELD

•Oppède (7½ miles/12 km).
•Fontaine-de-Vaucluse (7½ miles/12 km).

MBVF NEARBY
•Roussillon (5½ miles/9 km).
•Ménerbes (7 miles/11 km).
•Venasque (9½ miles/15 km).

Vaucluse (84)
Population: 1,666
Altitude: 1,171 ft. (357 m)

**TOURIST INFO—
DESTINATION LUBERON**
04 90 72 02 75
destinationluberon.com

Gourdon

Between sea and sky

Perched above the Vallée du Loup, in the middle of the Préalpes d'Azur regional nature park, Gourdon looks out over the waters of the Mediterranean. Built on an isolated rock to defend against Saracen invasions in the 8th-10th centuries, Gourdon has often served as a stronghold. A first fortress was constructed in the 9th century. In the 12th century, the castle was built, overlooking the whole valley. Sheltered by the imposing fortress, the village is crisscrossed by infinitely narrow streets, showcasing its restored houses, the Romanesque Église Saint-Vincent, and numerous artisan shops. At the far end of the village stands its showpiece: the Place Victoria. Immortalized by Queen Victoria's visit in 1891, this panoramic viewpoint offers a breathtaking vista. In the late 19th century, the village spread to the hamlet of Pont-du-Loup, at the foot of the rock, in the Loup valley, where the climate was more conducive to growing aromatic plants.

 HIGHLIGHTS

Place Victoria: Panoramic viewpoint of the Côte d'Azur.
Église Saint-Vincent (12th century).
Galerie de la Mairie: Exhibitions (04 93 42 92 00).
Castle gardens: Designed by André Le Nôtre (1613-1700) (04 93 09 68 02).
Cascades du Saut du Loup (Gorges du Loup): Tour of waterfalls and viewpoint over the valley, May–Oct. (04 93 70 51 55).
Lavanderaies de la Source Parfumée: Fields of flowers and aromatic plants; guided group tour by a master gardener (04 93 09 68 23).

 ACCOMMODATION & EATING OUT

gourdon06.fr

 LOCAL SPECIALTIES

Food and Drink
Nougat and *calissons* (candy) • *Pain d'épice* (spice cake).
Art and Crafts
Perfumery • Soap making • Glassware.

 EVENTS

Aug.: Open-air theater festival (around 15th).
Nov.–Mar.: Theater festival, Pont-du-Loup (last Fri.).

 OUTDOOR ACTIVITIES

Paragliding • Walking: Chemin du Paradis and numerous marked trails.

 FURTHER AFIELD

• Gorges du Loup (5 miles/8 km).
• Grasse (8½ miles/14 km).
• Saint-Paul-de-Vence (16 miles/26 km).
• Côte d'Azur: Cannes, Antibes, Nice (17–22½ miles/27–36 km).

Alpes-Maritimes (06)
Population: 371
Altitude: 2,493 ft. (760 m)

TOURIST INFO—GOURDON
04 89 87 73 31
gourdon06.fr
agglo-sophiaantipolis.fr

Grignan

Letters from the Provençal Drôme

Lying between the Dauphiné and Provence, a short distance from the Enclave des Papes region, Grignan and its castle evoke new beginnings and the famous correspondence of Madame de Sévigné. Just as Grignan's houses seem to spring forth from the base of the imposing fortress, the history of the village is inseparable from that of its castle. The castle town, first recorded in the 12th century, developed at the behest of the Dauphiné's powerful Adhémar family. The village spread beyond the ramparts in the 16th century, when houses were constructed outside the walls, as well as the collegiate church of Saint-Sauveur. Later, major decorative improvements transformed the medieval fortress into the largest Renaissance château in southeastern France. From the castle's terraces, a superb view over the landscape of vineyards, lavender fields, and truffle-rich forest is a reminder that some of the best local produce in this part of the Drôme comes from Grignan.

 HIGHLIGHTS

Château de Grignan (11th-20th centuries): 16th–20th-century artworks, interactive exhibitions on the castle's architecture; self-guided and guided tours (04 75 91 83 50).
Collégiale Saint-Sauveur (16th century): 17th-century organ, Madame de Sévigné's tomb; self-guided tour.
Chapelle Saint-Vincent (12th-13th centuries): Contemporary stained-glass windows; self-guided tour all year round.
Colophon, Maison de l'Imprimeur: Museum of printing, typography workshops (04 75 46 57 16).
Jardin Sévigné: Gardens with hedge maze.
Village: Guided tours with tourist info center; guided tours of the "botanical village" by the Grignan, Pierres et Roses Anciennes association, end Apr.–early Jun. (04 75 46 56 75).

 ACCOMMODATION & EATING OUT

Hotel-restaurants
♥ Le Clair de la Plume**** (04 75 91 81 30).
♥ La Ferme Chapouton**** (04 75 00 01 01).
♥ La Bastide de Grignan*** (04 75 90 67 09).
Gîtes
♥ La Maison d'Ambrine***** (06 32 32 65 98).

 LOCAL SPECIALTIES

Food and Drink
Truffles • Goat cheeses • AOP Grignan-les-Adhémar and Côteaux du Tricastin wines.

Art and Crafts
Artist metalworker • Painter • Ceramics • Pottery • Textile designer • Metal sculptor.

 EVENTS

Market: Tues. 8 a.m.–12 p.m., Place du Mail.
Jan.-Feb.: Truffle and wine events (end Jan.–early Feb.).
May: Village fair (2nd Sun.).
Jul.-Aug.: Festival de la Correspondance (early Jul.); costumed evening markets.

 OUTDOOR ACTIVITIES

Horseback riding • Walking.

 FURTHER AFIELD

•Enclave des Papes: Grillon, Valréas, Visan, Richerenches (2½–9½ miles/4-15 km).
•Tricastin villages: Clansayes, Saint-Paul-Trois-Châteaux, Saint-Restitut (9½–12 miles/15-20 km).
•Nyons (14 miles/23 km).
•Montélimar (16 miles/25 km).

 MBVF NEARBY
•La Garde-Adhémar (10 miles/16 km).
•Le Poët-Laval (19 miles/30 km).

Drôme (26)
Population: 1,600
Altitude: 623 ft. (190 m)

TOURIST INFO—PAYS DE GRIGNAN - ENCLAVE DES PAPES
04 75 46 56 75
grignanvalreas-tourisme.com

Hell-Bourg
(Commune of Salazie)

Creole heritage at the heart of the "intense island"

On the southern side of the Cirque de Salazie amphitheater—the natural entrance to the "peaks, cirques, and ramparts" designated as a UNESCO World Heritage Site—Hell-Bourg devotes itself to Creole tradition, lifestyle, and hospitality. The Cirque de Salazie (a volcanic caldera) sets the scene for Hell-Bourg: ravines plunge into the Rivière du Mât and waterfalls flow down the rock face covered with lush vegetation that is maintained by the humidity of the trade winds blowing in from the Indian Ocean. The Hell-Bourg area was long a refuge for slaves fleeing the plantations on the coast, and was not colonized until 1830. With the discovery, the following year, of therapeutic springs, Hell-Bourg became a fashionable spa that was frequented by the island's well-to-do families every summer. Thatched huts gave way to villas adorned with pediments and mantling, surrounded by verandas opening onto gardens with bubbling fresh-water fountains.

 HIGHLIGHTS

Tour of Creole huts: Guided tour by Freddy Lafable (06 92 15 32 32) or Guid'A Nou (06 92 86 32 88); self-guided tour with audio guide (rental from tourist info center, 02 62 46 16 16).

Villa Folio and its garden: 19th-century Creole house, visitor interpretive center. Guided tours for individuals and groups (02 62 47 80 98 / 06 92 22 22 98).

Old thermal spa: Guided or self-guided tour (02 62 46 16 16).

Mare à Poule d'Eau: Explore the tropical flora and fauna of one of La Réunion's most beautiful stretches of water. Guided tour with Guid'A Nou (06 92 86 32 88).

Landscaped cemetery: Exceptional view of the Piton d'Anchaing and the center of the volcanic caldera.

• **Escape game**: Discover the village through an urban escape game (06 92 46 16 16).

• **Kér Maron**: Guided tour to discover the heart of the Maron kingdom: Creole stories, traditional picnic, nature workshops (06 92 45 48 54).

 ACCOMMODATION & EATING OUT

ville-salazie.fr

 LOCAL SPECIALTIES

Food and Drink
Creole produce.
Art and Crafts
Chayote straw braiding.

 EVENTS

Jul.: Fête du Chouchou, chayote fruit festival.
Aug.: CIMASA trail (last weekend).
Oct.: La Mascareignes trail (weekend around 20th).

OUTDOOR ACTIVITIES

Walking (60 miles/100 km of trails) • Rock climbing • Canyoning • Trail station dedicated to nature sports.

FURTHER AFIELD

• Natural and heritage sites of Salazie: Bé-Maho viewpoint, Mare à Poule d'Eau, Voile de la Mariée, old magma chamber at Bras Marron (2-10 miles/3-16 km).
• Bras-Panon: Vanilla cooperative (15½ miles/25 km).
• Grand-Îlet: Église Saint-Martin (18½ miles/30 km).
• Saint-André: Tamil temples, Parc du Colosse, Bois-Rouge sugar refinery, and Savanna rum distillery (25 miles/40 km).

La Réunion (974)
Population: 2,000
Altitude: 3,051 ft. (930 m)

TOURIST INFO—OFFICE DE TOURISME DE L'EST
02 62 46 16 16
reunionest.fr
ville-salazie.fr

Hunawihr

The colors of the vines

Situated on the Alsace wine route amid the vineyards, Hunawihr is a typical Alsatian village, bedecked with flowers. Hunawihr owes its name to a laundry-woman, Saint Huna; according to legend, she lived here in the 7th century with her husband, the Frankish lord Hunon. The church, dating from the 15th–16th centuries, contains 15th-century frescoes that recount the life of Saint Nicholas. Surrounded by a cemetery fortified by six bastions, it is built on the hill over-looking the village, whose attractions include the Fontaine Sainte Hune with its washhouse, the town hall (formerly the corn exchange), the Renaissance-style Maison Schickhardt, half-timbered houses, and bourgeois residences from the 16th and 19th centuries. Nature-lovers can visit the NaturOparC cen-ter for reintroducing storks and otters, and the butterfly garden, which are both magical places. Hunawihr is also famous for its marly-limestone terroir on which its vines thrive, particularly those of its *grand cru* Rosacker.

 **HIGHLIGHTS**

Church (15th and 16th centuries) **and fortified cemetery**: Saint Nicholas frescoes (15th century).
NaturOparC, Centre de Réintroduction des Cigognes et des Loutres: 12-acre (5-ha.) wildlife park dedicated to preserving storks, otters, and other local species (03 89 73 72 62).
Jardin des Papillons: Several hundred exotic butterflies from Africa, Asia, and the Americas, in a luxuriant garden (03 89 73 33 33).
Village: Guided tour of the church and village Jul.–Aug., Wed. 6.15 p.m. at the church; Randoland, discovery trail for kids aged 4–12 (03 89 73 23 23).
Grands Crus wine trail: Discovery trail all year round; guided tour with a winemaker and free tasting sessions in summer (03 89 73 23 23).

 ACCOMMODATION & EATING OUT

ribeauville-riquewihr.com

 LOCAL SPECIALTIES

Food and Drink
AOC Alsace wines, Crémant d'Alsace, and Alsace *grand cru* Rosacker (Gewürztraminer, Riesling, Pinot Gris) • Distilled spirits.

 EVENTS

Jun.: Marche Gourmand, 5-mile (8-km) walk with local produce and wine tasting.
Aug.: Hunafascht, Alsatian open-air evenings (1st Fri. and Sat.).

 OUTDOOR ACTIVITIES

Cycle touring • Walking • Mountain biking, 1 marked trail • Chemin de Compostelle (Saint James's Way) trail.

 FURTHER AFIELD

•Alsace wine route: Ribeauvillé, Bergheim, Kintzheim (3½–8 miles/3–13 km).
•Haut-Koenigsbourg (8½ miles/14 km).
•Colmar; Sélestat (9½ miles/15 km).

 MBVF NEARBY
•Riquewihr (1 mile/2 km).
•Eguisheim (12 miles/19 km).
•Mittelbergheim (23 miles/37 km).

Haut-Rhin (68)
Population: 587
Altitude: 935 ft. (285 m)

TOURIST INFO—PAYS DE RIBEAUVILLÉ ET RIQUEWIHR
03 89 73 23 23
ribeauville-riquewihr.com
hunawihr.fr

Hunspach

Authentic Alsace Verte

A typical village of the northern Alsace region, Hunspach features houses with white cob walls and half-timbering that showcase the carpenter's craft. At the end of the Thirty Years War, Hunspach had been almost entirely wiped out; it owes its salvation to French refugees and, in particular, to the Swiss immigrants who were granted farmland there. With wood and clay to hand, they built black-and-white half-timbered houses, just like those back home, and the village owes its picturesque charm to these buildings. With their hipped gables and tiled canopies, they make a lovely sight lined up along the main road and around the pink sandstone bell tower of the Protestant church. The balloon-shaped windowpanes of Hunspach work like distorting mirrors, giving passersby a false reflection and preventing them from peering inside. Behind their windows, the residents can see out without ever being seen.

 HIGHLIGHTS

Fort de Schoenenbourg-Ligne Maginot: World War II fortress built 1930–40, the most important construction on the Maginot Line in Alsace. Self-guided tours of the military blocks, command post, gallery, infantry casemates, etc. Accessible for those with reduced mobility (03 88 80 96 19).
Musée d'Antan and Kelsch'Idée boutique: History of the village and bygone rural life, presented in a converted barn (06 67 36 25 29).
Village: Guided tour in English, French, German, Spanish, and Russian, all year round (03 88 80 89 70); self-guided tour around the historic site (map available from tourist info center).

 ACCOMMODATION & EATING OUT

Guesthouses and Gîtes
♥ Maison Ungerer (03 88 80 59 39).

 **LOCAL SPECIALTIES**

Food and Drink
Wine • *Dickuechen* (brioche) • *Fleischnacka* (meat and pasta roulade) • Cheeses.
Art and Crafts
Painter • Alsatian objects • Kelsch fabric household linen.

 EVENTS

Jun.: Fête du Folklore (last weekend in spring).
Jul.-Aug.: Folklore and summer activities.
Dec.: Christmas country market (2nd Sun. of Advent).

 OUTDOOR ACTIVITIES

Walking: Trail around village • Horse-drawn carriage rides.

 FURTHER AFIELD

•Northern Vosges Regional Nature Park.
•Picturesque village route: Seebach, Hoffen, Hohwiller, Kuhlendorf, Steinseltz, Cleebourg (2-6 miles/3-10 km).
•Alsace wine route: Steinseltz, Oberhoffen-lès-Wissembourg, Riedseltz, Rott-Cleebourg, Wissembourg (4½-6 miles/7-10 km).
•Pottery-making villages: Betschdorf, Soufflenheim (5-11 miles/8-18 km).
•Germany: Palatinate region, Black Forest (6-25 miles/10-40 km).

Bas-Rhin (67)
Population: 637
Altitude: 525 ft. (160 m)

TOURIST INFO—ALSACE VERTE
03 88 80 89 70
alsace-verte.com

Lagrasse

An abbey in the heart of the garigue

Within the Corbières mountain range, where grapevines mingle with fragrant garigue (scrubland), Lagrasse is a rare bloom in Cathar country. Lagrasse's rich history is written in its narrow paved streets and in the images painted on the medieval ceilings of the Maison du Patrimoine. The village's venerable covered stalls now host craftspeople, artists, and designers. Terraces and markets enliven this little town, where people have enjoyed living since the 14th century. On the opposite bank of the Orbieu river stands the Benedictine abbey, founded in the 8th century. The oldest, mostly medieval part reveals the foundation stones, the dormitory, the cellar, and the bakery, and hosts concerts, exhibitions, and cultural events all year round. The other, private part is periodically open to visitors to meet the canons who now occupy the building, and to discover the cloister and gardens.

 **HIGHLIGHTS**

Abbaye Sainte-Marie (8th–18th centuries): Les Arts de Lire cultural center (public part), visits and events all year round (04 68 43 15 99). Self-guided tour on open days (private part; 04 68 58 11 58).

Église Saint-Michel (14th century): Gothic style, paintings by Giuseppe Crespi and Jacques Gamelin, 13th-century wood sculpture of the Virgin.

Maison du Patrimoine: Heritage center in a former presbytery, with 15th-century painted ceilings, exhibition on the painted ceilings of Languedoc-Roussillon (04 67 27 57 57).

Medieval village and Place de la Halle (14th century): Free access; guided individual and group tours by appt. (04 67 27 57 57).

 ACCOMMODATION & EATING OUT

Gîtes
♥ Le Studio Blanc (06 78 96 64 72).

 LOCAL SPECIALTIES

Food and Drink
Olive oil • Vinegar • Honey • AOC Corbières wines • Kina Karo (aperitif).

Art and Crafts
Antiques • Artisanal leather goods • Jewelry designer • Furniture designer • Soap making • Artist metalworker • Painters • Glass artist • Ceramists • Sculptor and caster • Stylist • Upholsterer.

 EVENTS

Market: Sat. 8 a.m. – 1 p.m., Place de la Halle.
May and Aug.: Les Banquets du Livre, literary and philosophy events, at the abbey.
Jul.: Les Abracadagrasses, world music festival (3rd weekend).
Sept.: Les Pages Musicales, chamber music festival.

 OUTDOOR ACTIVITIES

Fishing • Saint-Jean Lake (lifeguard Jul.–Aug.) • Hiking in the garigue: 2 marked circuits "Le Pied de Charlemagne" (3½ miles/6 km) and "Notre Dame du Carla" (6 miles/10 km).

 FURTHER AFIELD

• Wine estates (5 miles/8 km).
• Château de Villerouge-Termenès (8½ miles/14 km).
• Château de Termes (12½ miles/20 km).
• Canal du Midi and its villages (17 miles/27 km).
• Abbaye de Fontfroide (17½ miles/28 km).

Aude (11)
Population: 554
Altitude: 433 ft. (132 m)

TOURIST INFO—CORBIÈRES MINERVOIS
04 68 27 57 57
tourisme-corbieres-minervois.com

 **LOCAL SPECIALTIES**

Food and Drink
Armagnac • Floc de Gascogne aperitif • Free-range duck preserves (confit, foie gras) and pork • Organic wines.

 EVENTS

Jul.: Medieval fair (3rd weekend).
Jul.-Aug.: Evening markets; military encampment and medieval-themed events.

Larressingle

The land of Armagnac and the Captains of Gascony

Towering above the vines, the fortress-village of Larressingle cultivates the Gascon way of life. The village lies beyond a fortified gateway, just past a bridge straddling a green moat. It backs onto a crown of ramparts encircling the castle keep—for many years the residence of the bishops of Condom—and a high church with two naves. Larressingle was saved from ruin by the enthusiastic duke of Trévise, who created a rescue committee financed by generous American donors. Today the village boasts a delightful collection of heritage buildings that bear witness to the area's rich medieval past: the castle, dating from the 13th, 14th, and 16th centuries, which has three floors and a pentagonal tower, a fortified gateway, and the remains of its surrounding walls; the Romanesque church of Saint-Sigismond; and the charming and finely built residences, decorated with mullioned windows and topped with ocher tile roofs.

 HIGHLIGHTS

Medieval siege camp: Camp with siege engines for attack and defense, firing demonstrations of war machines (05 62 68 33 88).
Église Saint-Sigismond (12th century): Virgin and Child, contemporary stained-glass windows by the studio of Pierre-Rivière and glass painter Gallet, statue of Saint-Sigismond modeled on Aimé Millet's *Vercingetorix Monument*.
Village: Self-guided tour; paid guided tour daily in summer, weekends and public holidays in May; recreational tour for families 11 a.m. Wed.–Sun. Jun.–Sept.; group tours by appt. all year round (05 62 28 00 80).

 ACCOMMODATION & EATING OUT

tourisme-condom.com

 OUTDOOR ACTIVITIES

Walking: Route GR 65 and short marked trails.

 FURTHER AFIELD

• Condom (3 miles/5 km).
• Cluniac site of Mouchan and Château de Cassaigne (3½ miles/6 km).
• Abbaye de Flaran (6 miles/10 km).

 MBVF NEARBY

• Fourcès, Montréal (6 miles/10 km).
• La Romieu (10½ miles/17 km).

Gers (32)
Population: 210
Altitude: 469 ft. (143 m)

TOURIST INFO— LA TÉNARÈZE
05 62 28 00 80
tourisme-condom.com

Lautrec

Flavors and colors from the Pays de Cocagne

This medieval town in the heart of Tarn's Pays de Cocagne is the home of painter Toulouse-Lautrec's family. At the top of La Salette hill, which commands far-reaching views over the whole Casters plain and the Montagne Noire, there is a Calvary cross and a botanical trail where a castle once stood. For many years the village was the only fortified site between Albi and Carcassonne, and some of its ramparts remain. Its shady plane-tree promenades run alongside them, and each year Lautrec—the capital of pink garlic farming—holds garlic markets there. The gateway of La Caussade leads straight from the rampart walk to the central square, where a traditional Friday morning market is still held under the beams of its covered hall. The Rue de l'Église leads to the collegiate church of Saint-Rémy, with its pastel blue walls that long brought riches to Lautrec and earned it its reputation as a "land of milk and honey."

 HIGHLIGHTS

Clogmaker's workshop: Reconstruction of an old workshop, with vintage machines and tools (05 63 75 90 04 / 07 86 91 98 77).

Église Collégiale Saint-Rémy (14th–16th centuries): Marble altarpiece by Caunes-Minervois, sculpted lectern (17th century).

La Salette windmill: For opening hours: 05 63 97 94 41. By appt. offseason.

La Salette botanical trail: Self-guided walk to discover the region's plants and panoramic view of the area with viewpoint indicator.

Village: Guided group tour of 10+ people daily, by appt. (05 63 97 94 41).

ACCOMMODATION & EATING OUT

lautrectourisme.com

LOCAL SPECIALTIES

Food and Drink
Lautrec pink garlic, garlic specialties (bread, vinegar, pâté) • Duck foie gras.

Art and Crafts
Ceramist • Cabinetmaker • Leather goods • Pastel dyeing • Art galleries • Jewelry • Household linen • Clothing • Wooden objects.

EVENTS

Market: Fri. 8 a.m.–12 p.m., Place Centrale.
Jun.: Fête des Moulins, windmill festival and open-air rummage sale (3rd Sun.).
Aug.: Fête de l'Ail Rose, pink garlic festival (1st Fri. and Sat.); Festival of the Arts in Pays de Cocagne (penultimate weekend).
Oct.: Outilautrec, traditional tool and machine fair (1st weekend).

OUTDOOR ACTIVITIES

Aquaval water sports (mid-Jun.–late Aug.) • Cycling, horseback riding, and walking: Marked trails.

FURTHER AFIELD

• Lombers: Écomusée du Pigeon (5½ miles/9 km).
• Réalmont (7 miles/11 km).
• Castres (Musée Goya) and Le Sidobre (9½–13½ miles/ 15–22 km).
• Saint-Paul-Cap-de-Joux: Musée du Pastel and Château de Magrin (12½ miles/20 km).
• Albi, UNESCO World Heritage Site (18½ miles/30 km).

Tarn (81)
Population: 1,706
Altitude: 1,033 ft. (315 m)

TOURIST INFO— LAUTRÉCOIS – PAYS D'AGOUT
05 63 97 94 41
lautrectourisme.com
lautrec.fr

Lauzerte

A fortified town in Quercy Blanc

Lauzerte overlooks the surrounding valleys and hills of Quercy Blanc from atop a spur of land. It was once simultaneously a trading town, a stronghold, and a staging post along the Saint James's Way, the pilgrims' route to Santiago de Compostela. Many of the village's buildings speak to its illustrious past: the old fortifications, the 13th-century Église Saint-Barthélémy (restored on several occasions), houses that once belonged to local notables, and the Place des Cornières, the town's commercial and artistic center. Above ribbed or three-centered arcades, residences dating from the 15th to 18th centuries still expose their white limestone façades and colorful shutters to the sun; among them, the Maison de Vassel has the only half-timbered, brick-clad façade on the square. At the edge of the plaza is a colorful ceramic work by Jacques Buchholtz that lends an unusual contemporary touch to the medieval setting.

 HIGHLIGHTS

Église Saint-Barthélemy (13th–18th centuries): Paintings, stalls, Baroque altarpiece, painted paneling attributed to Joseph Ingres and students.
Jardin du Pèlerin: Life-size game of snakes and ladders on the theme of the pilgrimage to Santiago de Compostela.
Village: Thematic guided tours; evening tour by torchlight; escape room and treasure hunts (05 63 94 66 61/ 06 19 13 66 53).

 **ACCOMMODATION & EATING OUT**

quercy-sud-ouest.com

LOCAL SPECIALTIES

Food and Drink
Foie gras and duck products • Fruits, AOP Chasselas de Moissac grapes • Macarons.
Art and Crafts
Ceramists • Illuminator • Metalworker • Engravers • Leather goods • Weaver • Set designer • Metal sculptor • Art galleries.

 EVENTS

Market: Wed. a.m., Foirail; Sat. a.m., Cornières.
Jul.: Métalik' Art, metallic sculpture symposium (2nd weekend); pottery market (3rd weekend).
Jul.–Aug.: Musical gourmet market (Thurs.).
Aug.: Rencontres Musicales Européennes, music festival (2nd weekend).
Sept.: Place aux Nouvelles, book festival (2nd weekend).

 OUTDOOR ACTIVITIES

Horseback riding • Fishing • Walking: Route GR 65 on the Saint James's Way, and shorter walks.

 FURTHER AFIELD

•Saint-Sernin-du-Bosc: Romanesque chapel; Montcuq; Moissac (2½–15½ miles/4–25 km).

 MBVF NEARBY
•Tournon-d'Agenais (16 miles/26 km).
•Auvillar (21 miles/34 km).

Tarn-et-Garonne (82)
Population: 1,470
Altitude: 722 ft. (220 m)

TOURIST INFO—PAYS DE SERRES EN QUERCY
05 63 94 61 94
quercy-sud-ouest.com

Lavardens

A stone nave in the Gascon countryside

Like a ship moored on a rocky outcrop, the imposing Château de Lavardens towers over the green crests and troughs of central Gascony. Once the military capital of the counts of Armagnac, the medieval fortress of Lavardens was besieged and dismantled in 1496 on the order of Charles VII. The castle passed into the hands of the d'Albret and later the de Navarre families, and was granted by Henri IV to his friend Antoine de Roquelaure in 1585. At 69 years old, de Roquelaure began rebuilding the castle out of love for his young wife, Suzanne de Bassabat. The restoration work undertaken by the Association de Sauvegarde du Château de Lavardens since the late 1970s respects all the individuality of this outstanding architectural site: the spaces, the original ocher tiles and bricks of the rooms, the exterior galleries, and the squinch towers—a unique architectural feature. At the foot of this white-stone sentinel, charming 18th-century village houses line the cobbled streets bordered with hollyhocks.

 HIGHLIGHTS

Chapelle Sainte-Marie des Consolations: Medieval chapel with exceptional views over the village.
Castle (12th-17th centuries): Guardroom, ballroom, games room, chapel; exhibitions (05 62 58 10 61).
Église Saint-Michel (11th century): Pulpit, wooden stalls, late 15th-century stained glass.
Village: Guided tour by appt. (05 62 05 22 89); "Pass'en Gers" guided tours (pass-en-gers.fr).

 ACCOMMODATION & EATING OUT

auch-tourisme.com

 LOCAL SPECIALTIES

Food and Drink
Gers green lentils • Vin de Pays Côte de Gascogne.
Art and Crafts
Saddler and harness maker • Bladesmith • Metal artist •
Furniture restorer • Stonecutters.

 EVENTS

Jul.-Aug.: Evening markets.
Jul.: Rétromotion, classic and sports car show (late Jul.).
Sept.: Village festival (3rd weekend).

OUTDOOR ACTIVITIES

Walking: Marked trails.

FURTHER AFIELD

• Castéra-Verduzan (6 miles/10 km).
• Biran and Saint-Jean-Poutge: Castles, churches (10 miles/16 km).
• Auch: Cathédrale Sainte-Marie, Musée des Amériques (14 miles/23 km).

 MBVF NEARBY
• La Romieu (19 miles/31 km).
• Larressingle (20 miles/32 km).

Gers (32)
Population: 400
Altitude: 646 ft. (197 m)

TOURIST INFO—GRAND AUCH COEUR DE GASCOGNE
05 62 05 22 89
auch-tourisme.com

Lavardin

Grottoes and Gothic architecture

This village, near the birthplace of poet Pierre de Ronsard (1524–1585), has retained its fortified castle, its medieval charm, and its many legends. Lavardin became famous when it withstood Richard the Lionheart's attack in 1118, thanks to its castle's tiered defenses. However, the lords of the region were not in a position to fight back when they faced Henry IV—the king of Navarre—and his troops. Furious when his subjects refused to convert to Protestantism, the young king and the duke of Vendôme destroyed the fortresses of Montoire, Vendôme, and Lavardin. Today, the castle ruins command the village from the top of a limestone cliff. A tufastone Gothic bridge with eight arches spans the Loir river. Almost every period of history has left its mark on Lavardin, which blends troglodyte, Gothic, and Renaissance houses. White façades rub shoulders with half-timbered houses topped with flat tiles. Lavardin also boasts grottoes that are unique in France and steeped in legend.

HIGHLIGHTS

Castle (11th and 14th centuries): Lodge, outbuildings, drawbridge, grand staircase, guardroom, keep. Tours May–Sept., by appt. (06 81 86 12 80).
Église Saint-Genest (11th century): Murals from 12th and 16th centuries representing Christ's Baptism and Passion (02 54 85 07 74).
Musée de Lavardin: Village history and castle heritage. Tours May–Sept. (06 81 86 12 80).

ACCOMMODATION & EATING OUT

lavardin.net

EVENTS

Jan.: Fête de la Saint-Vincent (weekend around 20th).
Mar.: World Chouine (traditional card game) Championships (1st Sun.).
Jun.: Journée des Jardins, garden festival (1st Sun.).
Aug.: Flea market (mid-Aug.).

Dec.: Christmas market in the village streets and castle (1st weekend).

OUTDOOR ACTIVITIES

Walking: Routes GR 35, GR 335, and 3 marked trails • Randoland, discovery trail for kids aged 4–12.

FURTHER AFIELD

•Saint-Rimay: W3, wartime German tunnel and bunkers (2 miles/3 km).
•Troo: Collegiate church, cave-dwellers' settlement (5 miles/8 km).
•Thoré-la-Rochette: Tourist train (6 miles/10 km).
•Couture-sur-Loir: Manoir de la Poissonière, Ronsard's birthplace (9 miles/15 km).
•Vendôme: Château of the counts and dukes of Bourbon-Vendôme (11 miles/18 km).

Loir-et-Cher (41)
Population: 183
Altitude: 262 ft. (80 m)

TOURIST INFO—PAYS DE VENDÔME
02 54 77 05 07
vendome-tourisme.fr
TOWN HALL
02 54 85 07 74
lavardin.net

Lavaudieu

In God's valley

In the Middle Ages, Benedictine monks built a monastery in the Senouire valley, turning it into *la vallée de Dieu* (God's valley), which gave the village its name. Robert de Turlande, first abbot of La Chaise-Dieu abbey and later Saint Robert, founded the abbey at Lavaudieu in 1057. Nuns lived here until the French Revolution. It is the only monastery in Auvergne to have conserved its Romanesque cloister. Adorning the wall of the refectory, with its line of single or coupled columns, some of which feature carved capitals, is a 12th-century Byzantine-inspired mural. The 11th–12th-century church adjoining the monastery lost its steeple during the French Revolution. Inside, a 15th-century Pietà in polychrome stone sits alongside Italian-influenced murals of an allegory of the Black Death from the 14th century. In the center of the village, the Musée des Arts et Traditions Populaires de Haute-Loire displays a typical Auvergne interior.

 EVENTS

Market: Wed. 5–9 p.m., Jul.–Aug.
Jul.: Fête de la Barrique, traditional "barrel" festival (weekend after 14th).
Jul.–Aug.: Concerts at the abbey and exhibitions (abbayedelavaudieu.fr / 04 71 76 46 00).

OUTDOOR ACTIVITIES

Climbing • Walking: 3 marked trails.

HIGHLIGHTS

Abbey: Cloisters, refectory (12th-century mural); Église Saint-André (Pietà, murals) (04 71 76 46 00 / abbayedelavaudieu.fr).
Musée des Arts et Traditions Populaires: Reconstruction of a traditional Auvergne interior from bygone days (04 71 76 46 00 / abbayedelavaudieu.fr).

FURTHER AFIELD

• Brioude (5 miles/8 km).
• La Chaise-Dieu (24 miles/38 km).

 MBVF NEARBY

• Lavoûte-Chilhac (12½ miles/20 km).
• Blesle (19 miles/31 km).
• Usson (25 miles/40 km).

ACCOMMODATION & EATING OUT

Guesthouses
♥ La Maison d'à Côté (04 71 76 45 04).

 LOCAL SPECIALTIES

Art and Crafts
Essential oil distillery • Upholstery and ornamental gilding workshop.

Haute-Loire (43)
Population: 250
Altitude: 1,411 ft. (430 m)

TOURIST INFO—BRIOUDE SUD-AUVERGNE
04 71 76 46 00
tourisme-brioudesudauvergne.fr

Lavoûte-Chilhac

Lulled by the lapping Allier river

In the southern part of Auvergne, nestled in a bend of the Allier river, Lavoûte-Chilhac displays its Cluny architecture in a setting of unspoiled natural beauty. The name Lavoûte-Chilhac is derived from the Latin word *voltar*, which means "to turn or to go around," in reference to the Allier river that encircles the village. In the Middle Ages, Odilon de Mercoeur, the fifth abbot of Cluny, fell under the region's charm and established the Cluny priory of Sainte-Croix de la Volte here. A distinctive feature of the village is its two neighborhoods separated by the Allier. The first is home to the priory, while the second is located on the left bank, with 19th-century houses built against the rockface and protected by tall façades from violent surges in the river's water level. The 15th-century medieval bridge that connects the two neighborhoods is the only way across the Allier and offers a sweeping view of the river and the village.

 HIGHLIGHTS

Prieuré Sainte-Croix de la Volte (11th, 15th, and 18th centuries): Private property; possibility to visit garden.
Église Prieurale Sainte-Croix (15th century): 12th-century polychrome statue of Christ on the cross, 16th-century stalls, statuette of the Vierge Notre-Dame-Trouvée.
Maison des Oiseaux et de la Nature du Haut-Allier: Exhibitions; dioramas of 50 distinguished bird species (06 76 37 44 69).
Village: Guided tours (04 71 77 28 30); 2 routes with QR codes from tourist info center (04 71 77 46 57).

 ACCOMMODATION & EATING OUT

Restaurant
♥ Au Prieuré (04 71 77 87 37).

 LOCAL SPECIALTIES

Art and Crafts
Cabinetmaker • Iron sculptor.

 EVENTS

Market: Fri. 5:30 p.m.; Sun. 9 a.m.–12 p.m. in Jul.–Aug., Place des Anciens Moulins.
Jul.: Pilgrimage to Notre-Dame-Trouvée (1st Sun.); textile arts market (late Jul.).
Aug.: Loz'art, art and crafts market (mid-Aug.).

 OUTDOOR ACTIVITIES

Fishing • Swimming • Rafting • Canoeing and kayaking • Walking: Route GR 470, 18 short circuits, "Robe de Bure et Cotte de Maille" trail • Mountain biking: "Grande Traversée de la Haute-Loire," "Via Allier" routes • Moped and electric bike rental.

 FURTHER AFIELD

•Chilhac: Musée de Paléontologie Christian Guth (3 miles/5 km).
•Langeac (8 miles/13 km).
•Vieille-Brioude (11 miles/18 km).

 MBVF NEARBY
•Lavaudieu (12½ miles/20 km).
•Blesle (25 miles/40 km).

Haute-Loire (43)
Population: 280
Altitude: 1,785 ft. (544 m)

TOURIST INFO—LES GORGES DE L'ALLIER
04 71 77 46 57
lesgorgesdelallier.fr

Limeuil

Barges and boatmen— a bustling trading center

Where the Dordogne and Vézère rivers meet, the once-flourishing port of Limeuil is now a welcoming and shady bank. The village has lived through troubled times, defending itself against the Vikings and then, during the Hundred Years War, the English. Three fortified gateways remain from this period, and visitors pass through them to reach the village, which is built on a steep slope. Along the winding lanes, the houses show off their façades of golden stone decorated with coats of arms. Halfway up the hill, at the Place des Fossés, the castle comes into view—medieval in origin but renovated in the Moorish style, it is surrounded by gardens with a panoramic view of the confluence. Just a few steps away stands the Église Sainte-Catherine, with a choir dating from the 14th century. Down below, an arched double bridge straddles the Vézère and Dordogne rivers, and the Place du Port is a reminder that Limeuil was an important inland waterway center in the 19th century.

HIGHLIGHTS

Chapelle Saint-Martin (12th century): Frescoes.
Panoramic gardens: Castle gardens organized by theme (colors, sorcerers, water, arboretum etc.); thematic discovery trails (trees, landscape, river transport and seamanship); escape game garden (05 53 73 26 13).
Village: Self-guided tour (information panels).

ACCOMMODATION & EATING OUT

Campsites
♥ Les Poutiroux**** (05 53 63 31 62).

LOCAL SPECIALTIES

Food and Drink
Craft beer • Périgord apples and vin de pays.
Art and Crafts
Jewelry • Art gallery • Fashion • Painters • Pottery • Glassblower • Glass beadmaker.

EVENTS

Market: Sun. a.m, Place du Port (Jul.–Aug.).
Jul.: Local saint's day (weekend closest to 14th); pottery market (3rd weekend); Fête du Confluent (4th weekend).

OUTDOOR ACTIVITIES

Swimming (no lifeguard) • Canoeing and kayaking • Fishing • Walking, horseback riding, and mountain biking: Route GR 6, Boucle de Limeuil (8 miles/13 km) and Boucle du Lac Rouge (3 miles/5 km).

FURTHER AFIELD

• Cingle de Trémolat (6 miles/10 km).
• Les Eyzies (9½ miles/15 km).
• Sarlat (22 miles/35 km).

MBVF NEARBY
• Belvès (11 miles/18 km).
• Monpazier (17 miles/27 km).
• Beynac-et-Cazenac, Castelnaud-la-Chapelle (17½ miles/28 km).
• Saint-Léon-sur-Vézère (19 miles/31 km).

Dordogne (24)
Population: 330
Altitude: 164 ft. (50 m)

TOURIST INFO—LASCAUX - DORDOGNE VALLÉE VÉZÈRE
05 53 51 82 60
lascaux-dordogne.com

Locronan
Thread and stone

A historic weaving village dominated by granite, Locronan owes its name to Saint Ronan, the hermit who founded it. In the 6th or 7th century, while still haunted with memories of druidic cults, the forest of Névet became home to the hermit Saint Ronan. In the 15th century, thanks to the dukes of Brittany, Locronan became one of the jewels of Breton Gothic art. The priory church was built between 1420 and 1480, while the Chapelle du Pénity (15th-16th centuries), next to the church, houses Saint Ronan's recumbent statue. During the Renaissance, the village became famous for its weaving industry: it provided hemp canvas sails for the ships of the French Royal Navy, and the East India Company was a faithful client. The latter's former offices still stand on the village square, as well as 17th-century merchants' dwellings and residences of the king's notaries. Locronan's elegant Renaissance granite buildings regularly provide the backdrop for movies, including *A Very Long Engagement* (with Audrey Tautou and Jodie Foster).

 HIGHLIGHTS

Église Saint-Ronan (15th century): 15th-century stained glass, statues, treasure.
Chapelle du Pénity (15th-16th centuries): Statue of Saint Ronan in Kersanton stone (15th century).
Chapelle Notre-Dame-de-Bonne-Nouvelle (16th century): Modern stained-glass windows by Alfred Manessier; cross and communal washing place.
Musée d'Art et d'Histoire Charles Daniélou: history of the weaving profession in the 18th century; creation of traditional costumes; collection of Breton costumes and headpieces; paintings by 50 early 20th-century painters, temporary exhibitions (02 98 51 80 80).
Village: Guided tours for groups and individuals (02 98 91 70 14).

 ACCOMMODATION & EATING OUT

locronan-tourisme.bzh

 **LOCAL SPECIALTIES**

Food and Drink
Galettes • Breton cake • *Kouign amann*.
Art and Crafts
Watercolorist • Antiques • Ceramists • Leather and tin worker • Steel worker • Leather goods • Painters • Art photographer • Glassblowers • Weavers • Wood sculptors • Celtic bookshop.

 EVENTS

Market: Tues. a.m., Place de la Mairie.
Jul.: Pardon de la Petite Troménie, procession (2nd Sun.); Procession de la Grand Troménie, circular pilgrimage route (2nd–3rd Sun., every 6 years [next one in 2025]).
Jul.–Aug.: Les Marchés aux Étoiles, evening craft and local produce market (Thurs., mid-Jul.-mid-Aug.).

 OUTDOOR ACTIVITIES

Walking: Route GR 38 and marked trails (Névet forest, circular walk; wheelchair accessible) • Mountain biking (Névet forest).

FURTHER AFIELD

•Douarnenez (4½ miles/7 km).
•Quimper (9 miles/15 km).
•Châteaulin; Nantes–Brest canal (10 miles/16 km).
•Crozon peninsula (19 miles/30 km).
•Pays Bigouden; Pont-l'Abbé (24 miles/39 km).

Finistère (29)
Population: 790
Altitude: 476 ft. (145 m)

TOURIST INFO—LOCRONAN CORNOUAILLE
02 98 91 70 14
locronan-tourisme.bzh

Jun.: La Nuit Romantique (Sat. after summer solstice).
Jul.–Aug.: Farmers' market, some Wed. 6 p.m., Place des Forges.
Dec.: "Une Nuit à Bethléem," living Nativity scene.

  OUTDOOR ACTIVITIES

Canoeing and kayaking • Fishing • Walking • Mountain biking.

Lods

Born from the river

Traversed by the Loue river, which tumbles through the valley a few miles away, Lods is an ancient village of winegrowers and blacksmiths. This small village in the Doubs *département* long exploited the energy of the Loue, an underground river that is partly fed by the Doubs river. The iron forges lie idle now and Lods no longer produces grapes, but the village still has its 16th- and 17th-century winegrowers' houses with their spacious vaulted cellars, clustered higgledy-piggledy around the 18th-century church and its tufa-stone bell tower. The Musée de la Vigne et du Vin (vine and wine museum), which is housed in a beautiful 16th-century building, the old smithy on the other side of the river, and a historical trail through the village all tell the fascinating story of the blacksmiths and winegrowers who used to live here.

 **HIGHLIGHTS**

Église Saint-Théodule (18th century): Paintings.
Musée de la Vigne et du Vin: Museum retracing the life of the valley's winegrowers, collection of tools and utensils, in an authentic 16th-century winegrowers' house (06 89 06 21 27 / 03 81 90 91 11).
Village: Free guided tour in Jul.–Aug. (03 81 62 21 50); self-guided tour of the ethnological trail.

 ACCOMMODATION & EATING OUT

lods.fr

 LOCAL SPECIALTIES

Food and Drink
Jésus de Morteau smoked sausage • Trout • Mountain ham • Comté cheese • Cancoillotte cheese.
Art and Crafts
Pottery studio • Bric-a-brac stores.

FURTHER AFIELD

•Source of the Loue river; Pontarlier; Joux Fort; Lac de Saint-Point (6–31 miles/10–50 km).
•Ornans: Musée Courbet and Musée du Costume (7½ miles/12 km).

Doubs (25)
Population: 245
Altitude: 1,214 ft. (370 m)

TOURIST INFO—DESTINATION LOUE LISON
03 81 62 21 50
destinationlouelison.com
lods.fr

Loubressac

Pointed roofs in the Dordogne valley

From its cliff top, Loubressac commands a panoramic view of the valley of the Dordogne. Loubressac was razed during the Hundred Years War but was revived when the people of the Auvergne and Limousin returned, and it owes its current appearance to their efforts. Today, the flower-decked lanes converge on a shady village square, where the Église Saint-Jean-Baptiste, dating from the 12th and 16th centuries, stands tall. The limestone medieval houses topped with old tiles are illuminated by the warm glow of the sun. Dominated by its castle perched on a natural promontory, the village offers far-reaching views of the Dordogne and Bave valleys. Numerous walking trails, which start in Loubressac, crisscross the area, linking the surrounding villages. Taking one of these snaking paths leads the visitor past springs or prehistoric dolmens to emerge on the limestone Causse plateau nearby.

 HIGHLIGHTS

Église St-Jean-Baptiste (14th-16th centuries): Sculpted tympanum, several chapels and altarpieces.
La Ferme de Siran: Tour of the angora goat farm, documentary on mohair production (05 65 38 74 40).
Ferme Cazal – Le Rouquet: Goat breeding farm and cheese production (06 72 71 98 84).
Village: Guided tour organized by local culture group Le Pays d'Art et d'Histoire de la Vallée de la Dordogne Lotoise (05 65 33 81 36).

 ACCOMMODATION & EATING OUT

Hotels
♥ Le Cantou 354** (05 36 08 08 00).

 LOCAL SPECIALTIES

Food and Drink
Cabécou goat cheese • Walnut oil • Flour.
Art and Crafts
Handicrafts • Painters • Pottery• Textile and leather creations • Ceramics.

 EVENTS

May: Fête du Printemps, craft and local produce market (1st Sun.).
Jul.: Local saint's day (around 20th).
Aug.: Farmers' market and food-lovers' picnic (2nd Thurs.); flea market (4th Sun.).
Dec.: Christmas market (2nd Sun.).

 OUTDOOR ACTIVITIES

Walking • Mountain biking.

 FURTHER AFIELD

•Prudhomat: Château de Castelnau-Bretenoux (3½ miles/6 km).
•Gouffre de Padirac, chasm (3½ miles/6 km).
•Château de Montal; Saint-Céré (5½ miles/9 km).

 MBVF NEARBY
•Autoire (3 miles/5 km).
•Carennac (5½ miles/9 km).
•Beaulieu-sur-Dordogne (10½ miles/17 km).
•Curemonte, Rocamadour (14½ miles/23 km).
•Martel (18 miles/29 km).
•Collonges-la-Rouge (19 miles/31 km).
•Turenne (20½ miles/33 km).

Lot (46)
Population: 511
Altitude: 1,115 ft. (340 m)

TOURIST INFO—VALLÉE DE LA DORDOGNE
05 65 33 22 00
vallee-dordogne.com
loubressac.fr

Lourmarin

The Provence of Camus and Bosco

Standing at the mouth of a gorge in the Luberon allegedly clawed out by a dragon, Loumarin attracted writers Albert Camus and Henri Bosco, who rest in the shade of the cemetery's cypress trees. The rough gash created by the Aiguebrun river, traversed by an old shell bridge, is the sole (and ancient) route through the Luberon mountains. The village thus sprang up here, around a modest Benedictine monastery and simple castle, the Castellas, belonging to the lords of Baux-de-Provence. Surrounded by a plain dotted with fortified Provençal *mas* houses, where fruit and olive orchards mingle with vines, the village's winding streets display fountains and a cascade of sun-kissed rooftops around the Castellas (now a belfry and clock tower) and the Romanesque church of Saint-Trophime-et-Saint-André. A stone's throw away is the Protestant church, which recalls the tragic massacre of the Vaud people in the 16th century, survivors of which converted to Protestantism. Beyond it, the castle overlooks fields and terraced gardens.

 **HIGHLIGHTS**

Château de Lourmarin (15th and 16th centuries): First Renaissance castle in Provence, furnished throughout; collection of engravings and objets d'art (04 90 68 15 23).

Protestant church (19th century): Monumental organ attributed to Lyon organ maker Augustin Zieger. Included in village tour.

Romanesque church (11th century): Included in village tour.

La Ferme de Gerbaud: Guided tour of aromatic plant farm. Tastings Thurs., by appt. (06 45 42 57 12).

Village: Tour all year round, by appt.; recreational tour and evening tour in Jul.–Aug. (04 90 68 10 77).

 ACCOMMODATION & EATING OUT

destinationluberon.com

 LOCAL SPECIALTIES

Food and Drink
Aromatic plants • Olive oil • *Gibassiers* (traditional cookies) • AOC Côtes du Luberon wines.

Art and Crafts
Jewelry designers • Clothing designers • Metalworker • Art galleries • Household linen • Potters • Sculptors • Tools in Damask steel.

 EVENTS

Market: Fri. 8 a.m.–1 p.m., Place Henri-Barthélemy and Avenue Philippe-de-Girard; farmers' market with street food Tues. 5–8 p.m. (early Apr.–mid-Jun.), 6–9 p.m. (mid-Jun.–late Oct.).

Jun.: Festival Yeah, pop/rock/electro music festival (1st weekend).

Jul.-Aug.: Rencontres Méditerranéennes Albert Camus, book festival; craft fairs.

 OUTDOOR ACTIVITIES

Walking: PR and GR routes • "Le Luberon à vélo" cycle route.

 FURTHER AFIELD

• Fort de Buoux (6 miles/10 km).
• Combe de Lourmarin, gorge; Forêt de Cèdres, forest; Apt (7–10½ miles/11–17 km).

 MBVF NEARBY
• Ansouis (6 miles/10 km).
• Ménerbes, Roussillon (14 miles/23 km).
• Gordes (18 miles/29 km).

Vaucluse (84)
Population: 1,062
Altitude: 722 ft. (220 m)

**TOURIST INFO—
DESTINATION LUBERON**
04 90 68 10 77
destinationluberon.com

Lussan

A medieval epic in the Pays d'Uzès

Set on a rocky plateau high above the garigue (scrubland), the walls of Lussan bear traces of a rich medieval history. With its near-circular silhouette surrounded by ramparts, a panoramic view over the Cévennes and Mont Ventoux, and stone façades bleached by the Midi sunshine, Lussan is the archetypal medieval village of the Languedoc region. Only a few remains are left of the earlier castle, founded in the 12th century by local lords, but its 15th-century counterpart stands almost entirely intact in the heart of the village, proudly displaying its four round towers, including one belfry tower. Showcasing tall façades with distinctive *génoise* tiles along its narrow streets, Lussan tells the tale of the once-turbulent relations between Catholics and Protestants, who each have their own place of worship, and, more recently, the history of silk production, which is widespread in the region. On the outskirts of the village the impressive Concluses—immense gorges carved out by the Aiguillon river, make for a novel walk.

 HIGHLIGHTS

Castle (town hall): Historic 17th-century painted ceiling and ramparts; guided tour by appt. (04 66 72 90 58).
Jardin des Buis: Garden dedicated to wellbeing; a Mediterranean interpretation of *niwaki* (Japanese art of tree-sculpting) (04 66 72 88 93).
Forge: Restored former forge. Artists' studio and exhibition space, dedicated to craftsmanship. Visits all year round (06 72 47 39 22).
Concluses: Gorges cut by the Aiguillon river, walks in summer when the water has run dry; site and discovery trail.
L'Aiguillon d'Art: Walking trail through the village, via a series of artworks (06 72 47 39 22).

 ACCOMMODATION & EATING OUT

Gîtes
♥ Bastide de Lussan (06 66 26 46 62).

 LOCAL SPECIALTIES

Food and Drink
Goat and sheep cheeses • Truffles.
Art and Crafts
Pottery • Wrought ironwork • Art gallery.

 EVENTS

Market: Sun. 8 a.m.–1 p.m., Stade de Lussan (Jun. 10th–Sept. 10th).
Apr.: Art & Jardin festival (last Sun.).
Aug.: Festival de Lussan (1st fortnight); Lussan Se Livre, book festival (last Sun.).
Nov.–Mar.: Histoires de Clochers, free guided tours of villages in the Pays d'Uzès, by a certified lecturer guide.

 OUTDOOR ACTIVITIES

Walking: 155 miles (250 km) of marked trails (see map-guide "Garrigues et Concluses autour de Lussan") • Horseback riding • Mountain biking.

 FURTHER AFIELD

• Grotte de la Salamandre, cave (7½ miles/12 km).
• Uzès: Cité des Évêques; tour of the castles of the Pays d'Uzès (11–18 miles/18–29 km).
• Alès (19 miles/30 km).

 MBVF NEARBY

• La Roque-sur-Cèze (12½ miles/20 km).
• Montclus (16 miles/25 km).

Gard (30)
Population: 499
Altitude: 978 ft. (298 m)

TOURIST INFO—PAYS D'UZÈS PONT DU GARD
04 66 22 68 88
uzes-pontdugard.com
mairie-lussan.fr

Lyons-la-Forêt

Village in a glade

Standing in the middle of one of the most beautiful beech groves in Europe, in Normandy's largest forest, Lyons showcases an attractive blend of flowers, half-timbered façades, and pink bricks. Gallo-Roman in origin, Lyons-la-Forêt stretches along the Lieure river. The church of Saint-Denis (12th–16th centuries) and the historic Benedictine and Cordelier convents watch over the river, with its ancient watermills. Right at the heart of Lyons-la-Forêt, the village center encircles an old feudal mound (where ruins of the castle in which Henry I of England died are still visible) and the square where "Le Fresne" (a beautiful house where the composer Maurice Ravel used to stay) is situated. A stone's throw away, the faded but elegant Place Benserade—named for a court poet of Louis XIV—is home to an iconic 18th-century covered marketplace, still in use several times a week. The 18th-century former bailiwick court inside the town hall is one of the village's main attractions.

 HIGHLIGHTS

Hôtel de Ville: Law court and 13th-century prison cell (02 32 49 31 65).
Village: Guided tours for groups and individuals by appt. (02 32 49 31 65).

ACCOMMODATION & EATING OUT

lyons-andelle-tourisme.com

 LOCAL SPECIALTIES

Food and Drink
Local Normandy produce.
Art and Crafts
Bric-a-brac store • Fashion accessory and interior decoration designers • Decorative objects • Weaver • Painters.

EVENTS

Market: Thurs., Sat., and Sun. 8.30 a.m.–1.00 p.m.
May: Foire à Tout, village fair (1st).

Pentecost: Craft fair.
Jul.: Fête de la Fleur, flower festival (1st weekend).
Oct.: Fête de la Saint-Denis (mid-Oct.).

 OUTDOOR ACTIVITIES

Horseback riding • Walking: 17 marked trails • Nordic walking • Fishing • Mountain biking: 3 trails.

 FURTHER AFIELD

• Abbaye de Mortemer; châteaux de Fleury-la-Forêt, de Heudicourt, de Vascoeuil, and de Martainville; Abbaye Notre-Dame de Fontaine-Guérard; Musée de la Ferme de Rome (3–12½ miles/5–20 km).
• Château Gaillard; Château de Gisors (15½–18 miles/25–29 km).
• Rouen (22 miles/35 km).

 MBVF NEARBY

• Gerberoy (23 miles/37 km).

Eure (27)
Population: 709
Altitude: 312 ft. (95 m)

TOURIST INFO—LYONS ANDELLE
02 32 49 31 65
lyons-andelle-tourisme.com

Le Malzieu-Ville

A Gévaudan stronghold

Known as the "Pearl of the Valley," Le Malzieu-Ville is a fortified medieval town in the historical province of Gévaudan. Le Malzieu-Ville built up its fortifications—ramparts, defensive towers, keeps, and monumental gates—to protect it during the Hundred Years War and project an impression of power. Yet a few centuries later the village faced the tumults of the Wars of Religion. Massacres, imprisonments, executions, and destruction ensued, followed by a terrible fire in 1631 that seemed to sound the death knell for Le Malzieu-Ville. But the village rose from the ashes: it began reconstruction work, assisted by Italian masons who came to lend a hand, as can be witnessed in some of the splendid stone doorways. Today, Le Malzieu-Ville offers visitors all the charms of a lively historic village at the heart of a magical landscape within the valley of the Truyère river.

 HIGHLIGHTS

Village: History trail; interactive "hunt of the Beast of Gévaudan"; guided tour.
Tour de l'Horloge (13th-century clock tower): Panoramic view. Self-guided tour in peak season., Mon.–Sat.; guided group tour by appt.
Tour de Bodon (13th century): Panoramic view; exhibition gallery and tourist info center.
Couvent des Ursulines: Former convent converted into a museum; 17th-century monastic cell; religious vestments and liturgical objects. Self-guided tour in peak season, Mon.–Sat.; guided group tour by appt.
Église Collégiale Saint-Hippolyte (11th, 16th, and 19th centuries): Our Lady of Apcher statue, treasury of liturgical objects, polychrome statue of Christ. Self-guided tour; tour of the treasury Thurs. p.m. in peak season; guided group tour by appt.
For all highlights: 04 66 31 82 73.

 ACCOMMODATION & EATING OUT

le-malzieu-ville.fr

 **LOCAL SPECIALTIES**

Food and Drink
Coupétade (bread pudding) • Wines • Chocolate • *Aligot* (cheesy potatoes) • Blueberries • Charcuterie • Mountain honey.
Art and Crafts
Designer • Artisanal leather goods • Pottery • Sheepskin accessories • Art gallery.

 EVENTS

Market: Tues. 9 a.m., Avenue Pierre Rousset.
May: Les Médiévales du Malzieu (Ascension weekend).
Aug.: Rencontres Musicales du Malzieu (early Aug.); Journée de la Bête, dedicated to the Beast of Gévaudan (last Fri.).
Sept.: Trail Margeride, cross-country run (2nd weekend).

 OUTDOOR ACTIVITIES

Walking: GR 4: Margeride circular trail, PR trail • Mountain biking circuits • Via Ferrata • Rock climbing • Tree-climbing • Lake • Skate park.

 FURTHER AFIELD

• Saint-Chély-d'Apcher: Musée de la Métallurgie (5 miles/8 km).
• Saint-Alban-sur-Limagnole: Château, Scénovision (6 miles/10 km).
• Mont Mouchet: Musée de la Résistance (10½ miles/17 km).
• Réserve des Bisons d'Europe de la Margeride (13½ miles/22 km).
• Musée Fantastique de la Bête du Gévaudan (19 miles/31 km).

Lozère (48)
Population: 750
Altitude: 2,831 ft. (863 m)

TOURIST INFO—MARGERIDE EN GÉVAUDAN
04 66 31 82 73
margeride-en-gevaudan.com
le-malzieu-ville.fr

Marcolès

A medieval town in southern Auvergne

Located in the very heart of Cantal's Châtaigneraie region, Marcolès has maintained the heritage and bustling commerce of a medieval stronghold. The outgrowth of a 10th-century Benedictine priory, Marcolès had, by the 16th century, grown to become a *bonne ville*—a town that benefited from the protection of the French king—and a popular stopover on the road leading from the mountains of Auvergne to the Midi. A stroll past the remains of the fortified outer wall and through the town's *carriérons*, or narrow streets, reveals the character and heritage that remain from this period: granite houses with roofs of *lauze* (schist tiles) or barrel tiles, and stately residences behind whose mullioned windows craftspeople and merchants are busy at work. The high point of any visit is to be found in the heart of the town, at the Gothic church of Saint Martin, with its rich statuary. Surrounded by wooded countryside and chestnut forests, Marcolès also has much to offer those in search of outdoor activities.

 **HIGHLIGHTS**

Église Saint-Martin (15th century): 15th-century polychrome stone statues, 14th-century wood statue-reliquary of Saint Martin, frescoes, 17th-century crucifix (04 71 46 94 82).
Clogmaker's workshop and forge: Traditional workshop from 1925 and demonstrations; forge from the 1930s (original hearth and tools). Tours by appt. (06 63 07 05 10).
Village: Self-guided heritage trail (informative panels, leaflet, and interactive digital map; 04 71 46 94 82); guided group tours of the village, church, and artisan workshops, tastings (Les Esclops association, 06 63 07 05 10); family treasure hunts for kids aged 6+ (04 71 46 94 82).

 ACCOMMODATION & EATING OUT

Hotel-restaurants
♥ Auberge de la Tour**** (04 71 46 99 15).

 LOCAL SPECIALTIES

Food and Drink
Mead.
Art and Crafts
Potters • Clogmaker • Painter • "Galoche du Cantal" clogs.

 EVENTS

Jul.: Les Nuits de Marcolès, storytelling and music (4th week)
Aug.: Criterium Cycliste International (1st Wed.); Lez'Arts de la Rue, street arts festival (15th).
Nov.: Art and craft market (2nd weekend)

 OUTDOOR ACTIVITIES

Walking and mountain biking • Cycling.

 FURTHER AFIELD

•Boisset: Château d'Entraygues; Maurs: Medieval town; Montsalvy: Medieval town and Puy de l'Arbre; Aurillac (8–15 miles/13–24 km).
•Lac de Saint-Étienne-Cantalès (17 miles/27 km).

 MBVF NEARBY
•Conques (21 miles/34 km).

Cantal (15)
Population: 610
Altitude: 2,257 ft. (688 m)

TOURIST INFO
04 71 46 94 82
chataigneraie-cantal.com

Martel

A gastronomic stopover in Quercy

Built on the limestone plateau in Haut Quercy with which it shares its name, Martel is a genuine architectural and gastronomic treasure steeped in southern calm. Nicknamed "the city of 7 towers," Martel emerged from the intersection of trade routes running north to south and east to west. The village is also located on the pilgrimage route to Rocamadour, which contributed to its development. Fortified with a double wall erected in the 12th and 14th centuries to protect it from numerous conflicts, medieval Martel remained the capital of the Quercy portion of the Vicomté de Turenne for five centuries and became a wealthy merchant town. In the 19th century, the village's proximity to the Dordogne was a strategic advantage: near the river's banks, barge captains unloaded salt and wine from western France. Renowned for truffles, an exceptional product of Martel's terroir, the village is also classified as a Site Remarquable du Goût for its walnuts.

 HIGHLIGHTS

Palais de la Raymondie (13th–14th centuries): Museum of the Gallo-Roman site Uxellodunum, exhibitions on the history of Martel (06 84 07 60 24 / 05 65 37 30 03).

Église Saint-Maur (11th century): Fortified Gothic church rebuilt in the 14th century, sculpted tympanum, 131-ft. (40-m) bell tower.

Haut Quercy tourist train "Le Truffadou": 8-mile (13-km) round-trip tour on the railroad used to transport truffles during the interwar period (05 65 33 22 00).

Reptiland: Vivarium-aquarium with one of the largest reptile collections in Europe (05 65 37 41 00).

Village: Self-guided tour with booklet; evening guided tours in summer and recreational tours (05 65 33 81 36); guided tour by tourist train (daytime and evening) in peak season (05 65 33 65 99).

 ACCOMMODATION & EATING OUT

Hotel-restaurants
♥ Domaine Les Falaises*** (05 65 27 18 44).

 LOCAL SPECIALTIES

Food and Drink
AOP Périgord walnuts • Walnut oil • Truffles • Duck products • Lavender.
Art and Crafts
Art galleries • Antiques • Ceramist • Painter • Enameler • Stained-glass artist • Bookbinder.

 EVENTS

Market: Wed. and Sat. a.m., Halles de Martel, Place des Consuls.
Dec.–Feb.: Truffle market (1st Sat.).
Jul.–Aug.: Dances under Les Halles (Wed. nights).
Jul.–Sept.: Gourmet market (once a month).

 OUTDOOR ACTIVITIES

Swimming in the Dordogne at Plage de Gluges • Canoeing and kayaking • Walking • Mountain biking • Paragliding.

 FURTHER AFIELD

- Creysse (4½ miles/7 km).
- Brive-la-Gaillarde (19 miles/30 km).

 MBVF NEARBY
- Carennac (10 miles/16 km).
- Turenne (10½ miles/17 km).
- Curemonte (12 miles/19 km).
- Loubressac (16 miles/26 km).
- Autoire (17 miles/27 km)
- Rocamadour (18 miles/29 km).
- Beaulieu-sur-Dordogne (19 miles/30 km).

Lot (46)
Population: 1,660
Altitude: 787 ft. (240 m)

TOURIST INFO-VALLÉE DE LA DORDOGNE
05 65 33 22 00
vallee-dordogne.com

Ménerbes

Tranquility and beauty in the Luberon

Perched on a ridge clinging to the side of the Luberon mountains, Ménerbes looks down over vines and cherry trees. It has been inhabited since prehistoric times, as La Pichoune dolmen (funerary monument)—unique in Vaucluse—attests. But it was during the Middle Ages and the Renaissance that the village acquired its historic buildings, such as the abbey of Saint-Hilaire or the Carmelite convent. In a symphony of luminous, golden stone, very fine 16th- and 17th-century residences are dotted along the fortified rocky spine, facing the Vaucluse mountains. The citadel, reinforced after a siege to protect the inhabitants, strikes an imposing silhouette at one end of the village. Visitors can also admire the castelet where Nicolas de Staël lived; the old vicarage; the former residence of General Robert, and later Dora Maar; and the Hôtel d'Astier de Montfaucon, a former hospice that today houses the Maison de la Truffe et du Vin du Luberon.

 **HIGHLIGHTS**

Abbaye Saint-Hilaire (13th century): Former Carmelite convent; chapel, cloisters, chapter house, refectory (Apr.-Nov.).
Maison de la Truffe et du Vin (17th-18th centuries): Showcase and boutique for truffles and wines of the Luberon (04 90 72 24 94).
Maison Jane Eakin: House/museum of the American painter (1919-2002). Tours in summer by appt. (04 90 72 21 80).
Musée du Tire-Bouchon: Collection of more than 1,200 corkscrews from the 17th century to the present, located at the Domaine de la Citadelle (04 90 72 41 58).
Botanical garden: 6 terraces from the 18th century.
Chapelle Notre-Dame-des-Grâces (18th century).
Chapelle Saint-Blaise (18th century).
Église Saint-Luc (16th century).
Dolmen de la Pichoune: Neolithic funerary monument.

 ACCOMMODATION & EATING OUT

menerbes.fr

 LOCAL SPECIALTIES

Food and Drink
Fruit and vegetables • Luberon truffles • AOC Côtes du Luberon wines.
Art and Crafts
Interior decoration • Fashion • Art photographer • Pottery • Ironworker • Painters.

 EVENTS

Market: Thurs. 9 a.m.–12 p.m. (Apr.-Oct.).
Jul.-Aug.: Les Musicales du Luberon; La Strada, open-air Italian cinema (late Jul.-early Aug.).
Aug.: Fête de la Saint-Louis (3rd weekend).
Dec.: Truffle market and concert (last weekend).

 OUTDOOR ACTIVITIES

Walking: Marked trails • Cycling: "Autour du Luberon à Vélo," Luberon by bike (regional nature park) • Mountain biking.

 FURTHER AFIELD

•Cavaillon; Apt; Avignon (10–25 miles/16–40 km).

MBVF NEARBY
•Gordes (7 miles/11 km).
•Roussillon (10 miles/16 km).
•Lourmarin (13½ miles/22 km).
•Venasque (15 miles/24 km).

Vaucluse (84)
Population: 1,014
Altitude: 735 ft. (224 m)

TOURIST INFO—PAYS D'APT LUBERON
04 90 72 21 80
luberon-apt.fr
menerbes.fr

candles) • Interior decoration • Bookshop • Art gallery • Paintings and sculptures • Lighting • Watercolorist.

 EVENTS

Jul.–Aug.: Jazz de Minerve (Tues.); festival of travel photography.

OUTDOOR ACTIVITIES

Swimming • Walking: Route GR 77 and 2 marked trails.

Minerve

Vines and stone

Nestling on a spur emerging from the deep gorges carved by two rivers, Minerve is a stone ship beached in the garigue (scrubland). Inhabited for 6,000 years, this wine-growing village owes its impregnable position to the two gorges of the Briant and Cesse rivers that enclose it. Backing onto the castle and protected behind its ramparts, Minerve resisted Simon de Monfort's crusading army for several weeks in 1210. Its 11th-century Église Saint-Étienne houses the oldest altar in France. A stele near the church and the street named Rue des Martyrs keep alive the memory of 180 Cathars burned at the stake after their surrender. The "Candela"—the corner of a wall rising toward the sky—is all that remains of the castle, which was demolished in the 17th century. At the edge of the village, a path leads down from the southern postern to the Cesse, which remains dry for much of the year, and the stone bridges that cross it.

 HIGHLIGHTS

Musée Archéologique et Paléontologique (archaeology and paleontology museum): Permanent and temporary exhibitions (04 68 91 22 92).
Musée Hurepel: History of the Cathars and the Crusades told through original figurines and miniature decors (04 68 91 12 26).
Village: Guided group tour only and by appt. of the village, ramparts, and church, with its early Christian altar (04 68 91 81 43).

 ACCOMMODATION & EATING OUT

minervois-caroux.com

 LOCAL SPECIALTIES

Food and Drink
Goat cheeses • AOC Minervois wines • Olive oil.
Art and Crafts
Artisanal products (jewelry,

FURTHER AFIELD

•Lac de Jouarres (11 miles/18 km).
•Caunes-Minervois (16 miles/26 km).
•Narbonne (20 miles/32 km).
•Lastours (25½ miles/41 km).
•Carcassonne (29 miles/47 km).
•Oppidum d'Ensérune, archaeological site; Béziers (28 miles/45 km).

Hérault (34)
Population: 104
Altitude: 745 ft. (227 m)

TOURIST INFO—MINERVOIS AU CAROUX
04 68 91 81 43
minervois-caroux.com
minerve-occitanie.fr

Mirmande

Hilltop orchard in the Rhône valley

Mirmande clambers up the hill to the Église Sainte-Foy, from where there are far-reaching views of the Rhône valley and the Vivarais mountains. The tall façades of Mirmande scale the north face of the Marsanne massif, emerging from the ancient ramparts and overlapping each other to seek protection from the Mistral. Dominating the Tessonne valley, where thousands of fruit trees bloom in spring, this jewel in the Drôme valley is a maze of lanes, cobblestones, and steps, all ablaze with flowers. At the very top stands the delightful 13th-century Église Sainte-Foy. Although Mirmande stopped breeding silkworms at the end of the 19th century—several old silkworm nurseries keep the memory of this prosperous industry alive—the village was given a new lease on life thanks to its fruit production, as well as to the initiatives of two individuals: the cubist painter and writer André Lhote (1885–1962), who created his summer school here, and the geologist Haroun Tazieff, who was mayor from 1979 to 1989.

 HIGHLIGHTS

Église Sainte-Foy (12th century): Exhibitions and concerts.
Chareyron orchard: Self-guided tour daily.
Village: Guided group tour Mar.–Oct., by appt. (04 75 63 10 88).

 ACCOMMODATION & EATING OUT

valleedeladrome-tourisme.com

LOCAL SPECIALTIES

Food and Drink
Seasonal fruit, vegetables, and fruit juice • Drôme vins de pays.
Art and Crafts
Jewelry designer • Painters • Sculptors • Art galleries • Silkscreen printer • Pottery • Glassmaking • Interior decoration • Antiques • Dressmaker.

 EVENTS

Market: Sat. 9 a.m.–1 p.m.
Mar.: Nature trail (last weekend).
Oct.: Rare plant and garden fair (2nd Sun.).
Dec.: Torchlight walks; Nativity scenes in village.

 OUTDOOR ACTIVITIES

Walking • Mountain biking.

 FURTHER AFIELD

• Cliousclat, pottery village (1 mile/2 km).
• Montélimar (12½ miles/20 km).
• Forêt de Saoû (20 miles/32 km).
• Vallée de la Gervanne (22 miles/35 km).

 MBVF NEARBY
• Le Poët-Laval (21 miles/34 km).
• Grignan (25 miles/40 km).
• La Garde-Adhémar (26 miles/42 km).

Drôme (26)
Population: 553
Altitude: 640 ft. (195 m)

TOURIST INFO—VALLÉE DE LA DRÔME
04 75 63 10 88
valleedeladrome-tourisme.com
TOWN HALL
04 75 63 03 90

Mittelbergheim
The fine wines of Zotzenberg

On the wine route in Alsace, at the foot of Mont Sainte-Odile, Mittelbergheim combines exceptional architectural unity, hospitality, and the art of wine-making. Mittelbergheim was founded by the Franks near Mont Sainte-Odile, and was dedicated to this patron saint of Alsace. For many years it belonged to nearby Andlau Abbey, erected in the 9th century by the wife of Emperor Charles le Gros. Glowing with vibrant colors in fall and wild tulips in springtime, the village is surrounded by vineyards from its base (where the Rhine Plain begins) to the Zotzenberg vineyard on the hilltop. Here, the Sylvaner grape is grown, among other varieties, making some of the very best *grand cru* wines. The façades of the houses lining the village streets form harmonious perspectives; dating from the 16th and 17th centuries, they are superbly preserved, adorning the streets with their eye-catching pink sandstone frontages.

 HIGHLIGHTS

Former oil mill (18th century). **Mémoire de Vignerons, Musée Viticole**: Museum conserving wine-producing heritage. Free self-guided tour Sun. afternoon Jul.–Oct.; guided group tour of 4+ people by appt. (03 88 08 00 96).
Mittelbergheim-Zotzenberg wine trail: Signposted walk (panels made by artists presenting the 7 Alsatian grape varieties and comic strips illustrating the work of a winegrower).
Village: Guided tour by appt.; self-guided tour (information panels, map available from town hall; 03 88 08 92 29).

 ACCOMMODATION & EATING OUT

paysdebarr.fr

 LOCAL SPECIALTIES

Food and Drink
Honey • AOC Alsace and *grand cru* Zotzenberg Sylvaner wines.
Art and Crafts
Ceramic sculptures • Cabinetmaking • Graphic creations.

 EVENTS

Jul.: Fête du Vin, wine festival (last weekend).
Jul.-Aug.: Sommermarik, local produce market (Wed. evening).
Oct.: Fête du Vin Nouveau, new wine festival (2nd weekend).
Dec.: Bredelmarik, market for Alsatian Christmas cakes (1st Sun.).

 OUTDOOR ACTIVITIES

Walking: Route GR 5 and Chemin de Compostelle (Saint James's Way), marked trails • Mountain biking.

 FURTHER AFIELD

• Alsace Wine Route: Barr (1 mile/2 km), Obernai (6 miles/10 km).
• La Seigneurie (1 mile/2 km).
• Mont Sainte-Odile (9½ miles/15 km).
• Sélestat (12½ miles/20 km).
• Strasbourg (22½ miles/36 km).

 MBVF NEARBY
• Bergheim (18½ miles/30 km).

Bas-Rhin (67)
Population: 580
Altitude: 722 ft. (220 m)

TOURIST INFO—PAYS DE BARR
03 88 08 66 65
paysdebarr.fr

Moncontour

Born of revolution

In a spot where two green valleys meet, Moncontour is girdled by its imposing medieval ramparts. The village was founded in the 11th century as part of the defenses for nearby Lamballe, capital of Penthièvre. Despite being damaged in numerous battles during the Middle Ages and partly dismantled during the French Revolution by order of Richelieu, the walls still boast eleven of its original fifteen towers, together with the Saint-Jean postern. Echoing its Finistère neighbor Locronan, from the 18th century until the Industrial Revolution Moncontour developed around the production of *berlinge* (wool and linen cloth), which was exported to South America and the Indies. Standing out in this granite-and-slate setting, the grand mansions, town hall, and Église Saint-Mathurin are reminders of this prosperous era. At the end of the 18th century, during the Chouannerie uprisings against the Revolutionary government, the republican General Hoche established his headquarters in a mansion on the Place Penthièvre.

 **HIGHLIGHTS**

Église Saint-Mathurin (16th and 18th centuries): Historic 16th-century stained-glass windows.
Jardin d'Hildegarde: Medieval vegetable and flower garden. Open Sun. in summer (02 96 93 63 50).
Théâtre du Costume: Permanent exhibitions on knights in the Middle Ages, and costumes from Louis XII (1498–1515) to 1900 (Carolyne Morel, 06 81 87 33 40).
Village: Heritage walk, "The medieval fortress" (90 mins). Guided tours for individuals in summer (Tues. a.m.), and all year round by appt. for groups; carriage rides Mon. in summer (02 57 25 22 22).

 ACCOMMODATION & EATING OUT

capderquy-valandre.com

 LOCAL SPECIALTIES

Food and Drink
Rocher de Moncontour (chocolate).
Art and Crafts
Pottery • Ceramist • Dressmaker-hatmaker• Bead artist • Stylist • Costume designer • Painter • Résidence des Arts (art and craft exhibitions and residencies).

 EVENTS

Market: Tues. 4:30–7:30 p.m., by the church.
May: Urban mountain-bike downhill race (1st Sun.).
Jul.–Aug.: Les Remparts Font du Bruit, music festival (Tues evening).
Aug.: Festival Dell Arte, street art (last weekend).
Dec.: Ménestrail, cross-country trail (1st Sat.).

 OUTDOOR ACTIVITIES

Walking • Horseback riding • Mountain biking • Nordic walking • Fishing.

 FURTHER AFIELD

•Plémy (3 miles/5 km).
•Hénon, Quessoy, and Trébry: Parks and residences of Ancien Régime notables (3½–5 miles/6–8 km).
•Lamballe: Haras National, equestrian center; Musée Mathurin Méheut, museum on the artist; collegiate church (10 miles/16 km).
•Saint-Brieuc (16 miles/26 km).

Côtes-d'Armor (22)
Population: 800
Altitude: 394 ft. (120 m)

TOURIST INFO—CAP D'ERQUY VAL ANDRÉ
02 57 25 22 22
capderquy-valandre.com

Monestiés

Old stones in France's unspoilt southwest

Situated between Albi and Cordes-sur-Ciel, cradled in a bend of the Cérou river, Monestiés overlooks a pristine landscape and bears witness to its rich past. The once-fortified medieval village grew up around the Église Saint-Pierre, a seat of religious and political power from the 10th century. Its first appearance in written records dates back to 936. The name "Monestiés" seems to derive from the word for "monastery" and thus would suggest that the village belonged to a nearby religious foundation. It has retained its historic maze of narrow streets lined with old residences. Throughout the village, half-timbered houses, doors with carved lintels, and corbeled arcades and houses display a warm and harmonious simplicity. One of these buildings—an old townhouse from the 15th century—today houses the Bajén Vega museum, dedicated to the work of two exiled Spanish artists who made their home in the Tarn.

 HIGHLIGHTS

Chapelle Saint-Jacques (16th century): 15th-century statuary in polychrome limestone representing the 3 last Stations of the Cross. Guided tour and 3D tour with immersive sound effects (05 63 80 14 02).
Musée Bajén Vega: Paintings by Francisco Bajén and Martine Vega; mini-museum for toddlers (05 63 76 19 17).
Église Saint-Pierre (10th and 16th centuries): Monumental 17th-century altarpiece and 18th-century painting.
Village: Guided group tour of 15+ people Apr.–Oct. by appt. (05 63 80 14 02).

 ACCOMMODATION & EATING OUT

monesties.fr

LOCAL SPECIALTIES

Food and Drink
Honey • Lamb • Rabbit • Vegetables.

Art and Crafts
Luthier and bow maker • Pottery.

 EVENTS

May: European Night of Museums (3rd Sat.)
Jun.: Fête de l'Âne, donkey festival (early Jun.); La Nuit Romantique (Sat. after summer solstice).
Jul.–Aug.: Evening farmers' market (Thurs. 5:30 p.m.).

 OUTDOOR ACTIVITIES

Horseback riding • Fishing • Walking and mountain biking: Marked trails • Botanical trail • Water sports: La Roucarié lakeside leisure park.

 FURTHER AFIELD

•Cap'Découverte-Le Garric, Cagnac-les-Mines: Musée-Mine Départemental; Albi; Gaillac (6–17 miles/10–27 km).

 MBVF NEARBY
•Cordes-sur-Ciel (9½ miles/15 km).
•Najac (18½ miles/30 km).
•Castelnau-de-Montmiral (21½ miles/35 km).

Tarn (81)
Population: 1,360
Altitude: 689 ft. (210 m)

TOURIST INFO—SÉGALA TARNAIS
05 63 76 19 17
monesties.fr
tourisme-tarn-carmaux.fr

Monflanquin

A Tuscan air

French writer Stendhal (1783–1842) called the landscape around Monflanquin in the southwest of France "a little Tuscany." Founded in 1256 by Alphonse de Poitiers, brother of Louis IX (Saint Louis), Monflanquin is one of about three hundred fortified towns or villages that were typically built by the kings of France and England or the counts of Toulouse, who were fighting for control of the southwest of France. At the end of the 14th century, the village became the center of a bailiwick and was enclosed within ramparts punctuated by fortified gates and topped with towers. The ramparts were destroyed in 1622 by royal proclamation after the clashes of the Wars of Religion. Monflanquin has nevertheless retained its characteristic checkerboard street plan. At the heart of the village, the Place des Arcades features a broad colonnade supported by stone pillars; it contains stunning residences, including the House of the Black Prince. From the Cap del Pech, there is a spectacular view over the Lède valley.

 **HIGHLIGHTS**

Musée des Bastides: History of medieval fortified towns; recreational interactive tour, activities for kids (05 53 36 40 19).
Village: Discovery tour of the fortified town with Janouille la Fripouille, a medieval troubadour, by appt. (05 53 36 40 19). Geocaching trail "Tales and Legends" (Tèrra Aventura app.).
Pollen, contemporary art hub and artists' residence: Exhibitions, lectures, and events (05 53 36 54 37).

 **ACCOMMODATION & EATING OUT**

coeurdebastides.com

LOCAL SPECIALTIES

Food and Drink
Foie gras • Cheeses • Organic produce • Beer • Hazelnuts • Prunes • Wine.
Art and Crafts
Jewelry • African crafts • Art galleries • Sculptors • Soap making.

 EVENTS

Market: Thurs. a.m., Place des Arcades; in summer, small market Sun. a.m. and farmers' market Thurs. evening.
Jul.: Baroque music festival (late Jul.).
Aug.: Les Médiévales, medieval festival (13th–15th).
Sept.: Les Foulées Monflanquinoises, organized runs for all ages (1st Sun.).

 OUTDOOR ACTIVITIES

Horseback riding • Fishing • Walking • Mountain biking.

 FURTHER AFIELD

•Gavaudun: Castle (7 miles/11 km).
•Saint-Avit: Musée Bernard-Palissy (7½ miles/12 km).
•Châteaux de Biron and de Bonaguil (10½–14½ miles/17–23 km).

 MBVF NEARBY
•Villeréal (8 miles/13 km).
•Penne-d'Agenais (12½ miles/20 km).
•Monpazier (13½ miles/22 km).

Lot-et-Garonne (47)
Population: 2,352
Altitude: 594 ft. (181 m)

TOURIST INFO—COEUR DE BASTIDES
05 53 36 40 19
coeurdebastides.com

Monpazier

An iconic fortified town

Eight hundred years after its foundation, Monpazier retains its original street plan and remains an excellent example of a medieval *bastide* (fortified town). It was founded in 1284 by Edward I, king of England. Despite the hardships caused by the Hundred Years War, famine, and epidemics, Monpazier is remarkably well preserved. Amid the three hundred or so *bastides* of the southwest, Monpazier's singularity and exemplarity as a masterpiece of architecture and urban planning led architects Viollet le Duc and Le Corbusier to consider it a model for all fortified towns. Crisscrossed by *carreyras* (streets) and *carreyrous* (alleys), the village is laid out around the delightful Place des Cornières. Perfectly square, it is lined with 13th-century buildings and surrounded by 14th- and 18th-century arcades. Among the superb medieval structures are the central covered market; the Église Saint-Dominique with its square bell tower; the chapter house; the Dîmes barn, and three fortified gates.

 HIGHLIGHTS

Bastideum - Musée de Monpazier: History and way of life of local fortified towns; medieval garden, traditional games, escape game, events, Apr.–late Oct. (05 53 57 12 12).
Église Saint-Dominique (13th and 15th centuries): Stalls.
Village: Guided group tour by appt.; evening tour by torchlight Mon. 9:30 p.m. in Jul.–Aug. (05 53 22 68 59).

 ACCOMMODATION & EATING OUT

Hotels
♥ Hôtel Edward 1er **** (05 53 22 44 00).
♥ Le Chevalier Bleu (05 53 63 50 97).

 LOCAL SPECIALTIES

Food and Drink
Périgord specialties • Wine.
Art and Crafts
Jewelry • Turned wood • Ceramics • Bookbinding • Gilding on wood • Framing •

Clock maker • Leather goods • Marquetry • Painting • Photographer • Glass painting • Glassblowing • Stained glass • Wall hangings • Upholstery fabrics.

 EVENTS

Market: Thurs. 7 a.m.–1 p.m.; mushroom market every afternoon in fall.
May: Art and crafts fair (Ascension weekend); Fête des Fleurs, flower festival.
Jul.: Cycling after dark (last Thurs.).
Aug.: Eté Musical en Bergerac, music festival (early Aug.).

 OUTDOOR ACTIVITIES

Walking.

 FURTHER AFIELD

•Abbaye de Cadouin (10 miles/16 km).

 MBVF NEARBY
•Belvès (10 miles/16 km).
•Monflanquin (13½ miles/22 km).

Dordogne (24)
Population: 502
Altitude: 650 ft. (198 m)

TOURIST INFO—BASTIDES DORDOGNE-PÉRIGORD
05 53 22 68 59
pays-bergerac-tourisme.com
monpazier.fr

Montbrun-les-Bains

Thermal treatments at the gateway to Provence

At Montbrun, situated between the Lure and Ventoux mountains, the region of Drôme takes on Provençal features, with lavender, linden trees, and aromatic plants. Tiered on the steep sides of a hill, the high façades of Montbrun are pierced with windows like arrow slits. They stand as the last line of defense protecting the imposing remains of a historic medieval castle. Rebuilt during the Renaissance, the castle was looted during the French Revolution. From the Place de l'Horloge and its belfry as far as the Sainte-Marie gate, narrow cobblestone alleyways lead from fountain to fountain, and to the 12th-century church, which houses a splendid Baroque altarpiece and several paintings, including *Coronation of the Virgin* by Pierre Parrocel. At the foot of the village, thermal baths in a modern building benefit from a spring that the Romans used; the waters help respiratory and rheumatic ailments, and improve fitness.

HIGHLIGHTS

Church (12th century): Baroque altarpiece, painting by Pierre Parrocel.
Thermes de Montbrun-les-Bains: Thermal spa, activities, thermal and beauty treatments (04 75 28 80 75).
Village: Guided tour Tues. 3 p.m. Apr.–Oct. (5 p.m. Jul.-Aug.) by appt.; guided evening tour by torchlight Mon. 9:30 p.m. in Jul.-Aug. (04 75 28 82 49).

ACCOMMODATION & EATING OUT

baronnies-tourisme.com

LOCAL SPECIALTIES

Food and Drink
Goat cheese • Honey, herbs, and spices • Einkorn wheat • Organic produce.
Art and Crafts
Pottery• Perfumes and aromatic plants.

EVENTS

Market: Sat. 9 a.m.–12 p.m., Place de la Mairie; farmers' market Mon. 4–7 p.m. (Apr.–Oct.); summer market 5– 8 p.m. (Jul.-Aug.).
Sept.: Journée Bien-être au Naturel, plant and wellbeing fair (1st Sun.); local saint's day and fireworks (2nd Sat.).
Oct.: Fête de la Courge, pumpkin and squash festival (mid-Oct.).

OUTDOOR ACTIVITIES

Canyoning • Rock climbing • Via Ferrata • Horseback riding • Walking: GR route and 24 marked trails • Cycling • Mountain biking.

FURTHER AFIELD

• Sault (7½ miles/12 km).
• Buis-les-Baronnies (16 miles/26 km).
• Nyons (18½ miles/30 km).
• Vallée du Toulourenc; Vaison-la-Romaine (20 miles/32 km).
• Mont Ventoux (23½ miles/38 km).

Drôme (26)
Population: 451
Altitude: 1,969 ft. (600 m)

TOURIST INFO—BARONNIES EN DRÔME PROVENÇALE
04 75 28 82 49
baronnies-tourisme.com

Montclus

Between river and lavender fields

Sitting at a bend in the Cèze river, clothed in vineyards and lavender, Monclus exudes all the charm of a Languedoc village. Inhabited since prehistoric times, the site attracted fishing tribes to settle before it became Castrum Montecluso in the Middle Ages, earning its name from its hilltop position at the foot of a mountain. In the 13th century, both the abbey of Mons Serratus and an imposing fortified castle were built here. A few ruins of the old troglodyte Benedictine monastery remain, as well as a vast room hewn out of the rock, while the huge square tower of the castle still casts its long shadow over the village's pink-tiled roofs. From the Place de l'Église, narrow alleys, steps, and covered passageways punctuate the village. As visisters wander past the bright stone façades of lovingly restored residences, they catch occasional glimpses of lush green gardens tumbling down to the Cèze—a haven of peace and tranquility.

 HIGHLIGHTS

Church (19th century).
Castle: Main hall, Saint-Gilles spiral staircase. Open Jul.–Aug.; guided tour daily in Jul. (04 66 82 25 73).
Village: Guided tour in peak season (04 66 82 30 02).

ACCOMMODATION & EATING OUT

provenceoccitane.com

 LOCAL SPECIALTIES

Food and Drink
Honey • Olive oil • Lavender essence.
Art and Crafts
Painter • Carpenter • Ironworker.

EVENTS

Market: Provençal market Tues. a.m. (Jul.-Aug.).
Aug.: Local saint's day (1st weekend).

OUTDOOR ACTIVITIES

Swimming • Canoeing and kayaking • Walking • Horseback riding • Mountain biking.

FURTHER AFIELD

•Cornillon; Goudargues (6 miles/10 km).
•Bagnols-sur-Cèze: market, Pont-Saint-Esprit (15 miles/24 km).
•Grotte Chauvet 2, cave (18½ miles/30 km).
•Gorges de l'Ardèche (21 miles/34 km).

MBVF NEARBY
•Aiguèze (9½ miles/15 km).
•La Roque-sur-Cèze (12½ miles/20 km).
•Lussan (15½ miles/25 km).

Gard (30)
Population: 188
Altitude: 295 ft. (90 m)

TOURIST INFO—PROVENCE OCCITANE
04 66 82 30 02
provenceoccitane.com
village-montclus.fr

119

Montpeyroux

A labyrinth in sandstone

Perched on a mound to the south of Clermont-Ferrand and winding around its castle keep, the medieval village of Montpeyroux offers a panoramic view of the Auvergne volcanos. Sitting on the ancient Régordane Way linking the Auvergne with Languedoc, Montpeyroux exudes a southern flavor. For centuries, its inhabitants made their living from the vineyards and the arkose quarry. Arkose is a sandstone rich in crystalline feldspar, and it is this stone that makes the village's houses sparkle with golden glints. It was also used to build major Romanesque churches in the Auvergne, including Saint-Austremoine in Issoire and Notre-Dame-du-Port in Clermont-Ferrand. The vineyards of Montpeyroux disappeared at the end of the 19th century during the outbreak of phylloxera, and the quarry closed in 1935, heralding the village's decline. However, restoration work began in the 1960s, and Montpeyroux has been given a new lease on life thanks to the replanting of vines and the arrival of artists and artisans.

 HIGHLIGHTS

Montpeyroux tower (13th century): Paid visit Apr.–Oct. (04 73 96 62 68).
Église Notre-Dame (1846–1847).
Ferme Pédagogique de la Moulerette: Educational farm with 50 animal breeds; workshops and activities (06 30 92 48 35).
Village: Guided tour all year round by appt. (04 73 96 62 68).

 ACCOMMODATION & EATING OUT

montpeyroux63.com

LOCAL SPECIALTIES

Food and Drink
AOC Côtes d'Auvergne wines • Regional produce (store).
Art and Crafts
Ceramists • Art galleries • Picture framing workshop • Photographer • Artists •

Driftwood objects • Tattoo artist • Enameled lava • Pebbles • Soaps • Candles.

 OUTDOOR ACTIVITIES

Fishing • Walking: 2 marked trails, "L'Arkose" (5½ or 7½ miles/9 or 12 km) • Mountain biking • Rock climbing.

 FURTHER AFIELD

•Issoire (9½ miles/15 km).
•Clermont-Ferrand (12½ miles/20 km).
•Saint-Nectaire; Besse-en-Chandesse; Massif du Sancy (12½–25 miles/20–40 km).
•Abbaye de Mégemont (14½ miles/23 km).

 MBVF NEARBY
•Usson (15 miles/24 km).

Puy-de-Dôme (63)
Population: 360
Altitude: 1,499 ft. (457 m)

TOURIST INFO—AUVERGNE PAYS D'ISSOIRE
04 73 89 15 90
issoire-tourisme.com
montpeyroux63.com

Montréal

Ancient and medieval Gascony

Located between Haut- and Bas-Armagnac, and surrounded by vineyards, the *bastide* (fortified town) of Montréal stands in the heart of Gascony and the Ténarèze. In 1255, Alphonse de Poitiers, the brother of Louis IX (Saint Louis) built the first Gascon fortified town on a spur overlooking the Auzoue river. A grid of streets and cobbled lanes lead to the central square, which is lined with arcades on three sides. Built into the fortifications, of which a ribbed gate remains, the 13th-century Gothic Église Saint-Philippe-et-Saint-Jacques, with its flat, square bell tower, looks down on half-timbered houses. To the north, the pre-Romanesque Église Saint-Pierre-de-Genens features a reused Roman colonnade and a Chi-Rho (symbol for Christ) carved into the antique marble. With its Flamboyant Gothic floorplan and vaulting, the small chapel of Luzanet represents an architectural style rarely found in southwest France. The older, 4th-century Séviac Roman villa is a 70,000-sq.-ft. (6,500 m²) palace boasting sumptuous mosaics and thermal baths.

 HIGHLIGHTS

Collégiale Saint-Philippe-et-Saint-Jacques (13th century).
Église Saint-Pierre-de-Genens (11th century): Carved portal, white marble tympanum.
Chapelle de Luzanet (16th century): Chapel built on an ancient Gallo-Roman site, panoramic views over the vineyards.
Église de Routgès (13th century).
Séviac Gallo-Roman villa: Vast polychrome mosaic floor, thermal baths (05 62 09 71 38).
Site Paléontologique de Béon: Major European fossil site. Guided tour in summer and all year round for groups by appt. (05 62 28 00 80).
La Fabrique à Souvenirs (The memory factory): Discovery tour and activities, in the Armagnac-Gascogne vineyard, free admission (05 62 28 00 80).
Village: Guided tour of the fortified town by appt., all year round for groups (05 62 28 00 80); downloadable visit and treasure hunt, geocaching (05 62 28 00 80.

 ACCOMMODATION & EATING OUT

tourisme-condom.com

 **LOCAL SPECIALTIES**

Food and Drink
Preserves (foie gras, duck confit, etc.) • Cheese • Honey • Wine, Floc de Gascogne, and Armagnac.

Art and Crafts
Ceramist • Painters • Paintings on cardboard • Statues in reconstituted marble.

 EVENTS

Market: Fri. 8 a.m.–1 p.m, under the Arcades.
Late Mar.–early Apr.: European Artistic Craft Days.
Jul.–Aug.: Evening gourmet markets; *courses landaises* (traditional bull leaping and dodging) and village festival (1st fortnight Aug.).
Nov.: Flamme de l'Armagnac festival (3rd weekend).

 OUTDOOR ACTIVITIES

Fishing (Étang de Montréal) • Walking: GR 65 and PR routes.

 FURTHER AFIELD

• Vallée de l'Auzoue: Fourcès (3½ miles/6 km); Nérac (21 miles/34 km).
• Condom (9½ miles/15 km).

 MBVF NEARBY
• Larressingle (6 miles/10 km).
• La Romieu (18½ miles/30 km).
• Lavardens (25 miles/40 km).

Gers (32)
Population: 1,178
Altitude: 427 ft. (130 m)

TOURIST INFO—LA TÉNARÈZE
05 62 28 00 80
tourisme-condom.com

Montrésor

On the banks of the Indrois

Montrésor gets its name from the treasurer (*trésorier*) of the chapter house at Tours Cathedral, who had his estate here in the 10th century. In the early 11th century, the powerful count of Anjou, Foulques III, began to build a fortress at Montrésor to defend the approaches to the Touraine. Remains of the double ring of defenses are still visible. At the end of the 15th century, Imbert de Bastarnay (advisor to the French kings Louis XI, Charles VIII, Louis XII, and François I) built the present castle in the Renaissance style inside the fortress walls. He also had the collegiate church of Saint-Jean-Baptiste constructed. In 1849, the castle became the property of Xavier Branicki, a Polish count and friend of Napoléon III. He restored it and filled it with many works of art: sculptures by Pierre Vanneau, and paintings from the schools of masters such as Veronese, Kaplinski, and Winterhalter. Converted into a cultural center and exhibition space, Cardeux covered market, which was once the wool market, recalls village life in bygone days.

 HIGHLIGHTS

♥ **Castle** (11th-15th centuries): 15th-century fortifications; art collection, romantic gardens (02 47 19 27 50).
Collégiale Saint-Jean-Baptiste (16th century): Alabaster tomb with three recumbent statues, Annunciation by Philippe de Champaigne, stained-glass windows, 16th-century stalls, reliquary with the skullcap of Pope John Paul II.
Cardeux market (18th century): Permanent exhibition of gemmail stained glass and the history of Montrésor.
Village: Guided group tour only, by appt. (02 47 92 70 71).
Banks of the Indrois: Walking paths and information points along the river.

 ACCOMMODATION & EATING OUT

loches-valdeloire.com

 **LOCAL SPECIALTIES**

Food and Drink
Macarons • Rillettes • Montrésor wine.
Art and Crafts
Local crafts (Maison de Pays shop) • Bladesmith • Interior decoration • Mohair products.

 EVENTS

Market: Sat. a.m., in the covered market.
Jul.-Aug.: Illuminated trail with music and events on the banks of the Indrois (evenings); painters' and sculptors' fair (Aug. 15th).
Dec.: Christmas market (1st–20th).

 OUTDOOR ACTIVITIES

Fishing • Walking: 2 marked trails • Cycling • Horseback riding.

 FURTHER AFIELD

• Lac de Chemillé (1 mile/2 km).
• Chartreuse du Liget (2½ miles/4 km).
• Loches, Vallée de l'Indre (10½ miles/17 km).
• Beauval Zoo (12¼ miles/20 km).
• Château de Valençay (18½ miles/30 km).

Indre-et-Loire (37)
Population: 316
Altitude: 328 ft. (100 m)

TOURIST INFO—LOCHES TOURAINE - CHÂTEAUX DE LA LOIRE
02 47 92 70 71
loches-valdeloire.com
montresor.fr

Mushrooms • AOC Saumur, Saumur-Champigny, Crémant de Loire wines.

Art and Crafts
Antiques • Art galleries.

 EVENTS

Market: Sun. 8 a.m.-1 p.m., Place du Mail.
Mid-Jul.-mid-Aug.: Les Musicales de Montsoreau, music at castle and church.
All year round: Flea market (2nd Sun. of each month).

Montsoreau

The lady's castle

Sitting between Anjou and the Touraine, with the Loire on the horizon, Montsoreau is a place of history, gentle living, and harmony. Close to the royal abbey of Fontevraud, Montsoreau lies between the Loire and a hill, and grew up around its 15th-century castle. The village has conserved a rich heritage marked notably by the Loire river and Montsoreau's lady, Françoise de Maridor; Alexandre Dumas wrote tales about her passionate and fatal love affair with Bussy d'Amboise. Montsoreau has much to offer visitors, who can wander the village's flower-lined paths that climb toward the vineyards, and admire its white tufa-stone residences and immaculately tended gardens. Beyond the many courtyards and alleyways that extend an invitation to stroll, the Loire stretches into the distance, and the Saut aux Loups hillside hides historic troglodytic cave dwellings. A visit here is also an opportunity to taste some famous Saumur-Champigny and Crémant de Loire wines.

 HIGHLIGHTS

Castle (15th century): Museum of contemporary art (02 41 67 12 60).
Église Saint-Pierre-de-Rest (13th-18th centuries; 02 41 51 70 15).
♥ **Champignonnière Le Saut aux Loups**: Mushroom farm in troglodytic caves (02 41 51 70 30).
Maison du Parc Naturel Régional Loire-Anjou-Touraine: Flora and fauna exhibitions (02 41 38 38 88).
Marché des Vins de Loire: Wine tour in a troglodytic cave (02 41 38 15 05).
Village: Guided tour (02 41 51 70 22).

 ACCOMMODATION & EATING OUT

Campsites
L'Isle Verte**** (02 41 51 76 60).

 **LOCAL SPECIALTIES**

Food and Drink
Organic apples and pears •

 OUTDOOR ACTIVITIES

Fishing • Water sports on the Loire • Walking: Route GR 3, 1 marked trail, heritage trail from Montsoreau to Candes-Saint-Martin • Cycling: "La Loire à Vélo" and other trails • Horseback riding trail.

 FURTHER AFIELD

•Abbaye de Fontevraud; Saumur; Chinon (2½–12 miles/ 4–19 km).

 MBVF NEARBY
•Candes-Saint-Martin (½ mile/1 km).
•Crissay-sur-Manse (24 miles/39 km).

Maine-et-Loire (49)
Population: 440
Altitude: 108 ft. (33 m)

TOURIST INFO—SAUMUR VAL DE LOIRE
02 41 51 70 22
ot-saumur.fr | ville-montsoreau.fr

Mornac-sur-Seudre

A pearl in the marshes

Typical of Charente-Maritime, the little port of Mornac exposes the white façades of its houses trimmed with hollyhocks to the sun. During Gallo-Roman times, the attractions of the Seudre river turned the budding village of Mornac into a small fishing town on a hill near the present castle. As commerce developed, attractive low houses began to replace modest huts. Today, Mornac-sur-Seudre is a center of oyster farming as well as salt production, which can be discovered by visiting the salt marshes. Brimming with medieval charm, the old town is crisscrossed by alleys leading to the port. The Romanesque church, built in the 11th century over a Merovingian shrine, is topped by a fortified square tower and has a magnificent chevet.

 **HIGHLIGHTS**

Église Saint-Pierre (11th century): Medieval frescoes, reliquaries.
Seudre marshes: Guided biodiversity tour with the Huître Pédagogique association (06 83 71 34 87); boat tour (07 87 75 25 34).
Salt marsh tour: Meet salt producer Sébastien Rossignol (06 71 09 03 03).
Village: Guided tour (05 46 08 21 00).

 ACCOMMODATION & EATING OUT

royanatlantique.fr

LOCAL SPECIALTIES

Food and Drink
Oysters • Shrimps • Salt.
Art and Crafts
Artisanal leather goods • Jewelry • Bag, clothing, and accessories designer • Salt dough • Painters and sculptors • Pottery• Blowtorch glassmaker.

 EVENTS

Market: Wed., 8 a.m.–1 p.m, in the covered market.
Jul.–Aug.: Evening craft market (Thurs.); exhibitions at the port and church.
Aug. (depending on tide): Voiles de Mornac, annual gathering of traditional sailboats (late Aug.).
Sept.: Pottery market (last weekend).

 OUTDOOR ACTIVITIES

Seudre river cruises • Horseback riding • Canoeing and kayaking • Fishing • Walking: 3 marked trails.

 FURTHER AFIELD

•Saujon: Train des Mouettes, tourist steam train; Royan; La Palmyre: Zoo (6–9½ miles/10–15 km).
•Meschers-sur-Gironde: Grottes de Régulus, cliff-face cave dwellings (15 miles/24 km).

 MBVF NEARBY
•Talmont-sur-Gironde (18 miles/29 km).

Charente-Maritime (17)
Population: 860
Altitude: 16 ft. (5 m)

**TOURIST INFO—
DESTINATION ROYAN
ATLANTIQUE**
05 46 08 21 00
royanatlantique.fr

Artists' studios in former Carmelite convent.

EVENTS

Market: Fri. a.m., local produce and crafts, at covered market (Jul.-Aug.).
Late Mar.-early Apr.: European Artistic Craft Days.
Apr.: Natural wine fair (1st weekend); Fête des Plantes, plant fair (around 20th).
Jul.-Aug.: Haut Limousin festival (late Jul.-early Aug.).

Mortemart

The great and the good in Limousin

A small Limousin town with a glorious past, Mortemart resonates with ten centuries of history. Established on a marshy plain that gave the village its name (*Morte mortuum*, "dead sea"), Mortemart soon enjoyed its glory days. In 995, as a reward for his victorious defense of the neighboring town of Bellac, Abon Drut, lord of Mortemart, was authorized to build a castle on his land. In the 13th century, the seigneury of Mortemart was home to the famous Rochechouart-Mortemart family and was established as a peerage by Louis XIV in 1650. At the end of the 15th century, the castle was modernized with living quarters flanked by towers; part of the moat still remains. Carmelite and Augustinian monasteries, first constructed in 1330, were rebuilt at the end of the 17th century and bear witness to the important religious center founded by Cardinal Pierre Gauvain, who was from Mortemart. The 18th-century covered market, typical of the region, evokes the thriving trade that took place here.

HIGHLIGHTS

Château des Ducs (13th-15th centuries): Privately owned in part; accessible for walks around the old moat.
Carmelite convent (14th-17th centuries): monumental staircase and 17th-century murals; artists' studios.
Église de Saint-Hilaire de Poitiers (14th century): 14th-century polychrome statue of the Virgin; 15th-century stalls; 17th-century lectern, altarpiece; Counter-Reformation stained glass.
Market (17th-18th centuries).
Village: Guided group tour by appt. (05 55 68 12 79); Geocaching trail "The Dead Sea Cache" (Terra Aventura app.).

ACCOMMODATION & EATING OUT

mortemart.fr

 LOCAL SPECIALTIES

Art and Crafts
Poetry publisher •

OUTDOOR ACTIVITIES

Walking: 3 marked trails •
Golf de Mortemart (18 holes).

FURTHER AFIELD

•Monts de Blond, uplands (1-9½ miles/2-15 km).
•Nouic: Château du Fraisse (4 miles/6 km).
•Oradour-sur-Glane: Centre de la Mémoire (9½ miles/15 km).
•Bellac; Le Dorat (8-15½ miles/13-25 km).
•Saint-Junien (12½ miles/20 km).

Haute-Vienne (87)
Population: 124
Altitude: 984 ft. (300 m)

TOURIST INFO—PAYS DU HAUT LIMOUSIN
05 55 68 12 79
visitlimousin.com/haut-limousin
mortemart.fr

Moustiers-Sainte-Marie

The star of Verdon

Tucked in a notch in a crag at the entrance to the Gorges du Verdon, Moustiers continues a tradition of faience making. Located at the foot of two cliffs, at an altitude of nearly 2,000 ft. (600 m), and protected by the legendary star suspended above its rooftops, Moustiers owes its existence to a body of water and its fame to an Italian monk. The water is the Adou river: flowing from a spring in the Vaucluse, it shaped medieval Moustiers's reputation as a village of papermakers, potters, and drapers. In the 17th century, a monk from Faenza brought the secret of enameling to the village, and Moustiers became the capital of "the most beautiful and finest faience in the kingdom." The industry has been revived in recent years, and now over a dozen studios combine tradition with innovation, earning the village the label Ville et Métiers d'Art. On both sides of the river, golden-hued houses topped with Romanesque tiles huddle around small courtyards and line alleys linked by steps and vaulted passageways.

HIGHLIGHTS

Chapelle Notre-Dame-de-Beauvoir (12th and 16th centuries).
Parish church (12th and 14th centuries): Pre-Romanesque vault, nave from 14th and 16th centuries, Lombard bell tower.
Musée de la Faïence: History of faience ceramics from the 17th century to the present (collection of over 400 pieces); exhibitions (04 92 74 61 64).
Village: Guided tours for individuals Apr.–Oct. and groups all year round, by appt. (04 92 74 67 84).

ACCOMMODATION & EATING OUT

Hotels
♥ Le Colombier*** (04 92 74 66 02).
♥ La Ferme Rose*** (04 92 75 75 75).

LOCAL SPECIALTIES

Food and Drink
Cookies • Artisanal preserves, salted produce • Olive oil • Lavender honey • Honey beer.
Art and Crafts
Faience and ceramic workshops • Bladesmith • Glassmaker • Painter.

EVENTS

Market: Fri. 8 a.m.–1 p.m, Place de l'École; Wed. 6–11 p.m. in Jul.–Aug., Place de la Mairie.
Aug.–Sept.: Fête de la Diane (Aug. 31st–Sept. 8th).

OUTDOOR ACTIVITIES

Walking: Route GR 4 and 12 marked trails • Canyoning • Canoeing, kayaking, pedalo • Rock climbing • Paragliding • Mountain biking.

FURTHER AFIELD

• Lac de Sainte-Croix (3 miles/5 km).
• Grand Canyon des Gorges du Verdon; Castellane (6–28 miles/10–45 km).
• Riez (9½ miles/15 km).
• Valensole (20 miles/32 km).
• Gréoux-les-Bains health resort (21 miles/34 km).

Alpes-de-Haute-Provence (04)
Population: 730
Altitude: 2,100 ft. (640 m)

TOURIST INFO—MOUSTIERS-SAINTE-MARIE
04 92 74 67 84
moustiers.fr

Najac
Tumbling rooftops in the Aveyron

Set on a steep hill, the fortress of Najac dominates the village and wild gorges of this southern French region. A simple square tower in the 12th century, the Château de Najac was fortified a century later by Alphonse de Poitiers, last count of Toulouse and brother of Louis IX (Saint Louis). Its strategic position made it the linchpin of the valley and earned it a turbulent history. Belonging to the counts of Toulouse, then the kings of France, it suffered attacks over the centuries from the English, Protestants, and during the Croquant peasant revolts. In the 1200s, inhabitants suspected of being Cathars were sentenced by the Inquisition to build the Église Saint-Jean at their own expense. Its southern-French style of pointed arch makes it one of the first Gothic churches in the region. At the village's center, the long, narrow Place du Barry evokes the village's commercial activities: its stone or half-timbered houses from the 14th and 15th centuries feature arcades to shelter merchandise.

 HIGHLIGHTS

Royal fortress (12th and 13th centuries): Keep, Saint-Julien's Chapel (frescoes), governor's chamber (panoramic view from the terrace). Open Apr.–Oct. (05 65 29 71 65).
Église Saint-Jean (13th–14th centuries): Open daily (05 65 29 71 34).
Maison du Gouverneur: 13th-century house, newly renovated; events, exhibitions, and workshops for young people. Open Apr.–Oct., group tour by appt. (05 65 81 94 47).
Najac Muséum: Permanent collection of photos and postcards on life in Najac, archival documents (06 07 94 85 22).
Village: Guided tours Jul.–Aug., by appt. for groups offseason; torchlit guided tours; sensory tours and nature walks Jul.–Aug.; treasure hunt for kids (05 36 16 20 00).

 ACCOMMODATION & EATING OUT

bastides-gorges-aveyron.fr

 LOCAL SPECIALTIES

Food and Drink
Fouace de Najac (brioche) • *Gâteau à la broche* (spit cake) • *Astet najacois* (roast stuffed pork) • Cheeses • Chocolate.
Art and Crafts
Jewelry • Bladesmith • Potter.

 EVENTS

Market: Sun. 8 a.m.–1 p.m., Place du Faubourg.

Jul.: Sous les Toiles de Najac, open-air cinema festival (2nd week); Festival d'Autan (2nd fortnight).
Jul.–Aug.: Evening market (Wed.).
Aug.: Festival en Bastides, theater and street performances (1st week), village festival (3rd weekend).

 OUTDOOR ACTIVITIES

Canoeing and kayaking • Paddleboarding • Rock climbing • Tree climbing • Horseback riding • Fishing • Via Ferrata • Mountain biking • Walking: Route GR 36 and several marked trails.

 FURTHER AFIELD

•Villefranche-de-Rouergue and Villeneuve, fortified towns (13½–22½ miles/ 22–36 km).
•Saint-Antonin-Noble-Val (17½ miles/28 km).

 MBVF NEARBY

•Cordes-sur-Ciel (15½ miles/25 km).
•Monestiés (18½ miles/30 km).
•Sauveterre-de-Rouergue (26½ miles/43 km).

Aveyron (12)
Population: 700
Altitude: 1,115 ft. (340 m)

TOURIST INFO—BASTIDES ET GORGES DE L'AVEYRON
05 36 16 20 00
bastides-gorges-aveyron.fr

Navarrenx

A bastion in the Pyrenees

Situated at the place where the Gave d'Oloron river and the Saint James's Way meet, Navarrenx is one of the oldest towns in the old province of Béarn. Built as a *bastide* (fortified town) in 1316, Navarrenx enjoyed a number of privileges that helped it to expand. From 1538 onward Henri II d'Albret, king of Navarre, made important alterations in an attempt to protect this vital commercial center and crossroads from the Spanish. Italian architect Fabricio Siciliano was commissioned, and his work is still visible today in the historic stronghold. The impressive ramparts 33 ft. (10 m) high, from which you can see the Pyrenees, provide a magnificent view over the Gave d'Oloron, as well as over several bastions and military structures. The Gave d'Oloron, the longest salmon river in France, has also given Navarrenx its reputation as a "salmon capital," and freshwater fishermen still enjoy its bounties.

 HIGHLIGHTS

Centre d'Interprétation: Museum inside the former arsenal, dedicated to the history of Navarrenx (05 59 66 10 22).
La Poudrière: Permanent exhibition on gunpowder (05 59 66 10 22).
La Porte Saint-Antoine (16th–18th centuries).
Village: Self-guided tour with brochure (available from tourist info center); themed tour for individuals; guided group tour by appt.; model of the fortified town; interactive virtual reality visit (05 59 38 00 33).

 **ACCOMMODATION & EATING OUT**

tourisme-bearn-gaves.com

LOCAL SPECIALTIES

Food and Drink
Salted meats • Jams • Craft beers • Gave river salmon and trout.

Art and Crafts
Artist and interior decorator • Jewelry designer • Pottery • Photographer • Stylist and designer • Ceramics.

 EVENTS

Market: Wed. a.m., Place Darralde; summer market, Sun. a.m., town hall (Jun.–Sept.).
Easter weekend: Craft fair.
Aug.: Festival des Pierres Lyriques, classical music festival (1st fortnight); medieval festival (late Aug.).

 OUTDOOR ACTIVITIES

Walking: Route GR 65 and several marked trails • Mountain biking: 140 miles (225 km) of marked trails • Salmon and trout fishing (1st category) • Golf: 18-hole course.

 FURTHER AFIELD

• Château de Laàs and gardens (6 miles/10 km).
• Église de l'Hôpital-Saint-Blaise, UNESCO World Heritage Site (9½ miles/15 km).
• Sauveterre-de-Béarn (12½ miles/20 km).
• Orthez (14½ miles/23 km).

Pyrénées-Atlantiques (64)
Population: 1,053
Altitude: 394 ft. (120 m)

TOURIST INFO—BÉARN DES GAVES
05 59 38 00 33
tourisme-bearn-gaves.com

Noyers
Medieval Burgundy

On the doorstep of the vineyards of Chablis and the regional nature park of the Morvan, nestled in a bend of the Serein river, Noyers combines a remarkable medieval heritage with the amenities of a lively village in tune with the times. A stone's throw from Auxerre and Vézelay, Noyers invites visitors to travel back in time to centuries past. There is history in each stone here: in the church, chapels, castle ruins, cobbled streets and squares, half-timbered houses—home to winegrowers and the middle classes—mansions, and old tiled roofs. Still protected by ramparts studded with sixteen towers and three fortified gateways, the medieval village offers visitors a well-preserved ensemble set with water and greenery. The heart of the village beats to the rhythm of its crafts and commerce, but also its cultural and gastronomic riches: art collections, truffle market, concerts, and the Gargouillosium—a stone-carving festival, which provided the backdrop for the movie *La Grande Vadrouille*.

HIGHLIGHTS

Musée des Arts Naïfs et Populaires de Noyers (in the 17th-century college): Extensive collection of naive and folk art, including Hokusai's manga notebooks (03 86 82 89 09).

Site of the castle ruins: Discovery tour covering the themes of nature, history, and art; self-guided visit (03 86 82 66 06).

Église Notre-Dame (15th century): Flamboyant Gothic architecture; 16th-century stalls (03 86 82 66 06).

Village: Guided tours in Jul.-Aug. by appt. (03 86 82 66 06); carriage rides (06 26 29 12 48).

ACCOMMODATION & EATING OUT

destinationgrandvezelay.com

LOCAL SPECIALTIES

Food and Drink
AOC Chablis and Irancy wines, Crémant de Bourgogne sparkling wine • Farm produce (goat cheese, lamb, veal).

Art and Crafts
Contemporary art • Art galleries • Antiques• Ceramics • Medieval illuminator • Feathered masks • Wrought ironwork • Tapestry artist • Artisanal leather goods • Pottery • Painters • Upholsterer • Sculptors • Jewelry, clothing, and decorative object designer.

EVENTS

Market: Wed. 8 a.m.-1 p.m.; flea market Sat. a.m. (Jul.-Aug.).
Jul.: Grands Crus de Bourgogne festival (10th–20th).
Aug.: Festival Vallée et Veillée, world music festival (1st weekend).
Sept.: Illuminations as part of the Heritage Weekend (3rd weekend).
Oct.: Truffle market (Sun. before Nov. 1st).

OUTDOOR ACTIVITIES

Swimming (no lifeguard) • Fishing • Walking: 3 marked trails.

FURTHER AFIELD

• Prieuré de Vausse; Buffon: Foundry; Fontenay Abbey (9½–25 miles/15-40 km).
• Chablis (12½ miles/20 km).

MBVF NEARBY
• Montréal (11 miles/18 km).
• Vézelay (25 miles/40 km).

Yonne (89)
Population: 612
Altitude: 620 ft. (189 m)

TOURIST INFO—GRAND VÉZELAY
03 86 82 66 06
destinationgrandvezelay.com

Oingt

(Commune of Val-d'Oingt)

A golden nugget in the heart of vineyards

Overlooking the Beaujolais vineyards, Oingt is a jewel amid the *pierres dorées* (golden stones), rich in iron oxide, found in this region. Built on a ridge dominating the Roman roads between Saône and Loire, this former Roman *castrum* saw its heyday in the Middle Ages. It was around the year 1000 CE that the Guichard d'Oingt lords, powerful *viguiers* (judges) for the count of Le Forez, built a motte-and-bailey castle and its chapel here, and in the 12th century a keep was added. Today, the fortified Nizy gate at the entrance to the village provides the first sign of its medieval past. Houses with yellow-ocher walls, where the play of light and shadow constantly changes, line the road leading to the parish church. Next to it are the remains of the castle's residential buildings and keep, which have now been converted into a museum.

 HIGHLIGHTS

Tower (12th century): Museum of the village's history, panoramic terrace with viewpoint indicator. Guided tour (04 72 52 97 33).

Les Apéritifs de la Tour: Tasting of the estate's wines with commentary, included in the tour of the tower (04 74 07 27 40).

Église Saint-Matthieu (10th century): 12th-century polychrome sculptures, Stations of the Cross, Pietà, pulpit; liturgical museum.

Musée de la Musique Mécanique et de l'Orgue de Barbarie: Display of old objects (collection of 60 instruments) and music demonstrations (04 72 52 97 33).

Maison Commune (16th century): Exhibition of works by regional artists (painters, sculptors, ceramists), Apr.–Oct. (04 72 52 97 33).

Village: Guided tour with the museum, by appt. (04 72 52 97 33); "Dans la peau d'un artiste" guided tour to meet local craftsmen (includes visit of Tour de Oingt; 04 74 07 27 40).

ACCOMMODATION & EATING OUT

destination-beaujolais.com

LOCAL SPECIALTIES

Food and Drink
AOC Beaujolais wines.
Art and Crafts
Calligrapher • Ceramist • Textile designer • Pottery• Stained-glass artist •

Art galleries • Jewelry • Watercolorist • Artists' collective.

EVENTS

Market: Thurs. 3–7 p.m., Place de Presberg,
Jul.: Rosé Nuit d'Eté, aperitif and concert (1st fortnight).
Sept.: Festival International d'Orgue de Barbarie et de Musique Mécanique, organ festival (1st weekend).
Nov.: Beaujolais Nouveau festival (3rd Thurs.).

OUTDOOR ACTIVITIES

Walking • Mountain biking: Marked trails.

FURTHER AFIELD

•Beaujolais wine route.
•Pays des Pierres Dorées: Golden stone villages, known as "little Tuscany" (2½–12½ miles/4–20 km).
•Villefranche-sur-Saône (8½ miles/14 km).
•Lyon (22 miles/35 km).

Rhône (69)
Population: 671
Altitude: 1,804 ft. (550 m)

TOURIST INFO—
DESTINATION BEAUJOLAIS
04 74 07 27 40
destination-beaujolais.com

Olargues

The natural charm of the Languedoc

Situated in a bend in the Jaur river, Olargues provides walks flavored with history at the heart of the Haut-Languedoc regional nature park. At the foot of Mont Caroux, the "mountain of light," Olargues combines the coolness of Massif Central rivers with the sunshine of the South, and its landscapes of chestnut and cherry trees with vineyards and olive groves. Although this exceptional site has been occupied since prehistoric times, it was in the 12th century that lords in the region built a castle, fortified village, and bridge over the Jaur here; the latter is one of the biggest bridges of its type in Europe. It leads visitors to discover the village's *calades* (decorative cobblestones), stone houses covered with barrel tiles rather than the traditional *lauzes* (schist tiles), the ruined ramparts, the covered stairway of the commandery, and the Église Saint-Laurent, whose bell tower—the only vestige remaining—was formerly a castle keep.

 HIGHLIGHTS

Centre Cebenna: Study center for the environment and sustainable development. Activities, nature tours for all ages, exhibitions, 3D projections (04 67 97 88 00).
Musée d'Arts et Traditions Populaires: Museum of village history, old tools, geology of the region, life-size reproduction of a forge, May–Sept. (04 67 97 70 79).
Village: Self-guided tour all year round and by appt. for groups; guided tour Mon. 6 p.m. in Jul. (04 67 23 02 21/ 04 67 97 06 65).

 ACCOMMODATION & EATING OUT

minervois-caroux.com

 LOCAL SPECIALTIES

Food and Drink
AOP Cévennes chestnuts and Olargues chestnut-based specialties • Wild plants and fruits.
Art and Crafts
Painter • Luthiers • Artisanal leather goods • Artists' and artisans' collective.

 EVENTS

Market: Sun. 8 a.m.–1 p.m., Place de la Mairie.
Aug.: Festibaloche, contemporary music festival (1st weekend); Autour du Quatuor, classical music festival with organ concert (mid-Aug.).

Nov.: Fête du Marron et du Vin Nouveau, chestnut and new wine festival (1st weekend after Nov. 1st).

 OUTDOOR ACTIVITIES

Swimming • Canoeing and kayaking • Canyoning and spelunking • Rock climbing • Walking: Via Tolosane leg of Saint James's Way • Mountain biking and hybrid biking • Passa Païs: Haut Languedoc greenway for walkers and cyclists (46½ miles/75 km).

 FURTHER AFIELD

- Le Caroux, massif; Gorges d'Héric (3½ miles/6 km).
- Gorges de l'Orb; Vieussan (5 miles/8 km).
- Monts de l'Espinouse (7½ miles/12 km).
- Saint-Pons-de-Thomières (11 miles/18 km).
- Roquebrun (12 miles/19 km).

Hérault (34)
Population: 500
Altitude: 600 ft. (183 m)

TOURIST INFO—MINERVOIS AU CAROUX
04 67 23 02 21
04 67 97 06 65
minervois-caroux.com

Parfondeval

Nature and history in the Thiérache

Surrounded by wooded countryside and home to red-brick houses with silver grey slate roofs, Parfondeval is a village typical of this region that remains characterized by farming life. During the reign of Louis XIII and Louis XIV, the villagers of Parfondeval built a fortified church dedicated to Saint Médard to defend themselves from hordes of brigands. The church is reached through an arch set into a house, then by passing between two turrets. The village's central square is partially occupied by a pond. In the early 20th century, the village had six others, where animals came to drink. Since then, a wetland with three new ponds awarded the label Mares Remarquables has been created and is accessible via the Sentier du Triton. Walking through the village, visitors see houses decorated with glazed or vitrified bricks in diamond shapes and half-timbered façades known locally as *bauchage*.

HIGHLIGHTS

Village: 1 mile (1.4 km) of signposted path; free audio guides available at restaurant/terrace Le Relais de la Chouette.
Église Saint-Médard (16th century): Self-guided tours daily. Free guided tour weekends 4.30–6.30 p.m. in Jul.–Aug.
La Maison des Outils d'Antan: Collection of 2,000 farming tools and everyday items from the 1900s (03 23 97 61 59).

ACCOMMODATION & EATING OUT

Restaurants
♥ Le Relais de la Chouette (03 23 99 39 27).

 LOCAL SPECIALTIES

Food and Drink
Cider and apple juice •
La Folie Douce (local aperitif with red berries).

EVENTS

Market: 1st Sat. of each month, 10 a.m.–1 p.m.
Jun.: Village festival (weekend following Fête de la Saint-Médard).
Aug.: Flea market (Sun. after 15th).
Oct.: Potironnade, guided walk and meal (around 20th).

OUTDOOR ACTIVITIES

Walking, horseback riding, and mountain biking: "Par le Fond du Val" and "Sentier du Triton" trails.

FURTHER AFIELD

• Aubenton (8 miles/13 km).
• Plomion: Fortified church (10 miles/16 km).
• Vervins: Musée de la Thiérache (15 miles/24 km).
• Saint-Michel: Benedictine abbey (17 miles/27 km).
• Guise: Fortified castle (28 miles/45 km).

Aisne (02)
Population: 160
Altitude: 725 ft. (221 m)

TOURIST INFO—PAYS DE THIÉRACHE
03 23 91 30 10
tourisme-thierache.fr

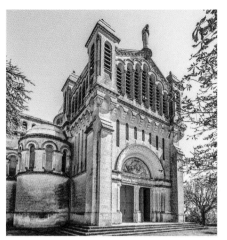

Penne-d'Agenais

A stronghold in the Lot valley

Standing on a rocky crest, Penne-d'Agenais overlooks the hills of the Pays de Serres and the Lot valley. Located in the southwest, this town was once occupied by the Gauls, as its Celtic name suggests: *penn*, also spelled *pen*, means "ridge or overhang." Due to its elevated position, the village was a strategic stronghold, used to keep watch over the Lot region and its valley. In the 12th century, Richard the Lionheart, king of England, fortified the Penne castle, which now lies in ruins. Over the centuries, Penne-d'Agenais has been the stage of many conflicts, including the Albigensian Crusade, in 1212; the Hundred Years War; and clashes between Catholics and Huguenots in the 16th century. A medieval charm fills the village's narrow streets, where the many local craftspeople display their skills. The impressive dome of the sanctuary of Notre-Dame-de-Peyragude, a pilgrimage site on the Saint James's Way, rises above the village and affords a remarkable panoramic view of the Lot and buildings embellished with Sarrasine arcades.

HIGHLIGHTS

Sanctuaire Notre-Dame de Peyragude (19th–20th centuries): Mosaic and oratory dedicated to the Virgin Mary; stained glass by Jacques Leuzy; Stations of the Cross by Henry Lafai.

Village: Map available from tourist info center; guided tour of the village and sanctuary by specialist Maria Garrouste, Tues. 10 a.m. in Jul.–Aug., by appt. (06 11 59 33 90).

 ACCOMMODATION & EATING OUT

Guesthouses
♥ Norpech ▮▮▮
(06 83 42 16 58).

LOCAL SPECIALTIES

Food and Drink
Prunes • Truffles: ♥ France Truffes (06 10 03 35 85) • Craft beers • Saffron.

Art and Crafts
Coppersmith • Metal sculptor • Weaver • Artisanal leather goods • Glassblowing workshop • Ceramist • Stained-glass artist • Wood turner • Tempera artist • Hybrid community space.

EVENTS

Market: Sun. 8 a.m.–1 p.m., at the port; gourmet market Thurs. 7 p.m. (Jul.–Aug.)
Late Mar.–early Apr.: European Artistic Craft Days.
Jul.: Fête de la Tourtière, flaky pastry festival (2nd Sun.); Penne'Art, contemporary art festival (last weekend).

Early Aug.: Fête de la Lumière, festival of light.

OUTDOOR ACTIVITIES

• Étangs Ferrié: Catch-and-release fishing, water sports • Walking: Routes GR 65 and GR 652, and 5 marked trails • Boating • Paddleboarding.

FURTHER AFIELD

• Fumel (13 miles/21 km).
• Agen (22 miles/35 km).

MBVF NEARBY

• Pujols-le-Haut (10 miles/16 km).
• Tournon-d'Agenais (11 miles/18 km).
• Monflanquin (18 miles/29 km).

Lot-et-Garonne (47)
Population: 2,341
Altitude: 689 ft. (210 m)

TOURIST INFO—FUMEL VALLÉE DU LOT
05 53 71 13 70
tourisme-fumel.com

Pérouges
The cobblestones of Ain

At the top of a hill, the medieval village of Pérouges forms a circle around its main square, which is shaded by a 200-year-old linden tree. Long coveted for its prosperity, due to its weaving industry, and for its strategic position overlooking the plain of the Ain river, the town was ruled by the province of Dauphiné, then the region of Savoy, before becoming French at the dawn of the 17th century. Despite being besieged several times, Pérouges has retained an exceptional heritage inside its ramparts, which was saved from ruin in the early 20th century. The fortified church, with its ramparts, arrow-slits, and keystones bearing the Savoyard coat of arms, is one of its principal treasures. Surrounded by attractive corbeled and half-timbered residences, and shaded by its "tree of freedom" planted in 1792, the Place du Tilleul reflects several centuries of history with its narrow cobblestone streets that lead off the square. With no fewer than 83 historically listed buildings, Pérouges forms a unique architectural ensemble.

 HIGHLIGHTS

Fortified church (15th century): Stone and wooden statues (Saint George and Virgin with cloak).
Maison des Princes: Museum of art, traditions, and history of Old Pérouges; watchtower; medieval garden.
Maisons Cazin (14th century): Art exhibitions.
La Maison des Arts Contemporains: Exhibitions (04 74 46 04 92).
Village: Free tour with audio guide (mobile app). Guided tours for individuals and groups; themed "murder" tour Jul.–Aug.; accessible tours for those with vision impairment. Limited accessibility on cobble paving (09 67 12 70 84).

 ACCOMMODATION & EATING OUT

perouges.org

 LOCAL SPECIALTIES

Food and Drink
Galettes de Pérouges • Chocolates • Bugey wine.
Art and Crafts
Antiques • Ceramist • Costumer • Enameler • Painter • Illustrator • Pottery • Bookbinding • Stained-glass artist • Silkscreen printer • Sculptors in wood.

 EVENTS

Late Mar.–early Apr.: European Artistic Craft Days.
Jun.: Medieval festival (2nd weekend).
Late Jun.–early Jul.: Printemps de Pérouges, music festival.
Dec.: Christmas market (2nd weekend).

 **OUTDOOR ACTIVITIES**

Walking: 4 marked trails.

 FURTHER AFIELD

• Villars-les-Dombes: Bird sanctuary (10½ miles/17 km).
• Ambérieu-en-Bugey: Château des Allymes (11 miles/18 km).
• Grottes de la Balme, caves (12½ miles/20 km).
• Ambronay: Abbey (13 miles/21 km).

Ain (01)
Population: 1,273
Altitude: 919 ft. (280 m)

TOURIST INFO—PÉROUGES BUGEY
09 67 12 70 84
perouges-bugey-tourisme.com
perouges.org

 EVENTS

Market: Wed. morning and evening in summer, Place des Promenades.
May: Festi Pesmes, art and gastronomy festival (Sat. and Sun., around mid-May).
Jul.: C'Rock-en-Île, rock festival (1st weekend); Fête de l'Île festival (3rd Sun.).
Jul.–Aug.: Rendez-Vous du Terroir, guided tour of village and food tasting.
Aug.: Fête de la Saint-Hilaire (1st weekend).

Pesmes

A village with a prosperous past

On the banks of the Ognon river, Pesmes bears witness to the work of winemakers, the glory days of the old lords of the town, and the heyday of Franche-Comté's metalworking industry. At the end of an avenue of hundred-year-old plane trees, the sight of the gap-toothed castle, with houses nestling at its feet, and of the impressive ramparts reflected in the calm waters of the river takes one's breath away. Founded in the Middle Ages on the route leading from Gray to Dole, and coveted for its strategic position, the town was by turns Frankish, Germanic, Burgundian, and Spanish, before becoming French during the reign of Louis XIV (1643–1715). At that time, it was a major trading post that brought together merchants and burghers. The village reflects this rich past: along the streets and the alleyways, where grand residences and winemakers' houses rub shoulders, visitors can discover the Église Saint-Hilaire with its imperial bell tower, the castle ruins, and the Loigerot and Saint-Hilaire gateways.

 HIGHLIGHTS

Château de Pesmes (15th–18th centuries).
Église Saint-Hilaire (12th–17th centuries): 16th-century triptych and statues, altarpiece, paintings, 17th-century organ case.
Hôtel Châteaurouillaud (15th–16th centuries).
Musée des Forges: Collection of machines and tools in the former workshops, forge-owner's house (06 79 85 59 87).
Village: Guided tour (03 84 65 18 15).

 ACCOMMODATION & EATING OUT

tourisme-valdegray.com

 LOCAL SPECIALTIES

Food and Drink
Pesmes honey and mead • Local products from Franche-Comté and Burgundy.
Art and Crafts
Ceramist • Engraver • Wrought ironworker • Sculptor.

 OUTDOOR ACTIVITIES

Water sports • Canoeing and kayaking • Paddleboarding • Fishing.

 FURTHER AFIELD

• Vallée de l'Ognon: Malans (Île Art sculpture park); Acey (abbey); Marnay (3–12½ miles/5–20 km).
• Moissey; Forêt de la Serre, forest; Dôle; Gray: Musée Baron Martin; Musée de l'Esperanto (6–12½ miles/10–20 km).
• Grotte d'Osselle, cave; Arc-et-Senans: Saline Royale, saltworks (18½–28 miles/30–45 km).

Haute-Saône (70)
Population: 1,092
Altitude: 689 ft. (210 m)

TOURIST INFO—VAL DE GRAY
03 84 65 18 15
03 84 31 24 38
tourisme-valdegray.com

Peyre

(Commune of Comprégnac)

A vertiginous viaduct

Clinging to a sheer cliff where the original church was built, Peyre overlooks the Tarn downstream of Millau. Beneath the plateau of the Causse Rouge, dotted with *caselles* (drystone shelters) whose *lauze* (schist tile) roofs once protected shepherds and winegrowers, the lower village with its maze of narrow, cobbled, stepped streets descends steeply toward the river. The top of Peyre stretches out at the foot of a high tufa cliff with a corbeled overhang that towers above the village. Fortified in the 17th century to serve as a refuge for residents of the parish, it has retained brattices and murder holes that bear witness to its defensive history. Recently restored as a venue for concerts and exhibitions, the church is bathed in changing light diffused by its glass and crystal stained-glass windows. It now faces another symbol of modernity: the P2 pier of the Millau Viaduct, which, surging upward from the Tarn, makes this viaduct the tallest bridge in the world.

 HIGHLIGHTS

Église Saint-Christophe (11th–17th centuries): Partially dug into the rock face. Contemporary art exhibitions Jun.–Sept.
Village: Guided tour from Jul. 1 to 3rd weekend in Sept., by appt. (05 65 60 02 42).
Colombier du Capelier, Comprégnac (14th century): Self-guided tour.
Maison de la Truffe, Comprégnac: Presentation of truffle cultivation and typical architecture from the Causses (06 86 84 38 95 / 06 71 88 44 27).

 ACCOMMODATION & EATING OUT

millau-viaduc-tourisme.fr

LOCAL SPECIALTIES

Food and Drink
Truffles and truffle-based produce.

Art and Crafts
Interior decoration, tableware • Potter.

 EVENTS

Jun.: Choeurs de Peyre, choral concerts.
Jul.: Fête de la Saint-Christophe (last weekend).
Mid-Jul.–mid-Aug.: Festival de la Vallée et des Gorges du Tarn.
Dec.: Truffle festival at Comprégnac and local produce market (weekend before Christmas).

 OUTDOOR ACTIVITIES

Aire de Loisirs des Pyramides (leisure park) • Walking.

 FURTHER AFIELD

• Millau (5 miles/8 km).
• Castelnau-Pégayrolles; Saint-Léon: Micropolis, insect museum; Chaos de Montpellier-le-Vieux, blockfield (12½–17 miles/ 20–27 km).
• Gorges de la Dourbie (13–24 miles/21–39 km).

Aveyron (12)
Population: 100
Altitude: 1,214 ft. (370 m)

TOURIST INFO— MILLAU GRANDS CAUSSES
05 65 60 02 42
millau-viaduc-tourisme.fr
www.compregnac12.fr

 Art and Crafts
Soap made from goat milk.

 EVENTS

Good Friday: La Granitola procession with the Confrérie Saint Antoine Abbé de Piana.
Jul.: Rencontres Interconfréries, Mass and procession (last Sun.).
Aug.: Festival with Mass and procession in the village (15th)

Piana

A natural splendor on the Isle of Beauty

At the entrance to the magnificent Calanques de Piana ("Calanche" in Corsican)—listed as a UNESCO World Heritage Site—stands Piana, overlooking the Gulf of Porto. The site of Piana was inhabited intermittently from the late Middle Ages until the early 16th century, but the founding of the current village dates to the 1690s. Twenty years later, the village had 32 households, and the Chapelle Saint-Pierre-et-Saint-Paul was built on the ruins of a medieval oratory. It was decided that another, larger church should be built; it was completed in 1792 and was dedicated to Sainte-Marie. Its bell tower, which was finished in the early 19th century, is a replica of the one at Portofino, on the Ligurian coast. It was on the sandy beach at Arone, near Piana, on February 6, 1943, that the first landing of arms and munitions for the Corsican Maquis (Resistance fighters) took place, delivered by the submarine *Casabianca* from Algeria.

 HIGHLIGHTS

Parish church (Baroque style): Polychrome wooden door, frescoes, miniature portraits by Paul-Mathieu Novellini (09 95 27 84 42).
Chapelle Saint-Pierre-et-Saint-Paul: Piana's previous parish church, restored in 2022.
Chapelle Sainte-Lucie (hamlet of Vistale): Byzantine-style frescoes, panoramic view of the Gulf of Porto.
Calanche di Piana: UNESCO World Heritage Site.
Ficajola marina and fishermen's huts.

 ACCOMMODATION & EATING OUT

ouestcorsica.com

LOCAL SPECIALTIES

Food and Drink
AOC Brocciu cheese • Charcuterie • Goat cheese • Honey.

 OUTDOOR ACTIVITIES

Swimming • Walking: Several trails in the Calanche and to the tower of Capo Rosso.

FURTHER AFIELD

• Scandola: Nature reserve (6 miles/10 km, access by sea from Porto or via a walking trail).
• Porto (7½ miles/12 km).
• Cargèse (12½ miles/20 km).
• Evisa and Gorges de la Spelunca: Rocky trail (12½ miles/20 km).
• Forêt d'Aïtone, forest (18½ miles/30 km).

Corse-du-Sud (20)
Population: 480
Altitude: 1,437 ft. (438 m)

TOURIST INFO—OUEST CORSICA
04 95 27 84 42
ouestcorsica.com

Le Poët-Laval

On the roads to Jerusalem

Surrounded by lavender and aromatic plants, this village was once a commandery. Le Poët-Laval, bathed in Mediterranean light, emerged from a fortified commandery of the order of the Knights Hospitaller—soldier-monks watching over the roads to Jerusalem. At the summit of the village, on a steep slope of the Jabron valley, stands the massive keep of the castle, built in the 12th century. Rebuilt in the 13th and 16th centuries, and topped with a dovecote, it has been restored and now hosts exhibitions. Of the Romanesque Saint-Jean-des-Commandeurs chapel, situated below the castle, there remains part of the nave and the chancel, topped by a bell gable. At the southwestern corner of the ramparts, the Renaissance façade of the Salon des Commandeurs harks back to the order's heyday in the 16th century, before the village rallied to Protestantism, as evidenced by the former Protestant church—now a museum—near the Grand Portail.

HIGHLIGHTS

Castle (12th, 13th, and 16th centuries): Permanent exhibition on the reconstruction of the village and temporary exhibitions, May–Sept. (04 75 46 44 12).
Centre d'Art Rochecolombe: Exhibitions, concerts (09 75 73 10 50).
Musée du Protestantisme Dauphinois: Former 16th-century residence turned into a Protestant church in the 17th century. History of Protestantism in Dauphiné; collections of contemporary mosaics (04 75 46 46 33).
Village: Paid guided tour Wed. a.m. Jul.–Aug. by Les Amis du Vieux Poët-Laval association (estelledevred@gmail.com); offseason group tours by appt. (amisvieuxpoetlaval.fr)

ACCOMMODATION & EATING OUT

lepoetlaval.org

LOCAL SPECIALTIES

Art and Crafts
Pottery • Jewelry and clothing designer • Art galleries.

EVENTS

Jul.: 3-day local saint's festival in Gougne (last weekend).
Aug.: Les Musicales du Poët-Laval, chamber music festival (early Aug.).

OUTDOOR ACTIVITIES

Walking: Routes GRP "Tour du Pays de Dieulefit," GR 965 (start of the Sentier International des Huguenots), and 2 short marked trails • Horseback riding • Mountain biking.

FURTHER AFIELD

• Dieulefit: Maison de la Céramique (2½ miles/4 km).
• Comps: 12th-century church (6 miles/10 km).

MBVF NEARBY

• Grignan (16 miles/26 km).
• Mirmande (21 miles/34 km).
• La Garde-Adhémar (24 miles/39 km).

Drôme (26)
Population: 1,007
Altitude: 1,007 ft. (307 m)

TOURIST INFO—PAYS DE DIEULEFIT-BOURDEAUX
04 75 46 42 49
dieulefit-tourisme.com
lepoetlaval.org

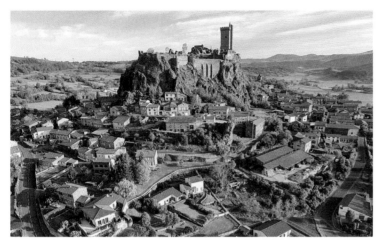

LOCAL SPECIALTIES

Food and Drink
Farmhouse produce • Flour • Artisanal pasta • Whisky from Auvergne.
Art and Crafts
Artisanal leather goods • Soapmaker: ♥ Savonnerie La Rose Trémière (06 03 88 57 31).

 EVENTS

Market: Thurs. evening, Place de l'Église (Jul.-Aug.).
Jul.: Village festival (around 15th).
Aug.: Medieval festival.
Dec.: Christmas market (3rd weekend).

 OUTDOOR ACTIVITIES

Walking: Chemin de Compostelle (Saint James's Way), Chemin Saint-Michel.

 FURTHER AFIELD

•Le Puy-en-Velay; Cascade de la Beaume; La Chaise-Dieu (4–23 miles/6.5–37 km).

 MBVF NEARBY
•Arlempdes (23 miles/37 km).

Polignac

Fortress of the "mountain kings"

Perched on a basalt outcrop near Puy-en-Velay, the powerful fortress of the lords of Polignac and the village below enjoy panoramic views over the Meygal and Mézenc mountains. According to legend, this volcanic hill was home to a temple to Apollo during Gallo-Roman times, indicating its importance back then. Texts dating back to 934 make mention of a public fortress that served to defend the town of Puy-en-Velay. But it was thanks to the Polignac family that the village developed during the 11th century. In order to establish their power in the region, the family created an imposing defensive system: a 105-ft. (32-m) keep, 2,625 ft. (800 m) of ramparts, and six fortified gates to reach the 7½-acre (3 ha.) hilltop. In 1533, Polignac had a royal visit from Francis I. During his stay, the king of France fell in love with the view from the village and dubbed the Polignac family "kings of the mountains."

 HIGHLIGHTS

♥ **Fortress**: Gardens, keep, defensive systems, and panoramic view of the Velay region. Self-guided tours (via QR code) and guided tours Feb.-Nov.; thematic tours in summer; treasure hunt guidebook for kids aged 5–12; tours for those with vision and hearing impairment and learning difficulties (04 71 04 06 04).
Église Saint-Martin (11th century): Constructed from volcanic breccia and renovated in the 19th century; chancel decorated with frescoes and a statue of Saint Anne. Self-guided tour (tour guide available).
Village: Heritage discovery trail "Les Charrirous" (leaflet and QR code), volcano discovery trail "Roche de Flayac."

 ACCOMMODATION & EATING OUT

mairiedepolignac.fr

Haute-Loire (43)
Population: 2,905
Altitude: 2,460 ft. (750 m)

TOURIST INFO—PUY-EN-VELAY
04 71 09 38 41
lepuyenvelay-tourisme.fr
mairiedepolignac.fr

AUVERGNE-RHÔNE-ALPES

Pradelles

Taking the Stevenson trail

Protecting pilgrims and mule-drivers on the Régordane Way, Pradelles was the "stronghold of the high pastures" in the 11th century. Overlooking the Haut Allier valley, with the Margeride mountains to the west, Mont Lozère to the south, and the Tanargue range to the east, Pradelles was long a stronghold surrounded by ramparts. A stopping place on the Régordane Way linking the Auvergne to the Languedoc, the village was also a crossroads for pilgrims traveling to Le Puy-en-Velay or Saint-Gilles-du-Gard, and for merchants bringing in salt, oil, and wines from the south by mule. Throughout the ages, Pradelles' high façades have thus seen generations of travelers, including Saint Jean-François Régis—who, in the 17th century, preached the Catholic faith in lands bordering the Cévennes that had been won over by Protestantism—the 18th-century highwayman and popular hero Louis Mandrin, and, more recently, Robert Louis Stevenson, who, with his donkey, traveled the route that now bears his name.

 HIGHLIGHTS

Parc du Chat Botté: Theme park combining local stories and traditions; games and activities for the whole family (04 71 00 87 87).
Village: Guided tour Mon. in Jul.–Aug., by appt. (meeting place in front of tourist info center; 04 71 00 82 65).

ACCOMMODATION & EATING OUT

lesgorgesdelallier.fr
pradelles43.fr

LOCAL SPECIALTIES

Food and Drink
Salted meats and fish.

 EVENTS

Jul.: French national day, concert and fireworks (14th)
Aug.: Saint-Laurent fair (1st Sun.); Corso Fleuri, procession of floral floats for local saint's day (15th).

 OUTDOOR ACTIVITIES

Fishing • Horseback riding • Walking: Routes GR 70 (Stevenson Trail), GR 470 (Sources et Gorges de l'Allier et de la Loire), and GR 700 (Régordane Way); marked trails • Vélo-rail (pedal-powered railcars) • Mountain biking.

 FURTHER AFIELD

•Langogne: Lac de Naussac, water sports base (4½ miles/7 km).
•Lac de Coucouron (7½ miles/12 km).
•Lac du Bouchet; Devès, volcanic field (12½–21½ miles/20–35 km)
•Le Puy-en-Velay (21½ miles/35 km).

 MBVF NEARBY
•Arlempdes (10½ miles/17 km).

Haute-Loire (43)
Population: 545
Altitude: 3,796 ft. (1157 m)

TOURIST INFO—GORGES DE L'ALLIER
04 71 00 82 65
lesgorgesdelallier.fr
pradelles43.fr

Prats-de-Mollo-la-Preste

The colors of Catalonia

At the foot of Mont Canigó and the Pic de Costabonne, Prats-de-Mollo-la-Preste combines the austerity of a fortified town with the bright colors of the Catalan south. In 982, monks built a church on the site, establishing the village of Prats-de-Mollo. The town was given ramparts in the 14th century and prospered in the 16th century thanks to its cloth weaving industry. Once a Spanish territory, the Vallespir region, formerly a viscounty, became part of France under the Treaty of the Pyrenees in 1659. To control the region, and particularly the Col d'Ares, Louis XIV ordered Vauban to build Fort Lagarde (1677-1682). In 1853, Napoleon III was a patient at La Preste, known for its thermal waters and treatments; the spa was annexed to Prats-de-Mollo by decree in 1956. Surrounded by a lush forest and a nature reserve, the village, which is located on the Spanish border, is lined with houses inspired by Catalan Baroque art.

HIGHLIGHTS

Fort Lagarde (17th century): Panoramic view of the village. Tours for individuals, guided tours, and interactive tours, Jul.–Sept. (04 68 39 70 83).
Église Sainte-Juste-et-Sainte-Ruffine (10th century): Rich furnishings from the 17th–19th centuries; self-guided tours Fri.–Sun., 2–6 p.m.; open daily in summer.
Chapelle Saintes-Juste-et-Ruffine (17th century): Stained glass and paintings by Jean Lareuse, open daily.
Ermitage Notre-Dame-du-Coral (17th–18th centuries): Small statue of the Virgin Mary (13th century), altarpieces (17th–18th centuries).
Centre d'Interprétation Transfrontalier de La Verneda: Presentation of cross-border artistic and historical heritage in the Catalan valleys of Tech and Ter; multimedia space, exhibitions; tours (04 68 83 99 49).
Tour de Mir (13th century): Former signal tower (5,053 ft./(1,540 m altitude) offering a panoramic view.
Village: Self-guided tour (map available at tourist info center); guided tour Fri. 3:30 p.m. (04 68 39 70 83).
Theatrical tour of Fort Lagarde or the medieval town: Sun. at 8:30 p.m., Jul.–Aug.
Preste spa: Water treatments, thermal baths (04 68 87 88 60).

ACCOMMODATION & EATING OUT

Hotel-restaurants
♥ Le Bellevue*** (04 68 39 72 48).

 LOCAL SPECIALTIES

Food and Drink
Craft beers • *Boles de picolat* (Catalan dish) • Catalan charcuterie • Farmhouse cheese • Honey.
Art and Crafts
Bladesmiths • Blacksmith • Painter • Sculptor.

EVENTS

Market: Fri. 8 a.m.–1 p.m., Place du Foirail.
Feb.: Fête de l'Ours, Bear carnival (1st weekend of local school vacation).
Jul.: Village festival (21st).
Aug.: Alegria d'Amunt, Catalan festival (3rd weekend).

OUTDOOR ACTIVITIES

Walking • Fishing: 4 routes • Mountain biking: 4 trails.

FURTHER AFIELD

• Arles-sur-Tech (7½ miles/12 km).
• Réserve Naturelle de Prats-de-Mollo-la-Preste (14 miles/23 km).
• Céret (20 miles/32 km).
• Camprodon, Spain (20 miles/32 km).

Pyrénées-Orientales (66)
Population: 1,155
Altitude: 1,886 ft. (575 m)

TOURIST INFO—SUD CANIGO
04 68 39 70 83
pratsdemollolapreste.com
sudcanigo.com

Pujols-le-Haut

(Commune of Pujols)

A former stronghold in the Albi region

Perched on a hill overlooking the Lot valley, Pujols has survived through the centuries, preserving its medieval charm. The exceptional site of Pujols has attracted the attention of many would-be conquerors—from early pre-history, through the Hundred Years War and the troubles of the Middle Ages to the French Revolution—but this ancient fortress has nonetheless retained much of its architectural heritage. In addition to part of the outer wall and the castle, there remain two fortified gates, one of which serves as the bell tower to the old seigniorial chapel of Saint-Nicolas. The Église Sainte-Foy has conserved its 16th-century wall paintings. On the village square, the covered market—built in 1850 with materials recovered from the Église Saint-Jean-des-Rouets—faces some fine late 13th-century half-timbered houses. The stone walls of the ground floor are topped with black oak beams interspersed with flat bricks.

 HIGHLIGHTS

Collégiale Saint-Nicolas (16th century): Former castle chapel, turned into collegial church in 1547; Flamboyant Gothic architecture.
Église Sainte-Foy (15th century): 16th-century murals.
Village: Guided group tour by appt. (05 53 36 78 69); guided tours and workshops for young people (09 64 41 87 73); guided tours with C. Joly, local storyteller (06 70 18 83 10).

ACCOMMODATION & EATING OUT

tourisme-villeneuvois.fr

LOCAL SPECIALTIES

Food and Drink
Walnuts, hazelnuts, and prunes and related products • Macarons and shortbread cookies.
Art and Crafts
Painters • Pottery • Toys •

Confrérie des Métiers d'Art (art workers' guild).

EVENTS

Market: Sun. 8 a.m.–1 p.m., Place Saint-Nicolas; gourmet market Wed. evening (Jul.–Aug.).
Jul.: Jazz festival (1st week).
Aug.: Couleurs du Monde, world dance and music festival (1st week); book sale (1st Sun.); potters' market (3rd Sun.).

OUTDOOR ACTIVITIES

Horseback riding • Fishing • Walking and mountain biking: Route GR 652 and many marked trails.

FURTHER AFIELD

• Grotte de Lastournelle, cave (3 miles/5 km).
• Agen (18 miles/29 km).

MBVF NEARBY
• Penne-d'Agenais (8½ miles/14 km).
• Monflanquin (14½ miles/23 km).
• Tournon d'Agenais (18½ miles/30 km).

Lot-et-Garonne (47)
Population: 3,717
Altitude: 614 ft. (187 m)

TOURIST INFO—GRAND VILLENEUVOIS
05 53 36 78 69
tourisme-villeneuvois.fr
pujols47.fr

Puycelsi

Forest fortress

At the edge of the Grésigne forest, Puycelsi watches over the Vère valley. Occupied since prehistoric times, then besieged by the Celts and later by the Romans, Puycelsi passed, in the late 12th century, into the ownership of the counts of Toulouse, who made it one of their favorite fortified residences. Due to its strategic position and its protective walls, the village was able to resist many sieges. Confined within its medieval fortifications, of which there remain more than 875 yards (800 meters) of ramparts and the Irissou double gate, Puycelsi offers splendid views over the Grésigne forest, the Vère valley, and the Causses du Quercy from its wall walks. At the heart of the village, the Église Saint-Corneille is bordered by a medicinal herb garden and surrounded by mostly 14th- and 15th-century houses, which combine stone with wood and brick beneath fine hollow-tile roofs.

 HIGHLIGHTS

Église Saint-Corneille (15th and 17th centuries): Statuary, altarpiece, 18th-century bell tower.
Research and conservation orchard: 20 acres (8 ha) of plots, 700 varieties of fruit trees, and 100 grape varieties from heirloom vines. Sale of fresh seasonal fruit. Guided tour in summer (05 63 33 19 41).
Village: Guided tour mid-Jul.–late Aug. (08 05 40 08 28).

 ACCOMMODATION & EATING OUT

la-toscane-occitane.com

 LOCAL SPECIALTIES

Food and Drink
Cookies and crackers • Fruits and fruit purées, juices, and sorbets • Honey • AOC Gaillac wines.
Art and Crafts
Artists and craftsmen collective • Ceramist • Painter-sculptor • Pottery • Soap making • Painting and modelmaking workshop.

 EVENTS

Jun.: Trail de Grésigne, trail running (4th Sun.).
Aug.: Medieval festival (mid-Aug.).

 OUTDOOR ACTIVITIES

Walking: Route GR 46, heritage walks, Grésigne forest.

 FURTHER AFIELD

• Gorges de l'Aveyron, from Bruniquel to Saint-Antonin-Noble-Val (7½–22 miles/ 12–35 km).
• Gaillac (13 miles/21 km).
• Caussade (15½ miles/25 km).

 MBVF NEARBY

• Castelnau-de-Montmiral (8 miles/13 km).
• Cordes-sur-Ciel (18½ miles/30 km).

Tarn (81)
Population: 463
Altitude: 981 ft. (299 m)

TOURIST INFO—LA TOSCANE OCCITANE GAILLAC, CORDES SUR CIEL ET CITÉS MÉDIÉVALES
08 05 40 08 28
la-toscane-occitane.com
puycelsi.fr

Riquewihr

The pearl of Alsatian vineyards

Producing wines that, for centuries, have matched the quality of its architecture, Riquewihr remains one of the finest examples of Alsatian heritage and lifestyle. Riquewihr is situated behind ramparts that are now besieged only by vines aligned in tight rows. Long linked to the duchy of Wurtemberg and given town status in 1291, it is today associated with excellence: that of the architecture of its residences, with their splendid inner courtyards, and of its powerfully aromatic wines, produced on the Sporen and Schoenenbourg hillsides. Walking along the narrow streets, the visitor never tires of admiring the large houses, which—from the richer bourgeois residences of the 15th and 16th centuries to more modest dwellings—are masterpieces of colorful half-timbered façades, flowerdecked balconies, decorated windowpanes, and "beaver-tail"-tiled roofs. Some of the old store signages are the work of Jean-Jacques Waltz (1873-1951), known as "Hansi": an Alsatian illustrator and caricaturist to whom the village has dedicated a museum.

HIGHLIGHTS

Musée du Dolder: History of the fortified medieval town from the 12th to the 17th centuries (03 89 58 44 08).
Tour des Voleurs and Maison de Vigneron: Former prison and its instruments of torture; interior of a 16th-century winegrower's house (03 89 58 44 08).
Grands crus wine trail: Self-guided visit all year round; guided tour with a winemaker, visit to the wine cellar, tastings in summer (03 89 73 23 23).
Signposted nature trail in Riquewihr Forest (03 89 73 23 23).
Village: Guided tour Mon. 4.30 p.m. in Jul.-Aug., followed by a drink; recreational walk for kids aged 4–12 (03 89 73 23 23); tour of the village and vineyard by tourist train (03 89 73 74 24).

 ACCOMMODATION & EATING OUT

ribeauville-riquewihr.com

LOCAL SPECIALTIES

Food and Drink
AOC Alsace and *grands crus* Schoenenbourg and Sporen wines • Beer and distilled spirits • Alsatian cookies • Honey • *La Riquewihrienne* (green sauerkraut).
Art and Crafts
Interior decoration • Art galleries.

EVENTS

Market: Fri. 8 a.m. – 12 p.m., Place Fernand Zeyer.
Jun.: International male choir festival (late Jun.).
Jul.-Aug.: Farmers' market (Tues. evening); winegrowers' open-air bar (Wed.–Sun.).
Dec.: Christmas market (daily).

OUTDOOR ACTIVITIES

Fishing • Walking: Route GR 5 and marked trails • Mountain biking.

FURTHER AFIELD

- Ribeauvillé (4½ miles/7 km).
- Kaysersberg (6 miles/10 km).
- Colmar (7½ miles/12 km).
- Haut-Koenigsbourg (15½ miles/25 km).

MBVF NEARBY

- Hunawihr (2 miles/3 km).
- Bergheim (5 miles/8 km).
- Eguisheim (10 miles/16 km).

Haut-Rhin (68)
Population: 1,008
Altitude: 728 ft. (222 m)

TOURIST INFO—PAYS DE RIBEAUVILLÉ ET RIQUEWIHR
03 89 73 23 23
ribeauville-riquewihr.com
riquewihr.fr

Rocamadour

A clifftop village on the road to Compostela

Built into the side of a cliff and nestled on a steep slope, Rocamadour overlooks the Alzou canyon and the Causse de Gramat. Dominated by the citadel and its ramparts, this internationally renowned medieval village and major pilgrimage site has been attracting worshippers and visitors for centuries. It was founded in the 9th century when a hermit named Saint Amadour settled in Quercy to engage in private prayer. Within the town's sanctuary, in one of seven chapels built around a parvis, stands a Black Madonna believed to induce miracles. Rocamadour has preserved its fortified gates and medieval layout featuring stone houses, churches, a defensive castle, and food-providing hamlets. In the Grotte des Merveilles, visitors can admire cave paintings and unusual rock formations. The village also shares its name with the famous goat cheese produced in the region—le Rocamadour.

 HIGHLIGHTS

Sanctuaire Notre-Dame de Rocamadour (12th century): 7 chapels; relic of Notre-Dame de Rocamadour; Basilique Saint-Sauveur; Saint-Amadour crypt (05 65 14 10 59).

Rocamadour ramparts (14th century): Panorama (admission fee).

Grotte des Merveilles: Prehistoric cave paintings dating back more than 20,000 years (05 65 33 67 92).

La Maison des Abeilles: Multimedia museum on bees (05 65 33 66 98).

Écoparc du Rocher des Aigles: Bird park featuring vultures, falcons, and parrots (05 65 33 65 45).

La Forêt des Singes: Wildlife park dedicated to safeguarding Barbary macaques (05 65 33 62 72).

Parc Durandal: Equestrian shows and medieval tournaments (06 19 39 18 00).

Village: Self-guided tour with illustrated booklet; guided tours (05 65 33 22 03); daytime and nighttime tours of the village by tourist train (05 65 33 65 99).

 ACCOMMODATION & EATING OUT

vallee-dordogne.com

 LOCAL SPECIALTIES

Food and Drink
AOP Rocamadour goat cheese (farm tours) • Foie gras • Truffles • Walnuts • Quercynois cookies• Amadour wine.

Art and Crafts
Bladesmith • Quercy lavender distillery (farm tours) • Soap making.

 EVENTS

May: Cheese festival (Pentecost Sun.).
Aug.: Sacred music festival (15th–26th).
Sept.: La Truffière aux Livres, book fair (1st Sun.); Les Montgolfiades, hot-air balloon festival (4th weekend).

 OUTDOOR ACTIVITIES

Walking: Routes GR 6, GR 46, GR 64, and GR 652; Chemin de Compostelle (Saint James's Way) • Mountain biking • Hot-air balloon flights.

 FURTHER AFIELD

• Couzou (4½ miles/7 km).
• Gramat (9½ miles/15 km).
• Gouffre de Padirac (11 miles/18 km).

 MBVF NEARBY
• Martel; Carennac (13 miles/21 km).
• Loubressac (15½ miles/25 km).

Lot (46)
Population: 617
Altitude: 915 ft. (279 m)

TOURIST INFO—VALLÉE DE LA DORDOGNE
05 65 33 22 00
vallee-dordogne.com

Rochefort-en-Terre

Brittany in flower

Halfway between the Gulf of Morbihan and "Merlin's Forest" (Brocéliande Forest), this village was once a *roche fort* (stronghold) that controlled the trading routes between land and sea. A medieval village that dates back to the 12th century, Rochefort-en-Terre is one of the oldest fiefdoms in Brittany. Its location, on a rocky outcrop surrounded by deep valleys, gave it a strategic position and a leading role. Traces of this rich history can be seen in the upper village, a legacy of a prosperous past with its old covered market, 12th-century collegiate church, ruins of the medieval castle of the counts of Rochefort, and the 17th–20th-century château, as well as the 16th- and 17th-century mansions with their richly embellished granite and shale façades. Rochefort-en-Terre became an artists' town in the early 20th century, thanks to the American portraitist Alfred Klots, and has retained its pictorial as well as its floral tradition.

 **HIGHLIGHTS**

Parc du Château: View of the remains of the medieval castle and of the 17th–20th-century château (02 97 26 56 00).
Collegiate church Notre-Dame de la Tronchaye (12th–14th centuries): Two stained-glass windows from 1926 and 1927, by the master glassmaker Roger Desjardin.
Naïa Museum: Museum and gallery of the arts of the imagination (07 76 69 36 51).
Village: Sightseeing tour of the Petite Cité; guided group tour by appt.; guided tour for individuals in Jul.–Aug., 11 a.m. Mon.–Fri. and 9 p.m. Mon.–Thurs.; in Dec., during Christmas illuminations, 4 p.m Tues.–Fri.; tour accessible for those with reduced mobility (wheelchairs available); visits to artists' studios (02 97 26 56 00).

 ACCOMMODATION & EATING OUT

Campsites
♥ Au Gré des Vents*** (02 97 43 37 52).

 LOCAL SPECIALTIES

Food and Drink
Breton shortbread, *kouign amann* (buttery cake) • *Pain d'épice* (spice cake) • *Galettes bretonnes* (butter cookies) • Honey • *Chouchen* (type of mead) • Cider • Apple juice.
Art and Crafts
Wooden handicrafts • Artisanal metalwork • Slate handicrafts • Artisanal candles • Pottery •

Embroidery • Ceramists • Jewelry designer • Sculptor • Leather goods • Painters • Soap making • Glassmaking.

 EVENTS

Jun.: Imaginambulles, comic strip festival (3rd weekend).
Jul.–Aug.: Local market.
Sept.: Marché fantastique (1st weekend).
Dec.: Christmas illuminations.

 OUTDOOR ACTIVITIES

Walking: Route GR 38 and marked trails around Rochefort • Moulin Neuf Aventure leisure park • Mountain biking.

 FURTHER AFIELD

•Questembert; St Jacut-les-Pins: Tropical Parc; La Vraie-Croix: 13th-century chapel; La Gacilly; Le Guerno: Branféré animal and botanical park (7–12 miles/11–19 km).

Morbihan (56)
Population: 630
Altitude: 164 ft. (50 m)

TOURIST INFO—ROCHEFORT-EN-TERRE
02 97 26 56 00
www.rochefortenterre-tourisme.bzh

La Roche-Guyon

A castle by the Seine

In a bend of the Seine carved into cliffs of chalk and flint, La Roche-Guyon mixes Île-de-France architecture with Normandy half-timbering. The village, which was originally troglodytic, consisted of *boves*: shelters carved out of the cliff face shared by animals and men. They are still in use, as dwellings, shops, and outhouses. The 12th-century keep is surrounded by a curtain wall and linked to the castle by an impressive secret passage more than 330 ft. (100 m) long. Built in the 13th century and remodeled in the 18th, the castle has retained its corner pepperpot turrets from its feudal past. The main building was completed with corner pavilions and terraces during the reign of Louis XV. Located on the main road between the castle and the Seine, the castle's kitchen garden—first created in 1697 and remodeled in the early 18th century—was restored in 2004 according to 18th-century plans.

 HIGHLIGHTS

Castle (13th–18th centuries): Guided and self-guided tours (salons, keep, chapels, bunker, and *boves*); activities for kids; cultural events (01 34 79 74 42).

Castle orchard and vegetable garden: Classed as "remarkable" by the Ministry of Culture. Free entrance during castle opening hours (01 34 79 74 42).

Église Saint-Samson (15th century): Marble statue of François de Silly, owner of the castle in the 17th century (01 34 79 70 55).

Heritage trail: Marked route to discover the built and natural heritage of the village.

Chemin des Peintres: Marked route to discover village views as painted by artists.

 ACCOMMODATION & EATING OUT

larocheguyon.fr

 LOCAL SPECIALTIES

Art and Crafts
Jewelry designer • Potter • Ceramist • ♥ Le Grain de Sel – Galerie Christian Broutin (06 82 74 53 37).

 EVENTS

May: Plantes, Plaisir, Passions, plant festival (1st weekend).
Ascension: Flea market.
Nov.: Wine fair (1st weekend) and Advent market (last weekend).

 OUTDOOR ACTIVITIES

Walking: Route GR 2, marked walks in forest and village • Mountain biking • Cycling: Veloroute "La Seine à Vélo."

 FURTHER AFIELD

•Haute-Isle: Troglodytic church; Vétheuil; Giverny: Claude Monet's house and gardens; Chaussy: Château de Villarceaux; Mantes-la-Jolie (2–10 miles/3–16 km).

Val-d'Oise (95)
Population: 479
Altitude: 394 ft. (120 m)

TOURIST INFO—LA ROCHE-GUYON
09 77 59 47 22
TOWN HALL
01 34 79 70 55
larocheguyon.fr

Mar.–Apr.: Most Beautiful Villages of France wine market.
May: Flower and garden decoration market (1st Sun.).
Jun.: Rodemack Solex (bike) Tour (mid-Jun.); Rodemack, Cité Médiévale en Fête (late Jun.).
Sept.: Flea market and rummage sale (1st Sun.).

 OUTDOOR ACTIVITIES

Walking • Mountain biking.

Rodemack

The little Carcassonne of Lorraine

Located near the borders of Luxembourg and Germany, Rodemack owes its nickname, "the little Carcassonne of Lorraine," to its impressive medieval heritage. In 907, Rodemack passed into the hands of the Abbot of Echternach and was influenced by German-Luxembourgish culture. A fief of the Luxembourg dynasty, the village existed in relative peace and experienced five centuries of prosperity. Arnould I, the first lord of Rodemack, built a castle on a spur overlooking the town. The edifice was modified over the centuries until it reached its current form. The village grew up around the 10th-century church, and fortifications were built in the 13th to 15th centuries. In 1815, during Napoleon's Hundred Days, Rodemack was defended by General Hugo, father of the poet Victor Hugo. A walk along the Ruelle de la Forge, Rue du Four, and Place de Gargants gives visitors the opportunity to discover its defensive walls and towers. The village itself is surrounded by a second wall with demi-lune (half-moon) towers and a gateway flanked by round towers.

 **HIGHLIGHTS**

Village: Guided group tour all year round, by appt. (03 82 56 00 02).
Citadelle à Rodemack: Park open daily 10:30 a.m.–5 p.m., May–Sept.
Jardin Médiéval (medieval garden): Open all year round.

ACCOMMODATION & EATING OUT

mairie-rodemack.fr

LOCAL SPECIALTIES

Food and Drink
Artisan beers and lemonade • Honey • Organic vegetables • Apple juice • Farm produce.

 EVENTS

Market: Le Noyer, large organic vegetable market, Sat. 9 a.m.–12 p.m., Route de Faulbach, and Wed. 5–8 p.m., ramparts car park. Sun.: free market 8 a.m.–12 p.m.

 FURTHER AFIELD

- Basse Rentgen: Château de Preisch (3 miles/5 km).
- Hettange-Grande: Nature reserve and Maginot Line fortification (6 miles/10 km).
- Sierck-les-Bains: Château des Ducs de Lorraine; Manderen: Château de Malbrouk (7½–12 miles/12–19 km).
- Schengen: Musée de l'Europe (10 miles/16 km).
- Thionville (11 miles/18 km).

Moselle (57)
Population: 1,379
Altitude: 594 ft. (181 m)

TOURIST INFO—CATTENOM ET ENVIRONS
03 82 56 00 02
tourisme-ccce.fr
mairie-rodemack.fr

La Romieu
At the crossing of the ways

Amid the simplicity and charm of the Gascon countryside, La Romieu with its collegiate church is a stopping place at the intersection of paths leading from Puy and Rocamadour to Santiago de Compostela. Taking its name from the Gascon word *roumiou*, meaning "pilgrimage," the village was founded in the late 11th century by Albert, a German monk returning from a pilgrimage to Rome. The area gained greater importance in the 14th century when the powerful Cardinal Arnaud d'Aux, cousin of Pope Clement V and a native of the village, established the collegiate church of Saint-Pierre here. This building, which has been on the UNESCO World Heritage list since 1998, survived the agonies of the Wars of Religion and the French Revolution, and today provides visitors with a remarkable example of Southern Gothic architecture. At its feet, the village blends in seamlessly. The arcaded village square and the houses with their bright stone façades typical of the region create a unified and graceful ensemble around the religious site.

HIGHLIGHTS

Collégiale Saint-Pierre (14th century): Church, cloisters, octagonal tower, sacristy with polychrome frescoes, bell tower. Self-guided and guided tours all year; combined ticket with Les Jardins de Coursiana (05 62 28 86 33).
Les Jardins de Coursiana: 15-acre (6-ha) English landscape garden, arboretum, kitchen garden, orchard, etc., classed as "remarkable" by the Ministry of Culture. Open Apr.–Oct. (05 62 68 22 80).
♥ **Gers Astronomie**: Astronomical observatory (06 45 49 43 75).
♥ **On Va Vers le Beau**: Café, bookshop, and coworking spaces (06 77 18 25 04).

ACCOMMODATION & EATING OUT

Campsites
♥ Le Camp de Florence**** (05 62 28 15 58).
Guesthouses
♥ La Maison d'Aux (05 62 28 14 89).

LOCAL SPECIALTIES

Food and Drink
Honey • Prunes • Apples • Strawberries • Melons • Garlic • Asparagus • Côtes de Gascogne wines.
Art and Crafts
Art galleries and artists' studios.

EVENTS

Market: local farmers' market Mon. a.m., Place Bouet (Jul.–Aug.).
May: Rose market (Sun. after 20th).
Jun.: L'Art au Mieux, art festival (mid-Jun.)
Jul.: Musique en Chemin, music festival (20th–23rd).
Sept.: Potters' market (2nd Sun.).

OUTDOOR ACTIVITIES

Walking: Routes GR 65, GR 652, and marked PR trails • Mountain biking: Marked trails • Spelunking: Karst trail.

FURTHER AFIELD

• Condom: Cathedral; Cassaigne: Castle; Valence-sur-Baïse: Flaran Cistercian abbey (7–12½ miles/11–20 km).

MBVF NEARBY

• Larressingle (10½ miles/17 km).
• Fourcès (15½ miles/25 km).
• Montréal (16 miles/26 km).

Gers (32)
Population: 573
Altitude: 614 ft. (187 m)

TOURIST INFO—GASCOGNE-LOMAGNE
05 62 64 00 00
gascogne-lomagne.fr
TOWN HALL
05 62 28 15 72
la-romieu.fr

La Roque-Gageac

Sheltered by a cliff

Surrounded by ancient mansions and crowned by cliffs, the village of La Roque-Gageac is reflected in the waters of the Dordogne river. An important stronghold in the Middle Ages, the village gained its fine residences, including that of humanist Jean Tarde (1561-1636), during the Renaissance. In the 19th century, it saw heavy traffic of *gabares* (flat-bottomed boats) on the Dordogne river that transported wines from Domme to Bordeaux. Sheltered by the south-facing cliffs, and overlooked by the 16th-century church, Mediterranean and tropical plants flourish along the village's streets and in its gardens. The yellow-stone façades and pitched roofs covered with brown tiles contrast with their green setting. The beauty and character of the houses of La Roque-Gageac can also be admired from a boat on the Dordogne.

HIGHLIGHTS

Jardin Exotique: Mediterranean and tropical plant garden. Free self-guided visit (05 53 29 40 29).
Bambousaie: Self-guided tour to discover different varieties of bamboo. Open 11:45 a.m.–7 p.m. (07 81 69 00 56).
Jardin de la Ferme Fleurie: Terraced gardens (romantic garden, grandmother's garden, wild garden, medicinal-herb garden; 05 53 28 33 39).
Village: Guided tour Jun.–Sept. (05 53 31 45 45).
Fort de la Roque-Gageac: Large ruined fortress with a panoramic view (05 53 31 04 08).

ACCOMMODATION & EATING OUT

sarlat-tourisme.com

LOCAL SPECIALTIES

Food and Drink
Foie gras • Périgord specialties.

Art and Crafts
Watercolorist • Painter-interior decorator.

 EVENTS

Market: Fri. 8 a.m.–1 p.m.
Aug.: Village festival (early Aug.); gourmet food market (Mon. after 20th).

 OUTDOOR ACTIVITIES

Swimming (no lifeguard) in the Dordogne • *Gabare* (traditional flat-bottomed boat) trips • Canoeing and kayaking • Fishing • Walking • Mountain biking • Cycling.

 FURTHER AFIELD

•Marqueyssac: Park and gardens (2½ miles/4 km).
•Sarlat (8 miles/13 km).
•Vallée de la Vézère (15½ miles/25 km).

 MBVF NEARBY

•Castelnaud-la-Chapelle (2 miles/3.5 km).
•Beynac-et-Cazenac (3 miles/5 km).
•Domme (3½ miles/6 km).
•Belvès (14½ miles/23 km).

Dordogne (24)
Population: 430
Altitude: 430 ft. (131 m)

TOURIST INFO—SARLAT PÉRIGORD NOIR
05 53 31 45 45
sarlat-tourisme.com

 OUTDOOR ACTIVITIES

Walking • Mountain biking • Swimming • Canoeing and kayaking • Fishing.

FURTHER AFIELD

- Cornillon; Goudargues (5 miles/8 km).
- Bagnols-sur-Cèze: Market (7½ miles/12 km).
- Gorges de la Cèze (9½ miles/15 km).

 MBVF NEARBY

- Montclus (9½ miles/15 km).
- Aiguèze (11 miles/18 km).

La Roque-sur-Cèze

Stone, vines, and water

Between Cévennes and Provence, surrounded by garigue (scrubland), La Roque-sur-Cèze has established itself on a rocky slope overlooking the Cèze river and the vineyards. Past the Pont Charles-Martel with its twelve arches, along steep, winding, cobbled streets, lies an endless jumble of buildings, rooftops, and covered terraces, whose sun-weathered stone walls and Genoese tiles give them a Tuscan feel. When visitors reach the summit of the village—after a little physical exertion—the ruins of the 12th-century castle and its Romanesque chapel are reminders of the strategic position that the site occupied in the Middle Ages on the Roman road leading from Nîmes to Alba. In sharp contrast to the serenity and aridity of the village are the waterfalls, rapids, and crevices of the Cascades du Sautadet, including the magnificent "giants' cauldrons"—cylindrical cavities carved out by the Cèze—which require caution but offer a refreshing place to relax in the wilderness.

 HIGHLIGHTS

Village: Historical trail; guided tour by appt. (04 66 82 30 02).
Church (19th century): Restored in 2013, contemporary stained-glass windows.
Chapelle du Presbytères: Exhibitions.
Les Cascades du Sautadet: Waterfalls.

ACCOMMODATION & EATING OUT

provenceoccitane.com

LOCAL SPECIALTIES

Food and Drink
AOC Côtes du Rhône wines.
Art and Crafts
Handcrafted santons and nativity figures and scenes.

 EVENTS

Aug.: Jam fair (weekend of 15th).

Gard (30)
Population: 177
Altitude: 295 ft. (90 m)

TOURIST INFO—PROVENCE OCCITANE
04 66 82 30 02
provenceoccitane.com
laroquesurceze.fr

Roussillon

The flame of the Luberon

Sparkling with colors in its verdant setting, Roussillon, just north of Marseille, is a jewel in the ocher massif. In Roman times, the ocher of Mont Rouge was transported to the port of Marseille, from where it was shipped to the East. Superseding silk farming, which was responsible for the village's rise in fortunes from the 14th century, the ocher industry developed in the late 18th century thanks to a local man, Jean-Étienne Astier. Since then, Roussillon has built its reputation on this brightly colored mineral. Today, ocher presents visitors with an almost infinite palette of hues in every narrow street and on numerous house fronts; it can also be seen in its natural setting, on the ocher trail, with its spectacular sites sculpted by water, wind, and humankind. On the Place de la Mairie—a lively meeting place for both locals and visitors—the Hôtel de Ville and the houses opposite date from the 17th century.

 **HIGHLIGHTS**

Ôkhra – Écomusée de l'Ocre: Guided tour on the manufacture, geology, and heritage of ocher; workshops and courses (04 90 05 66 69).
Sentier des Ocres (ocher trail): Mid-Feb.–late Dec. (04 90 05 60 25 or luberon-apt.fr).

 **ACCOMMODATION & EATING OUT**

roussillon-en-provence.fr

LOCAL SPECIALTIES

Food and Drink
Olive oil • Fruit juices • AOC Côtes du Luberon and Côtes du Ventoux wines.
Art and Crafts
Candles • Ceramists • Ocher-based handicrafts • Decorators • Fossils and minerals • Art galleries • Painters • Sculptors.

 EVENTS

Market: Thurs. 9 a.m.–12 p.m., Place du Pasquier.
Jul.: Beckett festival (late Jul.).
Jul.-Aug.: Fêtez le Cinema sous les Étoiles, outdoor film festival.
Aug.: Festival International de Quatuors à Cordes du Luberon, string quartet festival.
Sept.: Book fair (3rd weekend).

 OUTDOOR ACTIVITIES

Walking: Routes GR 6 and GR 97, and 4 marked PR trails • Hot-air balloon flights.

 FURTHER AFIELD

•Le Luberon; Apt (6–12½ miles/10–20 km).
•L'Isle-sur-la-Sorgue (17 miles/27 km).

 MBVF NEARBY

•Gordes (6 miles/10 km).
•Ménerbes (10½ miles/17 km).
•Lourmarin (14½ miles/23 km).
•Venasque (15 miles/24 km).

Vaucluse (84)
Population: 1,350
Altitude: 1,148 ft. (350 m)

TOURIST INFO—PAYS D'APT LUBERON
04 90 05 60 25
luberon-apt.fr
roussillon-en-provence.fr

Saint-Amand-de-Coly
(Commune of Coly-Saint-Amand)

An abbey in Périgord

Nestled at the intersection of three wooded valleys, the abbey at Saint-Amand-de-Coly watches over houses that are typical of the Périgord Noir region. The village owes both its name and its religious heritage to the monk Amand, who came to evangelize the Coly valley in the 6th century. The abbey was founded in the early 12th century and ensured Saint-Amand's prosperity for two centuries. With the Hundred Years War and the development of defense systems, the abbey church was considered the most beautiful fortified church in Périgord. The splendid 100-ft. (30-m) tall bell-tower porch, its huge Gothic arch, and its triple-arched door have a simple strength about them. Surrounding the site are houses and dovecotes in Sarlat stone with *lauze* (schist tile) roofs, along with an old tobacco-drying barn.

 HIGHLIGHTS

Abbey church (12th century): Guided tour Apr.–Oct., free and conscious participation (05 53 51 98 92). For groups, see lesamisdesaintamanddecoly.com.
La Ferme du Peuch: Walnut groves, harvesting, drying, and cracking of walnuts; tour of the oil press (05 53 51 27 87 / 06 76 72 79 62).
Signposted walk: Historical, nature, or recreational trails available at the Accueil Patrimoine Apr.–Oct. (05 53 51 98 92).

 ACCOMMODATION & EATING OUT

lascaux-dordogne.com

 LOCAL SPECIALTIES

Food and Drink
Walnuts • Walnut oil • Périgord *choconoiseries* (chocolate-covered walnuts).
Art and Crafts
Copperwork • Bladesmith • Stained-glass artist • Artists' studios.

 EVENTS

May: Faites l'Abbaye, activities around the abbey church.
Jul.: Saint-Amand Fait Son Intéressant, street performance festival (around 14th).
Jul.–Aug.: Local farmers' market with concerts and projections on the abbey (Tues., 6–10 p.m.); Périgord Noir classical music festival (late Jul.–mid-Aug.); village festival (Aug. 15).
Oct.: Marché aux Saveurs de l'Automne, fall produce market (last Sun.).

 OUTDOOR ACTIVITIES

Walking: 8 circuits • Horseback riding • Mountain biking: Base VTT Périgord Noir with numerous marked trails.

 FURTHER AFIELD

•Montignac; Prehistoric sites at Lascaux and Eyzies; Sarlat (5½–13½ miles/9–22 km).

 MBVF NEARBY
•Saint-Léon-sur-Vézère (12 miles/19 km).
•Vallée de la Dordogne: La Roque-Gageac (20 miles/32 km); Beynac-et-Cazenac and Castelnaud-la-Chapelle (21 miles/34 km); Domme (22 miles/35 km); Limeuil (29 miles/47 km).

Dordogne (24)
Population: 604
Altitude: 568 ft. (173 m)

ACCUEIL PATRIMOINE
05 53 51 98 92
colysaintamand.fr
TOURIST INFO—LASCAUX-DORDOGNE VALLÉE VÉZÈRE
05 53 51 82 60
lascaux-dordogne.com

Saint-Antoine-l'Abbaye

Miracles in medieval Dauphiné

Deep in a verdant valley surrounded by the Vercors massif, the Abbaye Saint-Antoine watches over the village that bears its name. The history of Saint-Antoine-l'Abbaye began in the 11th century, when Geilin, a local lord, brought back from his pilgrimage to the Holy Land the relics of Saint Anthony of Egypt. In around 1280, construction started on the abbey that was to house these famous relics, which were said to have the power to cure "Saint Anthony's Fire," a poisoning of the blood. Thanks to reconstruction work undertaken in the 17th century, visitors may still admire the abbey, considered to be one of the most remarkable Gothic buildings in the Dauphiné region. At the foot of this mighty building, the village bears living witness to the medieval and Renaissance eras: 15th–18th-century noblemen's houses in *molasse* stone with mullioned windows lead, via *goulets* (half-covered narrow streets), to old shops with half-timbered façades and the medieval covered market.

 **HIGHLIGHTS**

Abbey church (12th–15th centuries): Murals, Aubusson tapestries, wood paneling, 17th-century organ (04 76 38 53 85).

Abbey treasury: 17th-century ivory Christ, liturgical vestments. Guided tours only (04 76 38 53 85).

Musée de Saint-Antoine-l'Abbaye: History of the abbey and the order of the Hospitallers of Saint-Antoine; temporary exhibitions (04 76 36 40 68).

Medieval garden at the abbey: Medicinal herb, kitchen, and rose gardens (04 76 36 40 68).

Chapelle Saint-Jean-le-Fromental (12th century): Murals. Open weekends and public holidays in summer; guided group tour by appt. offseason (06 33 58 92 53).

Stonemason's workshop: Tour by appt. (04 76 36 44 12).

Village: Self-guided discovery trail "Le Sentier du Flâneur" (leaflet from tourist info center); guided group tours all year round, Apr.–Oct. for individuals (04 76 38 53 85).

 **ACCOMMODATION & EATING OUT**

tourisme.saintmarcellin-vercors-isere.fr

 LOCAL SPECIALTIES

Food and Drink
Honey • Mead • Hippocras (spiced wine) • *Pain d'épice* (spice cake) • Fruit wines.
Art and Crafts
Ceramics • Cabinetmaking • Leather goods • Soap making • Collective shop.

 EVENTS

Market: Local produce and crafts market, Fri. 4–7 p.m., Place de la Halle.
Jan.: Fête de la Truffe et Marché des Tentations, truffle festival (Sun. after 17th).
May: Rare flower and plant fair (3rd Sun.).
Jul.: Textes en l'Air, contemporary theater festival (last week).
Aug.: La Médiévale de Saint-Antoine, medieval festival.

 OUTDOOR ACTIVITIES

Miripili, l'Île aux Pirates theme park, Étang de Chapaize • Walking • Mountain biking.

FURTHER AFIELD

• Royans-Vercors paddle steamer (7½ miles/12 km).
• Saint-Marcellin; Pont-en-Royans; Romans-sur-Isère; Parc Naturel Régional du Vercors (8–14½ miles/13–23 km).

Isère (38)
Population: 1,197
Altitude: 1,247 ft. (380 m)

TOURIST INFO—SAINT-MARCELLIN VERSORS ISÈRE
04 76 38 53 85
tourisme.saintmarcellin-vercors-isere.fr

saint-antoine-labbaye.fr

Saint-Benoît-du-Sault

A priory on the edge of Limousin

Built on a granite spur, the village of Saint-Benoît-du-Sault stands at the entrance to the Occitan region. Enclosed by partially intact double ramparts, Saint-Benoît has preserved its medieval past in the form of a fortified gateway, a 14th-century belfry, and an old wall-walk. At the tip of the rocky promontory, a Benedictine priory offers a sweeping view over the valley. Majestic and sober, the church, from the first Romanesque period, contains carved capitals and an 11th-century baptismal font. At the heart of the village, 15th-and 16th-century houses line the narrow, often steep streets: the Portail and Maison de l'Argentier, with its carved lintel, are the most remarkable. Walking trails invite visitors to explore the village, built in the shape of an amphitheater overlooking the Portefeuille river, and the priory, which is reflected in the waters below, with a historically-listed dike.

 HIGHLIGHTS

Church (11th, 13th, and 14th centuries): Stained-glass windows from the 19th century and by contemporary master stained-glass maker Jean Mauret.
Priory: Open during exhibitions; tours of the dining terrace (02 54 47 41 44).
Village: Guided tours (02 54 47 67 95).

 ACCOMMODATION & EATING OUT

saint-benoit-du-sault.fr

 LOCAL SPECIALTIES

Food and Drink
Pâté Berrichon (egg pie) • Goat cheese.
Art and Crafts
Poetry and artists' book publisher • Engraver and painter • Ceramists • Contemporary art.

 EVENTS

Market: Thurs. and Sat. a.m. all year round.
Apr.: Pays de la Loire wine fair.
Jul.: Fireworks (14th); outdoor jazz (last Sun.).
Aug.: Interregional ram show (1st Wed.); classical and lyrical music festival (3rd week); local saint's day with evening show (15th).
Dec.: Brive goose, duck and capon produce fair (2nd Sun.).

 OUTDOOR ACTIVITIES

Fishing • Walking trails.

 FURTHER AFIELD

•Dolmens of Les Gorces and of Passebonneau (1–2 miles/2–3 km).
•Saint-Marcel: Musée Archéologique d'Argentomagus; Crozant: Fortress; Rosnay: Maison du Parc Naturel Régional de la Brenne (13½–23½ miles/22–38 km).

 MBVF NEARBY

•Gargilesse-Dampierre (15 miles/24 km).

Indre (36)
Population: 554
Altitude: 722 ft. (220 m)

TOURIST INFO— DESTINATION BRENNE
02 54 47 67 95
02 54 28 20 28
destination-brenne.fr
saint-benoit-du-sault.fr

155

Saint-Bertrand-de-Comminges

Ancient guardian of the Pyrenees

Saint-Bertrand-de-Comminges owes its name to the bishop who built its cathedral. Located at the foot of the Pyrenees, the village still contains the ruins of a Roman forum, established in 72 BCE by Pompey on his return from Spain. Considered to be King Herod's place of exile, the town grew up around a basilica in the 4th century before it was destroyed by the Vandals and then the Burgundians. Bertrand, bishop of Comminges, rebuilt the village from its ruins and installed an episcopal court there. Military in appearance, the Cathédrale Sainte-Marie, which was remodeled in the 14th century by the future pope Clement V, retains its 12th-century bell tower, its cloisters giving onto the Pyrenees, and its impressive portal. A rood screen stands in front of the choir and its 66 stalls and 16th-century episcopal throne. Fine houses from the 16th–18th centuries huddle around the cathedral. Circling the old town, the ramparts are punctuated by the Majou, Cabirole, and l'Hyrisson gateways.

 HIGHLIGHTS

Cathédrale Sainte-Marie (11th-14th centuries): Tympanum depicting the Adoration of the Magi, the Virgin and Child, and Saint Bertrand; 66 carved wooden stalls; 16th-century corner organ. Self-guided or guided tours, audio guides available (05 61 89 04 91).

Early Christian basilica: Ruins of a basilica whose foundations incorporate 28 sarcophagi in marble from the Pyrenees.

Chapelle Saint-Julien: 19th-century reconstruction of an ancient chapel.

Les Olivétains cultural and tourist center: Archaeological museum, bookstore, contemporary art exhibitions (05 61 95 44 44).

Musée du Blason et des Ordres de Chevalerie: History of the orders of chivalry; collection of over 2,000 coats of arms; collections of coins, illuminated manuscripts, medieval weapons. Tours by appt. (06 22 35 30 10).

Village: Guided group tour only, by appt. (05 61 95 44 44).

 ACCOMMODATION & EATING OUT

hautegaronnetourisme.com

 **LOCAL SPECIALTIES**

Food and Drink
Cassoulet and Mounjetado • Foie gras • *Porc noir de Bigorre* (rare-breed pork) • *Croustade* (flaky fruit pastry) • Barousse cheese • *Pistache de mouton* (lamb stew) • *Aïgo boulido* (Provençal soup) • Pétéram de Luchon (offal stew) • Alicuit de canard (duck stew) • Milhassou au potiron (pumpkin cake).

Art and Crafts
Jewelry • Fossils and minerals • Leather goods, saddlery • Umbrella maker • Blacksmith • Clogs.

EVENTS

Jul.: Les Médiévales (last weekend).
Jul.-Sept.: Festival du Comminges, classical music festival.

OUTDOOR ACTIVITIES

Walking: Route GR 656 and 2 marked trails.

FURTHER AFIELD

•Valcabrère: Basilica; Barbazan; Vallée de la Barousse, valley; Grottes de Gargas, caves; Montréjeau; Saint-Gaudens (1–10½ miles/2–17 km).

Haute-Garonne (31)
Population: 240
Altitude: 1,700 ft. (518 m)

TOURIST INFO— LES OLIVÉTAINS
05 61 95 44 44
hautegaronnetourisme.com

 EVENTS

Pentecost: Les Rencontres de Saint-Céneri, painting, sculpture, and photography festival.
Jul.: Saint Scène, music festival.
Aug.: Rummage sale (1st Sun.).

 OUTDOOR ACTIVITIES

Canoeing and kayaking • Fishing • Walking: Routes GR 36, GRP Tour du Mont des Avaloirs, several marked trails including via the Normandie-Maine regional nature park • Mountain biking.

 FURTHER AFIELD

•Saint-Léonard-des-Bois (3 miles/5 km).
•Alençon: Musée des Beaux-Arts et de la Dentelle, fine arts and lace museum (9½ miles/15 km).
•Forêt d'Écouves; Château de Carrouges; Parc Naturel Régional Normandie-Maine; Carrouges (12½–18½ miles/20–30 km).
•Bagnoles-de-l'Orne (25 miles/40 km).

Saint-Céneri-le-Gérei

A painter's paradise

Surrounded by nature, Saint-Céneri-le-Gérei lies in the heart of the Alpes Mancelles natural heritage site. The village was founded in the 12th century by Saint Céneri, an Italian hermit who created a monastery on the site, which the Normans later set on fire. Saint-Céneri-le-Gérei's charm lies in its stone houses perched on the bluff or nestled along the Sarthe river. The 11th-century Romanesque church boasts a ceiling that is one of a kind in France, and a little further on a 15th-century chapel secluded in the meadow keeps the legends of Saint Céneri alive. From the late 19th century, the village inspired many renowned painters, including Camille Corot (1796-1875) and Eugène Boudin (1824-1898). The walls of the Auberge des Soeurs Moisy, which they frequented, are still hung with charcoal portraits of artists and villagers sketched by candlelight.

 HIGHLIGHTS

Église Saint-Céneri (11th century): Murals from 12th and 14th centuries, pewter Stations of the Cross.
Chapel (15th century): Statue of Saint Céneri.
Auberge des Soeurs Moisy: Reception of the tourist info office early Apr.–late Sept. (02 33 80 66 33).
Village: Guided tour; guided bike tour (from 10 years old, 6-mile/10-km circuit); horse-drawn carriage tour Sat. in Jul.–Aug.; storytelling walk Jul.–Aug. (02 33 80 66 33).
Jardins de la Mansonière: 12 walled gardens; temporary exhibitions, workshops (02 33 26 73 24).

 ACCOMMODATION & EATING OUT

saintceneri.org

LOCAL SPECIALTIES

Art and Crafts
Painters • Sculptors.

Orne (61)
Population: 128
Altitude: 417 ft. (127 m)

TOURIST INFO—ALENÇON DESTINATION NORMANDIE
02 33 80 66 33
visitalencon.com
saintceneri.org

Saint-Cirq-Lapopie

A panoramic viewpoint over the Lot

Perched on an escarpment silhouetted against a background of tall cliffs, Saint-Cirq-Lapopie overlooks a bend in the Lot river. Controlling the Lot valley, which long enjoyed a flourishing trade in the transportation of goods by barge, the site of Saint-Cirq-Lapopie has been occupied since Gallo-Roman times. In the Middle Ages it became a powerful fortified complex that included the castles of the four dynasties that shared power here (Cardaillac, Castelnau, Gourdon, and Lapopie). Owing to its coveted strategic position, Saint-Cirq-Lapopie was constantly besieged over the centuries and its castles were mostly destroyed. Yet the village exudes an air of rare harmony, between its site, its architecture, and its landscapes. Numerous artists and writers succumbed to the magic of this place in the 20th century, including André Breton, who made the old Auberge des Mariniers his summer residence and ceased "wishing to be elsewhere."

 **HIGHLIGHTS**

Centre International du Surréalisme et de la Citoyenneté Mondiale – Maisons André Breton et Émile Joseph-Rignault: Located in the former homes of writer André Breton (knights' quarters with a tower built in the 12th-13th centuries) and collector Émile Joseph-Rignault (former seat of the archpriest of Saint-Cirq-Lapopie). Exhibitions, gardens, and spaces dedicated to poetry and surrealism; café-bookstore, concerts, screenings, workshops (ciscm.fr).

Maison Daura: Center for contemporary art, research, and artistic innovation; exhibition of artworks created during residency (05 65 40 78 19).

Village: Guided tours all year round (05 65 31 31 31); by appt. for groups (06 62 86 22 46 / 06 62 88 00 14).

 ACCOMMODATION & EATING OUT

cahorsvalleedulot.com

 **LOCAL SPECIALTIES**

Food and Drink
Duck foie gras • Walnuts • Truffles • Saffron • Cahors wine • Rocamadour cheese.
Art and Crafts
Artisanal leather goods • Jewelry • Hats • Ceramics • Tableware • Wooden toys • Paintings • Engraving • Sculpture • Wood turning • Clothing.

 EVENTS

Market: Farmers' market, Wed. 4–8 p.m., Place du Sombral (Jul.–Aug.).
Jul.: Village festival (weekend following Jul. 14th).

 OUTDOOR ACTIVITIES

Canoeing and kayaking • Walking: Route GR 36 and marked trails.

 FURTHER AFIELD

• Château de Cénevières (5½ miles/9 km).
• Vallée du Célé: Cabrerets, Pech Merle caves; Marcilhac (6–15½ miles/10–25 km).
• Causse de Limogne; Villefranche-de-Rouergue (9½–23½ miles/15–38 km).
• Cajarc; Figeac (12½–28 miles/20–45 km).
• Cahors (15½ miles/25 km).

Lot (46)
Population: 208
Altitude: 722 ft. (220 m)

TOURIST INFO—CAHORS VALLÉE DU LOT
05 65 31 31 31
cahorsvalleedulot.com

Saint-Côme-d'Olt

A pilgrims' stopping place on the Lot river

Located on the Saint James's Way in the fertile Lot valley, Saint-Côme-d'Olt is distinguished by its twisted spire and its delightful houses. Bordered on the south side by the green hills that overlook the basaltic mass of Roquelaure, and to the north by terraces of ancient vineyards, the village has grown up over time inside the circular ditches of the old medieval town, of which three fortified gates remain. The 16th-century church, whose twisted spire dominates the village, is Flamboyant Gothic in style. Its heavy carved-oak doors are reinforced with 365 wrought-iron nails. The Château des Sires de Calmont, built in the 12th century and remodeled in the 15th, has a Renaissance façade and two 14th-century towers. The narrow streets are still lined with old medieval shops and houses from the 10th and 16th centuries. The Ouradou, a building with an octagonal roof, was erected in memory of the victims of the 1586 plague.

HIGHLIGHTS

Chapelle des Pénitents (11th–12th centuries): Exhibition on Romanesque architecture and the White Penitents.
Église Saint-Côme-et-Saint-Damien (16th century): Twisted spire, 16th-century wooden Christ, 18th-century altarpiece, historically-listed 16th-century oak doors.
Village: Guided tour all year round by appt.; themed tours, discovery tour Jun.–Aug. (05 65 44 07 09).

ACCOMMODATION & EATING OUT

saint-come-olt.com

LOCAL SPECIALTIES

Art and Crafts
Jewelry • Potter • Artisanal shoemaker ♥ Aubrac Bottier, awarded "Living Heritage Company" label (06 85 02 70 42).

EVENTS

Market: Sun. 8 a.m.–1 p.m., town center.
May: La Transhumance Aubrac (Sun. nearest to 25th).
Jul.: Evening market (14th).
Aug.: Folk festival (2nd Sat.); evening market (Wed. before 15th); local saint's day (4th Sun.).

OUTDOOR ACTIVITIES

Canoeing and kayaking • Fishing • Walking: Route GR 65 and 10 marked trails • Mountain biking.

FURTHER AFIELD

•Flaujac, fortified hamlet (1 mile/2 km).
•Roquelaure: Castle, lava flow (2–3 miles/3–5 km).
•Espalion: Musée du Scaphandre; Calmont d'Olt, medieval castle; 11th-century Romanesque chapel of Perse; Pont Vieux, bridge; Chapelle des Pénitents (2½ miles/4 km).

MBVF NEARBY

•Estaing (8 miles/13 km).
•Sainte-Eulalie-d'Olt (12 miles/19 km).

Aveyron (12)
Population: 1,464
Altitude: 1,234 ft. (376 m)

TOURIST INFO—TERRES D'AVEYRON
05 65 44 10 63
terresdaveyron.fr
saint-come-olt.com

Saint-Guilhem-le-Désert

Romanesque architecture and wild nature

At the bottom of a wild gorge, the village of Saint-Guilhem encircles its abbey, one of the finest examples of early Romanesque architecture in the Languedoc. A stopping place on the Saint James's Way, Saint-Guilhem was, in the Middle Ages, a center of Christianity, where believers, Crusaders, and pilgrims came to pray and to venerate a piece of the True Cross. Although little remains of the original abbey, founded by Saint Guilhem in the 9th century, the present church is a gem of Romanesque architecture, listed as a UNESCO World Heritage Site. The heart of the village is the delightful Place de la Liberté. The impressive 150-year-old plane tree, fountains dating from 1907, and the arches of the 17th-century covered market make the square a magical place where people like to gather. Huddled together along the main street, picturesque houses with roofs finished in traditional pink barrel tiles are adorned with double Romanesque windows, Gothic lintels, and Renaissance mullions.

 **HIGHLIGHTS**

Abbaye de Gellone (11th, 12th, and 15th centuries): Abbey church; treasury (04 67 57 04 59).

Musée de l'Abbaye: Romanesque and Gothic sculptures, remains of the cloister (restored); film on the history of the abbey and its rebuilding (Apr.–Oct.), by appt. for groups (04 67 57 04 59).

Musée d'Antan: History of the village and its traditional trades, recounted through scenes featuring life-size santons (04 67 57 77 07).

Village and abbey: Guided group tour all year round, by appt. (04 67 56 41 97).

 ACCOMMODATION & EATING OUT

saint-guilhem-le-desert.com

 LOCAL SPECIALTIES

Food and Drink
Craft beers • Caviar • *Oreillettes* (cookies) • Olives and olive oil •Wine: ♥ Domaine La Voûte du Verdus (04 67 57 45 90).

Art and Crafts
Painters • Potters • Sculptors • Perfumers • Santon (crib figure) makers.

 EVENTS

Jan.: Fête de la Truffe et du Vin, truffle and wine festival (4th Sun.).
May: Les Marteaux de Gellone, medieval music festival (3rd and 4th weeks).

Jul.: Théâtre sous les Étoiles, open-air theater festival.
Sept.: Les Amis de Saint-Guilhem concert season.
Apr.–Dec.: Organ concerts, incl. traditional Christmas Day concert.

 **OUTDOOR ACTIVITIES**

Swimming • Fishing • Canoeing and kayaking • Walks for all levels • Spelunking.

FURTHER AFIELD

•Pont du Diable, bridge; Maison du Grand Site de France with wine cellar and Provençal farmhouse; Grotte de Clamouse, cave (2 miles/3 km).
•Saint-Jean-de-Fos: Argileum, pottery workshop (2½ miles/4 km).
•Cirque de Mourèze; Lac de Salagou; Villeneuvette (15½–16 miles/25–26 km).

Hérault (34)
Population: 250
Altitude: 292 ft. (89 m)

TOURIST INFO—SAINT-GUILHEM-LE-DÉSERT VALLÉE DE L'HÉRAULT
04 67 56 41 97 /
04 67 57 58 83
saintguilhem-valleeherault.fr
saint-guilhem-le-desert.com

Saint-Jean-de-Côle

Architectural symphony in Périgord Vert

Nestling in the hills, Saint-Jean-de-Côle is an inviting place to dream and meditate in an exceptional architectural setting. Overlooking the village square, the Château de la Marthonie has replaced the original fortress that was built here in the 12th century to defend the Périgord and Limousin borders. Burned down during the Hundred Years War, the latter made way for a 15th- and 16th-century building that combines Renaissance elegance and classical precision in its two wings, which share a magnificent straight-flight staircase. Adjoining a priory with cloisters and ambulatory, the Romanesque-Byzantine-style church was built between the late 11th and early 12th centuries. At the edge of the village, near the old mill, a humpback bridge with cutwaters spans the Côle river. This prestigious architectural ensemble is completed by the village's unusual little streets and old houses, some of which are half-timbered.

HIGHLIGHTS

Château de la Marthonie (12th, 15th, 16th, and 17th centuries): Guided tour of exterior, 16th-century staircases, and 17th-century salon (05 53 62 14 15).

Église Saint-Jean-Baptiste (11th–12th centuries): Wood paneling, paintings; interior sound and light show.

Priory (11th–12th centuries): Braille guide from tourist info center.

Village: Self-guided tour with multilanguage audio guide; treasure hunt for kids; guided tour; braille guides available (05 53 62 14 15).

ACCOMMODATION & EATING OUT

ville-saint-jean-de-cole.fr

LOCAL SPECIALTIES

Food and Drink
Trout: ♥ Pisciculture La Fon Pépy (07 84 01 46 17).

Art and Crafts
Ceramist • Art gallery • Painter.

EVENTS

May: Floralies, flower festival (weekend nearest to May 8).
Jul.-Aug.: Classical music concerts; street theater; Les Jeudis de l'Art, art exhibitions on Thurs.

OUTDOOR ACTIVITIES

Fishing • Walking, horseback riding, mountain biking: 10 ½-mile (17-km) greenway, marked trails, and railway-themed signposted trail • "Flow Vélo" cycle route.

FURTHER AFIELD

• Thiviers (4½ miles/7 km).
• Villars: Cave; Château de Puyguilhem; Abbaye de Boschaud ruins (5–7 miles/8–11 km).
• Limousin-Périgord regional nature park (6 miles/10 km).
• Brantôme (12½ miles/20 km).

Dordogne (24)
Population: 360
Altitude: 489 ft. (149 m)

TOURIST INFO—PÉRIGORD LIMOUSIN
05 53 62 14 15
perigord-limousin-tourisme.com
ville-saint-jean-de-cole.fr

Saint-Jean-Pied-de-Port

A fortified town in the Pays Basque

Situated on the banks of the Nive river, between the Basque coast and the Spanish border, this historically defensive site now watches over pilgrims on their way to Santiago de Compostela. At the end of the 12th century, the king of Navarre ordered a fortress to be built on a hill overlooking the Nive river, in the foothills of the mountains around Cize, in a bid to secure control of the main passage through the Pyrenees via Roncevalles. Shortly afterward, a new town emerged around the fortress. Its strategic position turned it into a military linchpin and thriving commercial center, as well as a site of religious importance on the Saint James's Way. This three-pronged identity can still be seen in the village's architecture: from the citadel (17th century) and the ramparts of the upper town (13th century), to the Porte Saint-Jacques—a UNESCO World Heritage Site—and the Église Notre-Dame-du-Bout-du-Pont, in pink sandstone from nearby Arradoy.

 **HIGHLIGHTS**

Citadel (17th century): Bastioned fortification overhauled by Vauban. Guided tour Mon. and Wed. in Jul.–Aug. (05 59 37 03 57).
Prison dite des Évêques (14th century): Medieval building used as a warehouse, then a prison. Permanent exhibition on the Basque sport of pelote and the Basque diaspora. Open Easter–late Oct. (05 59 37 00 92).
Église Notre-Dame-du-Bout-du-Pont (13th–14th centuries): One of the most important Gothic church buildings in the French Basque Country. Open every day.
Village: Guided group tour all year round by appt.; guided tour for individuals in Jul.–Aug. (05 59 37 03 57); self-guided tour with audio guide; tourist train tour Easter–late Oct. (05 59 37 00 92).

 ACCOMMODATION & EATING OUT

en-pays-basque.fr

 LOCAL SPECIALTIES

Food and Drink
AOP Ossau-Iraty cheese • AOC Irouleguy wine • AOC Kintoa Basque pork • Distilled spirits • Gâteau Basque • Macarons • Banka trout.
Art and Crafts
Artisan espadrille-maker • Potter • Gallery of local crafts.

 EVENTS

Market: Mon. 8 a.m.–1 p.m., Place des remparts; farmers' market Thurs. 9 a.m.–1 p.m., Place des remparts (Jun.– Sept.).
Aug.: Patron saint's day (around 15th); Citadelle en Scènes, theater festival (around 22nd).
Sept.: Irouleguy vineyard festival (2nd weekend).

 OUTDOOR ACTIVITIES

• Walking: Routes GR 10, GR 65, and several marked trails • Mountain biking: Grande Traversée du Pays Basque • Fly fishing.

 FURTHER AFIELD

• Saint-Jean-le-Vieux: Archaeological museum (3 miles/5 km).
• Esterençuby: Grottes d'Harpea, caves (5½ miles/9 km).
• Bidarray, frontier village (12½ miles/20 km).
• Espelette (22½ miles/36 km).

 MBVF NEARBY
• Ainhoa; La Bastide-Clairence (26½ miles/43 km).

Pyrénées-Atlantiques (64)
Population: 1,515
Altitude: 525 ft. (160 m)

TOURIST INFO—PAYS BASQUE
05 59 37 03 57
en-pays-basque.fr

Saint-Léon-sur-Vézère

A prehistoric treasure in the Vézère valley

Tucked away in a bend in the Vézère river, halfway between Lascaux and Les Eyzies, Saint-Léon is at the heart of this cradle of civilization. Occupied since prehistoric times, as evidenced in the remains of dwellings at Le Conquil, Saint-Léon is named after one of the first bishops of Périgueux. Located near a Roman road, the village was, until the arrival of the railway, a thriving port on the Vézère river, earning itself the name Port-Léon during the French Revolution. From the cemetery chapel at the village entrance, the road leads past the Château de Clérans and the Manoir de La Salle to a 12th-century Romanesque church with a *lauze* (schist tile) roof—one of the venues for the popular Périgord Noir music festival. Its floor plan resembles that of Byzantine churches. The Château de Chaban, dating from the Middle Ages to the 17th century, stands a stone's throw from the Côte de Jor nature site.

 HIGHLIGHTS

Dhagpo Kagyu Ling Buddhist study and meditation center: Main European center for the Kagyupa Buddhist tradition; classes, meditation, Buddhist philosophy courses (05 53 50 70 75).
Romanesque church (12th century): Frescoes.
Le Conquil prehistoric theme park: Dinosaur park and troglodytic site.
Donjon, Manoir et Jardin de la Salle (14th century): Square tower; medieval and Renaissance furniture; 300-year-old Lebanese cedar (26 ft./8 m). Self-guided tour daily Apr.–Nov. (05 53 42 72 88).

 ACCOMMODATION & EATING OUT

lascaux-dordogne.com

 LOCAL SPECIALTIES

Art and Crafts
Painters • Jewelry makers • Wood sculptor • Sculptors • Felt and glass work.

 EVENTS

Market: Gourmet and crafts market, Thurs. 6:30 p.m. in Jul.–Aug.
Jul.: Flea market (1st or 2nd Sun.).
Aug.: Périgord Noir music festival: concerts in the Romanesque church (mid-Aug.); village festival (2nd weekend).

 **OUTDOOR ACTIVITIES**

Canoeing and kayaking • Fishing • Forest adventure park • Horseback riding • Walking: Route GR 36, 3 marked trails • Hang gliding • Mountain biking.

 FURTHER AFIELD

•Côte de Jor: Panoramic view (2 miles/3 km).
•Vallée de l'Homme, prehistoric sites: Les Eyzies; Lascaux (2–9½ miles/3–15 km).
•Grotte de Rouffignac, cave (11 miles/18 km).
•Vallée de la Dordogne; Sarlat (18½–24 miles/ 30–39 km).

 MBVF NEARBY
•Saint-Amand-de-Coly (11 miles/18 km).

Dordogne (24)
Population: 432
Altitude: 230 ft. (70 m)

TOURIST INFO—LASCAUX-DORDOGNE VALLÉE VÉZÈRE
05 53 51 08 42 (peak season)
lascaux-dordogne.com
TOWN HALL
05 53 50 73 16
slve.fr

Saint-Quirin

Bell towers and hills in the Vosges mountains

At the foot of an amphitheater of hills, the village of Saint-Quirin is surrounded by the vast and game-filled Vosges forest, where beech and oak grow alongside spruce and larch. Higher up, the archaeological site of La Croix-Guillaume contains important Gallo-Roman remains from the 1st, 2nd, and 3rd centuries, which bear witness to the ancient culture of the peaks. Saint-Quirin is named after Quirinus, the military tribune of Rome who was martyred in 132 CE under the Emperor Hadrian. Many buildings testify to the village's glorious past: the priory and the Baroque priory church (1722), with its Jean-André Silbermann organ (1746), which is a listed historic monument, as well as the Église des Verriers—a beautiful Rococo-style edifice built in 1756 at Lettenbach. Below the church, the water from the miraculous spring was said to heal skin diseases through the intercession of Saint Quirinus. The village thus became a place of pilgrimage and devotion to its healing saint.

 HIGHLIGHTS

Priory church (18th century): Silbermann organ, relics of Saint Quirinus, large crystal chandelier.
High chapel (12th century): Stained-glass windows by Honer de Nancy.
Chapelle Notre-Dame-de-l'Hor at Métairies-Saint-Quirin (15th and 18th centuries): Statue of the Immaculate Conception, paintings.
Gallo-Roman archaeological site of La Croix-Guillaume: Guided tour with D. Heckenbenner (03 87 08 65 90).

ACCOMMODATION & EATING OUT

Gîtes
♥ Projet Z – Lodges (06 33 93 45 67).

🐓 LOCAL SPECIALTIES

Food and Drink
Honey • Salted meats and fish.

Art and Crafts
Artist • Sculptor • Glassmaker.

EVENTS

Market: Fri. 10:30 a.m.–12:30 p.m., town hall square; country market Jun.–Jul.
Apr.: La Ronde des Chevandiers, car rally (2nd Sat.).
May: Festival Rando Moselle, thematic walks and hikes.
Jul.: Music and firework display (14th).
Aug.: Barakozart music festival (last weekend).

🐾 OUTDOOR ACTIVITIES

Fishing • Walking: Route GR 5 and 5 "Moselle Pleine Nature" trails • Mountain biking.

📍 FURTHER AFIELD

• Abreschviller (3 miles/5 km).
• Sarrebourg: Chagall trail (10½ miles/17 km).
• Rhodes: Parc Animalier de Sainte-Croix, wildlife park (12½ miles/20 km).
• Massif du Donon; Col du Donon (13½ miles/22 km).
• Baccarat: Crystal glassmaking (25 miles/40 km).

Moselle (57)
Population: 754
Altitude: 1,050 ft. (320 m)

TOURIST INFO—SARREBOURG MOSELLE SUD
03 87 03 11 82
tourisme-sarrebourg.fr
03 87 08 63 98
saintquirin.fr

Saint-Robert

The hill of the Benedictines

Named after the founder of La Chaise-Dieu Benedictine abbey in the Auvergne, the village was built around a monastery founded by Saint Robert's disciples. The village stands on a hill, overlooking a landscape typical of southern Corrèze, on the site of an old Merovingian city. On the Saint-Robert plateau, the ruins of a curtain wall encircle the Benedictine monastery and its Romanesque abbey church. The stately cut-stone buildings, small castles, and houses with towers were, in their time, the residences of noblemen. Almost all of the fortified church's 12th-century structure has remained intact, with the exception of the nave. Scenes charged with biblical symbolism are engraved on the capitals, and a 13th-century life-size Christ carved in wood, brought back from Spain, testifies to the intensity of medieval faith. Saint-Robert, a city-state on the borders of Périgord, was itself the scene of violent religious clashes during the French Wars of Religion and the Fronde.

 HIGHLIGHTS

Église (12th century): 2 apses, square turret, and octagonal lantern.
Village: Old streets, panoramic view, miraculous fountain of Saint Maurice.

 **ACCOMMODATION & EATING OUT**

saintrobert.fr

 LOCAL SPECIALTIES

Food and Drink
Bread baked in a wood-fired oven • Walnut cake • Truffle and walnut groves.
Art and Crafts
Antiques • Flea market.

EVENTS

May and Nov.: Milk-fed veal prize-giving fair (2nd Mon.).
Jul.–Aug.: Festive markets (Fri. 7 p.m.); classical music festival (Jul. 15th–Aug. 15th).
Aug.: Local saint's day (15th).

Oct.: Fête du Vin Nouveau, new wine festival (2nd Sun.).

 OUTDOOR ACTIVITIES

Walking: 2 marked trails • Mountain biking: "Tour de la Corrèze" circuit.

 FURTHER AFIELD

• Église de Saint-Bonnet-la-Rivière and Yssandon site (7½ miles/12 km).
• Château de Hautefort (10 miles/16 km).
• Pompadour (13½ miles/22 km).
• Brive (15½ miles/25 km).

 MBVF NEARBY

• Ségur-le-Château (17 miles/27 km).

Corrèze (19)
Population: 300
Altitude: 1,148 ft. (350 m)

TOURIST INFO—BRIVE AGGLOMÉRATION
05 55 24 08 80
brive-tourisme.com
saintrobert.fr

Saint-Suliac

Between land and sea

With a panoramic view over the Rance estuary, Saint-Suliac is set in a beautifully unspoilt landscape. The impressive steeple of the Église de Saint-Suliac rises loftily above an old cemetery that represents a unique kind of churchyard in Haute Bretagne. The church stands in the center of a maze of narrow alleyways lined with fishermen's houses and low granite garden walls. Paths from the village lead to a variety of delightful attractions: the tide mill; the old salt marshes at Guettes, created in 1736; the standing stone of Chablé, dubbed the "Dent de Gargantua" (Gargantua's Tooth), and the intriguing remains of a Viking camp. The port, bustling with both fishing and pleasure boats, evokes Saint-Suliac's rich maritime history. This was a population of sailors, and the Vierge de Grainfollet (patron saint of Newfoundland), sitting above the village, bears witness to the heavy price that these coastal folk paid the sea in order to support their families.

 HIGHLIGHTS

Church (13th century): Stained-glass windows, wood carving, sailors' shrine.
La Maison des Collections: Museum on the history and traditional life of Bretons and fishermen (06 12 24 10 80).
Village: Guided tour in Jun.–Sept. (06 70 25 18 61).
Belvédère de l'Oratoire de la Vierge de Grainfollet: Panoramic viewpoint (village and Rance), accessible by coastal path (at low tide).

 ACCOMMODATION & EATING OUT

saint-malo-tourisme.com

 LOCAL SPECIALTIES

Food and Drink
Cider • Buckwheat galettes (pancakes) • Fish and shellfish • Cream and yogurt.
Art and Crafts
Watercolorist • Art gallery • Publisher • Dressmaking

workshop • Antique marine objects.

 EVENTS

Market: Tues. 4– 8 p.m, mid-Jun.–mid-Sept., Quai de Rance.
Aug.: Saint-Suliac Autrefois, historical event (1st weekend); Pardon de la Mer ceremony at Notre-Dame-de-Grainfollet (15th).
Sept.: Copeaux d'Abord, sea festival (last weekend).
Dec.: Christmas market and living Nativity scene (1st and 2nd weekends).

 OUTDOOR ACTIVITIES

Swimming • Fishing • Sailing • Horseback riding • Walking: Routes GR 34, GRP Tour du Pays Malouin, and 3 marked trails • Mountain biking.

 FURTHER AFIELD

• Saint-Malo (6 miles/10 km).
• Cancale (11 miles/18 km).
• Mont-Dol (12 miles/19 km).
• Dinan (13½ miles/22 km).
• Mont-Saint-Michel (18½ miles/30 km).

Ille-et-Vilaine (35)
Population: 961
Altitude: 69 ft. (21 m)

TOURIST INFO— DESTINATION SAINT-MALO BAIE DU MONT SAINT-MICHEL
02 99 56 66 99
saint-malo-tourisme.com
saint-suliac.fr

Saint-Véran

"Where hens peck at the stars"

The highest inhabited village in Europe—hence its motto—Saint-Véran lies at the heart of the Queyras regional nature park. As Saint-Véran has been accessible by road for little more than a century, the inhabitants had plenty of time to learn to pull together in this extreme environment (altitude of 6,699 ft./2,042 m). They battled floods, avalanches, and fires, and worked shale and larch in the Queyras to build the *fustes* and *casets* for sheltering animal fodder and livestock under protruding roofs. They also smelted copper, carved wood, tapped the water from the hillsides for their fountains, and harnessed the sun's rays for their brightly colored sundials. Moreover, they devised both winter and summer tourism, which capitalizes on the great outdoors while respecting their traditions. The mission crosses, erected in tribute to missionaries who came to convert this Queyras backwater, symbolize the area's fervent religious belief and practice, and form part of its heritage.

HIGHLIGHTS

Church (17th century): Stone lions, font.
Copper mine: Discovery tour of the site and exhibition at the old communal oven at Les Forannes.
Maison Traditionnelle: Traditional house inhabited and shared with animals until 1976; furniture, tools, etc. (04 92 45 82 39).
Musée Le Soum: The oldest house in the village (1641) (04 92 45 86 42).
Maison du Soleil et de l'Astronomie: Complex dedicated to solar observation, interactive experiences, themed visits, educational workshops (04 92 23 58 21 / saintveran-maisondusoleil.com).
Observatory (9,633 ft./2,936 m altitude): Tour of the dome and its equipment, discovery evenings by appt. (saintveran-maisondusoleil.com).
Village: Guided tour (registration at tourist info center or online).; guided group tour by appt. (04 92 45 82 21).

ACCOMMODATION & EATING OUT

Hotels
♥ Les Chalets du Villard*** (04 92 45 52 08).

 LOCAL SPECIALTIES

Food and Drink
Queyras honey.
Art and Crafts
Craft courses (plant collecting, lacemaking, weaving, knitting) • Bladesmith • Wood sculptors.

EVENTS

Jul.: Grand Raid du Queyras, trail running (2nd weekend); Franco-Italian pilgrimage to Clausis chapel (16th).
Jul.–Aug.: Sale of bread baked at the communal oven; star-gazing excursions.
Aug.: Trail des Étoiles, trail running (2nd weekend).

OUTDOOR ACTIVITIES

Astronomy • Rock climbing • Forest adventure course • Fishing • Walking, horseback riding, and hikes with donkey • Skiing: Alpine, cross-country, ski touring, snowshoeing • Mountain biking.

FURTHER AFIELD

- Molines-en-Queyras (3 miles/5 km).
- Château-Queyras (8½ miles/14 km).
- Aiguilles; Abriès (10–13 miles/16–21 km).
- Col d'Agnel and the Italian border (12½ miles/20 km).
- Guillestre; Mont-Dauphin (23½ miles/38 km).

Hautes-Alpes (05)
Population: 180
Altitude: 6,699 ft. (2,042 m)

TOURIST INFO—GUILLESTROIS ET DU QUEYRAS
04 92 45 82 21
lequeyras.com
saintveran.com

Sainte-Agnès

A balcony over the Mediterranean

Perched nearly 2,600 ft. (800 m) in the air, the highest coastal village in Europe affords a spectacular panoramic view over the Mediterranean from Cap-Martin to the Italian Riviera. Sainte-Agnès is a strategic site that has been fought over for centuries. Initially a fortified Roman camp, it was then the site of a defensive castle built in the 12th century by the House of Savoie, and in 1932-38 its fort was dug out of the rock to become the most southerly post on the Maginot Line, built to defend the Franco-Italian border. Today the village is valued for its unique location away from the crowds and concrete of the coast. The village has an authentic feel, with its crisscrossing cobblestoned alleyways—certain of which evoke legends of the presence of Saracens—secret vaults, and houses clinging to one another. The lofty ruins of the fortified castle now contain a medieval garden. From its highest point, a 360-degree panorama gives a superb contrast between the blue Mediterranean and, in winter, the snowy peaks of the Mercantour National Park.

 HIGHLIGHTS

Maginot Line fort: 6,500 sq. ft. (2,000 m²) of galleries, multimedia exhibition (04 93 35 84 58).

Église Notre-Dame-des-Neiges (16th century): Gilded wooden altar, 16th-century stone font, 17th-century statue of Saint Agnes, 16th- and 18th-century paintings, chandeliers from Monaco Cathedral.

Chapelle Saint Sébastien (17th century): Viewpoint and walking trails.

Castle site: Tour of the ruins and medieval garden, free admission 9 a.m.–5 p.m.; not accessible for those with reduced mobility.

 ACCOMMODATION & EATING OUT

menton-riviera-merveilles.fr

LOCAL SPECIALTIES

Food and Drink
Local jams.

Art and Crafts
Painter • Master glassmaker • Ceramist.

 EVENTS

Jan.: Mass and procession for Saint Agnes's Day.
May: Criterium Pedestre, walking rally (1st).
Jul.: Fête de la Lavande, lavender festival (4th weekend).
Sept.: Fête de la Saint Michel, open chapel (last Sun.).
Dec.: Fête de la Sainte Lucie, open chapel (13th).

 OUTDOOR ACTIVITIES

Mountain biking • Horseback riding • Walking.

 FURTHER AFIELD

• Hilltop villages of Castellar, Gorbio, Peille (3–12½ miles/ 5–20 km).
• Menton; Monaco; Nice (7–26½ miles/11–43 km).

 MBVF NEARBY
• Coaraze (24 miles/39 km).

Alpes-Maritimes (06)
Population: 1,336
Altitude: 2,559 ft.
(780 m)

TOURIST INFO—MENTON, RIVIERA ET MERVEILLES
04 83 93 70 20
menton-riviera-merveilles.fr
TOWN HALL
sainteagnes.fr

Sainte-Croix-en-Jarez

A monastery reborn as a village

Sainte-Croix-en-Jarez took root in a former Carthusian monastery, with the Pilat regional nature reserve as a backdrop. Driven out during the Revolution, the monks made way for villagers, and the former monks' cells subsequently housed a school, a town hall, and dwellings. The current church, with its decorated paneling, contains a reproduction of Andrea Mantegna's famous painting the *Martyrdom of Saint Sebastian*, as well as outstanding 15th-century carved stalls. In the medieval church there are wall paintings dating from the 14th century, while the monks' kitchen has conserved its monumental fireplace. Other features of the old monastery that have remained intact include a restored and furnished cell; the iron grille forged in 1692; the clock tower; the fortified façade, which was altered in the 17th century; the cloisters; and the grand staircase. In the hamlet of Jurieu, the village also boasts a 12th-century chapel and the megalithic site of Roches de Marlin.

 HIGHLIGHTS

Former charterhouse (13th century): Bakery, Brothers' court, cloisters, medieval church with 14th-century wall paintings, parish church, Fathers' court, kitchen, cells. Exterior walkway: hanging garden, covered paths. General and themed guided tours for groups and individuals; evening tours in Jul.–Aug. (04 77 20 20 81).

 ACCOMMODATION & EATING OUT

chartreuse-saintecroixenjarez.com

 LOCAL SPECIALTIES

Food and Drink
Charcuterie • Meat • Cheeses • Honey • Beers.
Art and Crafts
Local artisanal products (shop and information point).

 EVENTS

Pentecost: Traditional fair.
Jun.: Festin Musical, music festival (4th weekend).
Sept.: Les Musicales, classical music festival (2nd, 3rd, and 4th Sun.).
Oct.: Balade au Fil des Arts (1st Sun.); giant Cluedo (last Sun.).
Dec.: Provençal Nativity scene and Christmas activities (1st–31st).

 OUTDOOR ACTIVITIES

Fishing • Walking: 3 marked trails • Mountain biking.

 FURTHER AFIELD

- La Terrasse-sur-Dorlay (5 miles/8 km).
- Monts du Pilat (13½ miles/22 km).
- Saint-Étienne (18½ miles/30 km).
- Vienne (21½ miles/35 km).
- Lyon (28 miles/45 km).

Loire (42)
Population: 500
Altitude: 1,378 ft. (420 m)

TOURIST INFO—SAINTE-CROIX-EN-JAREZ
04 77 20 20 81
chartreuse-saintecroixenjarez.com

Sainte-Énimie

(Commune of Gorges du Tarn Causses)

Amid the wonders of the Tarn gorges

The Merovingian princess Énimie gave her name to the village: legend has it that she was cured of leprosy in spring waters here. The village is encircled by the cliffs of the limestone plateaus of Sauveterre and Méjean, through which the Tarn has gouged its gorges. Sainte-Énimie retains its distinctive steep alleyways, massive limestone residences that evoke its prosperous past, and half-timbered workshops and houses. The Romanesque church of Notre-Dame-du-Gourg contains some splendid statues from the 12th and 15th centuries. At the top of the village, the chapel of Sainte-Madeleine and a chapter house are all that remain of a Benedictine monastery. Below flows the Burle river, which is believed to have healing properties, and several paths lead to the cell to which Saint Énimie retreated. From here, there is a superb view of the village and the spectacular scenery of the Tarn, Jonte, and Causses gorges, all listed as UNESCO World Heritage Sites.

👁 HIGHLIGHTS

Église Notre-Dame-du-Gourg (13th-14th centuries): Statues, rich furnishings.
Refectory, known as the "salle capitulaire" (12th century).
Chapelle Sainte-Madeleine (13th century).
Hermit's hut: Semi-troglodyte hut over the natural grotto; viewpoint.
Village: Self-guided tour, heritage discovery trail available from tourist info center (04 66 45 01 14); guided evening tour Tues. 9 p.m. in Jul.–Aug.; self-guided tour with the Baludik app.

🍴 ACCOMMODATION & EATING OUT

cevennes-gorges-du-tarn.com

🐓 LOCAL SPECIALTIES

Food and Drink
Wines from Lozère and region • Cheeses • Charcuterie.

Art and Crafts
Jewelry designer • Potter.

📅 EVENTS

Market: Evening market Thurs. 6:30–11 p.m., main street.
Jul.: Comic and book festival (1st weekend); fireworks (14th).
Oct.: Village festival and pilgrimage (1st Sun.).

🤸 OUTDOOR ACTIVITIES

Canoeing and kayaking • Canyoning • Spelunking • Fishing • Swimming • Rock climbing • Adventure trail • Via ferrata and via cordata • Horseback riding • Walking • Mountain biking.

📍 FURTHER AFIELD

• Saint-Chély-du-Tarn (3 miles/5 km).
• Causse de Sauveterre; Causse Méjean: Grottes de Dargilan and Aven Armand, caves (5-11 miles/8-18 km).
• Castelbouc; Parc National des Cévennes (5½–6 miles/ 9–10 km).
• Quézac (11 miles/18 km).

Lozère (48)
Population: 400
Altitude: 1,591 ft. (485 m)

TOURIST INFO—GORGES DU TARN, CAUSSES ET CÉVENNES
04 66 45 01 14
cevennes-gorges-du-tarn.com

Sainte-Eulalie-d'Olt

Creativity and savoir faire in the Lot valley

Deep in the Lot valley, numerous artists and craftspeople are breathing life into the old stones of Sainte-Eulalie-d'Olt. This typically medieval village is laid out in a series of alleyways and small squares around the Place de l'Église. Wealthy residences from the 15th and 16th centuries are reminders of the village's prosperous past, and houses built in Lot shingle up until the 18th century abound in architectural details, with or without half-timbering. The church, cited in records in 909, has a Romanesque choir surrounded by impressive cylindrical columns, while the nave and the chapel are Gothic in style. Three apsidal chapels open off the ambulatory, and a reliquary chest contains two thorns supposedly from Christ's crown. Also worth seeing in the village are the Château des Curières de Castelnau, dating from the 15th century, and a corbeled Renaissance residence, with a façade that is punctuated with 14 windows.

 HIGHLIGHTS

Romanesque and Gothic church (11th, 12th, and 16th centuries): Relics.
Eulalie d'Art: Creative workshops, demonstrations, exhibition-sales, courses (05 65 47 82 68).
Musée-Galerie Marcel Boudou: Exhibitions in Jul.–Aug. (06 71 05 72 42).
Maison de la Chouette: Unique collection of owl-related objects. Open May–Sept. 10–11:30 a.m. / 3–6 p.m., or by appt. (06 88 98 83 00).
Village: Self-guided tour (map from tourist info center or Wivisites app.); guided tour for individuals Mon. and Fri. 5:30 p.m. Jun.–Sept., 6.30 p.m. in Jul. and Aug. (05 65 47 82 68).

 ACCOMMODATION & EATING OUT

Vacation village
♥ La Cascade*** (05 65 78 65 97).

 LOCAL SPECIALTIES

Food and Drink
Traveling home distiller (Nov. 1st-late Apr.) • Wood-baked levain bread • Organic chicken • Fruit farm.
Art and Crafts
Potter • Enamel carver • Glassblower • Jewelry designer • Painter • Sculptor • Dressmaker • Leaf painter • Bookbinder • Creator of wooden objects • Pearl artist.

 EVENTS

Market: Mon. a.m., Place de l'Église (Jul.-Aug.).
May: Marché des Senteurs et Saveurs, local produce market (1st Sun.).
Jul.: Historic procession of the Holy Thorn and local saint's day (2nd Sun.); En Vallée d'Olt, classical music festival (3rd and 4th weeks).
Nov.: Poule Un, charity auction (1st).

 OUTDOOR ACTIVITIES

Swimming • Canoeing and kayaking • Paddleboarding • Electric boats • Paddle boats • Fishing • Walking • Mountain biking • Waterbikes • Electric motorbikes.

 FURTHER AFIELD

• Parcs Naturels Régionaux des Grands Causses and de l'Aubrac (4 miles/6 km).
• Vimenet, fortified village (9½ miles/15 km).
• Sévérac-le-Château (18½ miles/30 km).

 MBVF NEARBY
• Saint-Côme-d'Olt (12 miles/19 km).
• Estaing (19 miles/31 km).

Aveyron (12)
Population: 391
Altitude: 1,345 ft. (410 m)

TOURIST INFO—CAUSSES À L'AUBRAC
05 65 47 82 68
causses-aubrac-tourisme.com

Sainte-Suzanne (Commune of Sainte-Suzanne-et-Chammes)

Beauty and rebellion

This medieval village, the "pearl of Maine," perched atop a rocky peak dominating the Erve valley, resisted attacks from William the Conqueror. When relics of Saint Suzanne (patron saint of fiancés) were brought back to Saint-Jean-de-Hautefeuille from the Crusades, the village was renamed in her honor. Atop a mound opposite the village, the site of Tertre Ganne, occupied by the earl of Salisbury's troops during the 1425 siege, offers a fabulous view of Sainte-Suzanne's striking profile. The keep partly survived this tumultuous period, but the double wall of 12th-century ramparts owes its present appearance to Guillaume Fouquet de La Varenne, comptroller general of posts, who also built the Renaissance lodge and took over ownership of the citadel from Henri IV. The hamlet of La Rivière, where the "Promenade des Moulins" winds, offers the loveliest vistas toward the medieval village.

 **HIGHLIGHTS**

Castle (17th century): Centre d'Interprétation de l'Architecture et du Patrimoine de la Mayenne, visitor center; exhibitions and activities (02 43 58 13 00).

Romanesque keep (11th century): Self-guided visit (interior staircases and gangways).

Moulin à Papier (15th–19th centuries): One of the last traditional paper mills in France, producing handmade paper. Guided tour, sale of artisanal paper (06 16 43 40 46 / 06 77 43 17 53).

Promenade des Moulins: Walk showing the charm of the many mills along the Erve river.

Camp des Anglais: Fortified camp, William the Conqueror's base during the siege of 1083–86, military fortifications. Self-guided tour (02 43 01 43 60).

Tertre Ganne: Panorama over the town (1½ miles/2 km).

Dolmen des Erves (2 miles/ 3 km): 6,500-year-old megalith.

 ACCOMMODATION & EATING OUT

coevrons-tourisme.com

 LOCAL SPECIALTIES

Art and Crafts
Candles • Painting, sculpture, and jewelry • Soap making • Bookstore and stationery.

EVENTS

Market: Sat. 8 a.m.–12 p.m., Place Ambroise-de-Loré.

May: Les 6 Heures de Sainte-Suzanne, race and sports festival.

Jul.: Fête du livre et du papier, book and paper festival (last Sun.).

Mid-Jul.–mid-Aug.: Les Nuits de la Mayenne, theater festival; medieval activities.

 OUTDOOR ACTIVITIES

Recreation area • Walking, horseback riding, and mountain biking trails (maps from tourist info center) • Pond fishing • Trail running routes • Cycle routes.

 FURTHER AFIELD

• Pays d'Art et d'Histoire Coëvrons Mayenne: Évron, Jublains, Mayenne (3–22 miles/5–35 km).

• Gué de Selle, lake and site (7½ miles/12 km).

• Grottes de Saulges – Musée de Préhistoire, caves and museum; Saint-Pierre-sur-Erve: Roman bridge and Moulin de Gô, watermill (10½ miles/17 km).

• Laval (22½ miles/36 km).

Mayenne (53)
Population: 1,267
Altitude: 525 ft. (160 m)

TOURIST INFO— LES COËVRONS
02 43 01 43 60
coevrons-tourisme.com

Salers

Volcanic grandeur and gastronomic delights

In the majestic scenery of the Monts du Cantal, Salers cultivates its geological beauty and the unique savors of its terroir. The seat of a baronetcy whose lords distinguished themselves in the First Crusade, the village was granted a license by Charles VII in 1428 to build ramparts, from which the Beffroi and La Martille gates survive. In 1550, Henri II established the royal bailiwick of the Hautes-Montagnes d'Auvergne here. On Place Tyssandier-d'Escous, the former bailiwick is surrounded by magistrates' residences, including Hôtel de Ronade, Maison de Flogeac, and Maison de Bargues. At the village's eastern end, the Barrouze Esplanade overlooks the Puy Violent peak and the Monts du Cantal. Acclaimed equally for meat and cheese, from Salers's own breed of cows, the village is a showcase for gastronomy in the Auvergne.

 HIGHLIGHTS

Église Saint-Mathieu: Romanesque-style portal and porch; Aubusson tapestries (17th century), Entombment (late 15th century), altarpieces, and paintings (04 71 40 72 33).
La Cave de Salers: Cheese-aging cellar specializing in AOP Salers cheese. Tours, exhibitions, and tastings; open all year round (04 71 69 10 48).
Village: Guided tour by tourist info center, Jun.–Sept., by appt. (04 71 40 58 08).

 ACCOMMODATION & EATING OUT

Hotel-restaurants
♥ Le Baillage*** (04 71 40 71 95).
♥ Hôtel des Remparts*** (04 71 40 70 33).

 LOCAL SPECIALTIES

Food and Drink
Carré de Salers (cookie) • Salers gentian aperitif • Salers meat • AOP Salers and Cantal cheeses.
Art and Crafts
Jewelry • Wooden toys • Lithographs and watercolors • Pottery • Wood carving • Glassworker • Bladesmith • Foundry • Horn carving • Prêt à porter fashion • Art photography • Basketry.

 EVENTS

Market: Wed. 8 a.m.–1 p.m., Place Tyssandier d'Escous.
May: Salon des Sites Remarquables du Goût, gourmet fair (1st); La Pastourelle, walking, running, and mountain biking races (3rd weekend).
Aug.: Journée de la Vache et du Fromage, cow and cheese festival (1st Wed.); Folklore gala (15th).

 OUTDOOR ACTIVITIES

Walking, cycling, and horseback riding trails in the Auvergne Volcanoes regional nature park • Rock climbing (La Peyrade).

 FURTHER AFIELD

• Aurillac (28 miles/45 km).
• Route du Puy Mary (2½–12½ miles/4–20 km).
• Route de Mauriac (3–10½ miles/5–17 km).
• Route de Saint-Paul-de-Salers (3½–19 miles/6–31 km).

 MBVF NEARBY
• Tournemire (16 miles/26 km).

Cantal (15)
Population: 317
Altitude: 3,117 ft. (950 m)

TOURIST INFO—PAYS DE SALERS
04 71 40 58 08
salers-tourisme.fr
salers.fr

Sancerre

The impenetrable fortress of Berry

Perched above hillsides covered in vineyards, Sancerre's majestic, former citadel stands on the edge of the Berry region, overlooking the Loire river running along the village below. In the 12th century, Étienne de Champagne, the first count of Sancerre, ordered the construction of a fortified castle at the top of the Piton de Sancerre, a hill in the Berry region. The medieval town developed at the foot of the castle, reinforcing its strategic position. Sancerre has known many conflicts over the centuries, including the Hundred Years War and the French Wars of Religion. In the 15th century, the town became a Protestant bastion and withstood a siege for several months. In 1621, its fortifications were destroyed, leaving nothing but the Tour des Fiefs, a vestige of the former stronghold's battered keep. Internationally renowned for its excellent wines, as well as for its cheese, the Crottin de Chavignol, Sancerre is a gastronomic destination in Berry.

 HIGHLIGHTS

Medieval town: Self-guided tour on the "Le fil d'Ariane" trail (information panels) or via the Wivisites app.; themed guided tours "Gourmande" (gourmet), "Éclairée" (enlightened), and "Privilege" (02 48 54 08 21).

La Maison des Sancerre: Interactive museum created by 350 Sancerrois winemakers, located in a 14th-century house. Animated relief map; 4D cinema; augmented reality; videos, garden; shop; tastings (02 48 54 11 35).

La Route des Vignobles: Spread over 14 towns and 7,200 acres (3,000 ha), the 106-mile (170-km) wine trail includes vineyard and château tours, and tastings (Bureau Inter-professionnel des Vins du Centre-Loire, 02 48 78 51 07).

 ACCOMMODATION & EATING OUT

tourisme-sancerre.com

 LOCAL SPECIALTIES

Food and drink
AOC Sancerre wine • AOP Crottin de Chavignol • *Croquets de Sancerre* (crunchy almond cookies) • *Lichou* (sweet almond cake).

Art and Crafts
Potters • Jewelry designers • Art galleries.

 EVENTS

Feb.: Bourges-Sancerre nighttime hike (3rd Sun.).

May: Wine fair; race in the vineyards; Jardins Suspendus, garden festival (Sun. nearest to 15th); farmers' market and craft market (Ascension Day).
Jun.: Trail de Sancerre, running race (mid-Jun.).
Oct.: Rallye des Vignobles Cosne-Pouilly-Sancerre, bike race (2nd weekend); Course Épicurienne Pouilly-Sancerre, running race.

 OUTDOOR ACTIVITIES

Fishing • Canoeing and kayaking • Walking: "Boucle de Chavignol" and other marked trails, trail running routes • Mountain biking: Several circuits and marked trails (see Sports Nature en Grand Sancerrois app.) • Cycling routes • Hot-air balloon flights.

 FURTHER AFIELD

• Pouilly-sur-Loire (9 miles/15 km).
• La Charité-sur-Loire (15 miles/25 km).
• Château de Guédelon; Aubigny-sur-Nère (25 miles/40 km).
• Bourges (28 miles/45 km).

Cher (18)
Population: 1,340
Altitude: 1,024 ft. (312 m)

TOURIST INFO—LE GRAND SANCERROIS
02 48 54 08 21
tourisme-sancerre.com

Sant'Antonino

In the skies over the Balagne

From its eagle's nest high above the Balagne, Sant'Antonino surveys the Mediterranean and Corsica's mountains. Although the Chapelle de la Trinité outside the village was built in the 12th century, families began to settle here only in the 15th century. They fused their homes together in the rock so that they became a protective wall to withstand invaders. The houses are so tightly packed that there was not enough space to build churches. Only the Chapelle Sainte-Anne is in the village itself; all the others, including the Chapelle de la Trinité and the parish church of L'Annonciade, were built in a meadow outside the village. Sant'Antonino is one of Corsica's oldest villages, with origins reputedly dating back to the 9th century. Stone reigns supreme here: in the tall façades of houses clinging on to the granite; in cobblestones mingling with rock in narrow, winding alleyways; in vaulted passageways leading to the old castle ruins. From here visitors can see right across the plain and the olive-planted hills of the Balagne.

 EVENTS

Sept.: Fête de Notre-Dame-des-Grâces (8th).
Aug.: Fête de la Saint Roch (16th).

 OUTDOOR ACTIVITIES

Donkey rides • Walking: 3 marked trails • Mountain biking.

Q FURTHER AFIELD

•Cateri, Lavatoggio (2½ miles/4 km).
•Aregno, Pigna (3–3½ miles/5–6 km).
•Lumio (7 miles/11 km).
•Villages of Corbara and L'Île-Rousse (10 miles/16 km).
•Calvi (10½ miles/17 km).

 HIGHLIGHTS

Église de l'Annonciade (17th century): 18th-century organ, historic paintings.
Chapelle de la Trinité (12th century).

 ACCOMMODATION & EATING OUT

balagne-corsica.com

 **LOCAL SPECIALTIES**

Food and Drink
Almonds • Citrus fruits • Jams • Wines, muscats • Olive oil • Corsican charcuterie and cheeses.
Art and Crafts
Jewelry designers • Raku ware • Paintings • Photographs • Minerals • Ceramics.

Haute-Corse (20)
Population: 141
Altitude: 1,624 ft. (495 m)

TOURIST INFO—CALVI BALAGNE
04 95 65 16 67
balagne-corsica.com

Saorge

Marvel of the Southern Alps

In the heart of the Roya valley, on the border with Italy, the towering façades of Saorge cling to the mountainside. Occupied since the Bronze Age, the small village of Saorge is renowned for its dramatic position surrounded by unspoiled natural landscapes. Its proximity with the Italian region of Liguria made it a major strategic stop on the ancient salt route between France and Italy. Once defended by three castles, Saorge was reputed to be impregnable. Today, the town, built on three levels connected by a maze of steep narrow streets and arched passageways, has something of a Tibetan village about it. Rising above the cascade of houses topped with purplish *lauzes* (schist tiles), the 17th-century former Franciscan convent, which became the Saorge monastery, is notable for its remarkable Baroque architecture. Saorge is also a major stop on the "Route du Baroque Nisso-Ligure," which begins in Nice and showcases historic organs in the Roya valley.

 HIGHLIGHTS

Monastère de Saorge (17th century): Garden, cloister, frescoes depicting scenes from the life of Saint Francis of Assisi (18th century); writers' residency since 2001. Self-guided or guided tours for individuals and groups; accessible for those with reduced mobility (04 93 04 55 55).

Église Saint-Sauveur and Chapelle Saint-Jacques or Les Pénitents Blancs (16th–17th centuries): 17th- and 18th-century altars and paintings, 19th-century organ.

Le Bain du Sémite: Natural pool (no lifeguard), located at the end of Bendola canyon; 25-minute walk.

Village: Self-guided tour, map from the tourist info center (04 93 04 51 23).

ACCOMMODATION & EATING OUT

menton-riviera-merveilles.fr

LOCAL SPECIALTIES

Food and Drink
AOC Nice olives • *Picore* (local brioche from Saorge) • Honey • Chestnuts • Heirloom fruits and vegetables.
Art and Crafts
Bookstore • Jewelry designer • Photographer.

EVENTS

Market: Sat. 8 a.m.– 12:30 p.m., Place George Clémenceau.
Jul.: Fête de la Tourte, traditional cake festival (4th Sat.).
Aug.: Festival de Musique Ancienne de la Roya, Baroque music festival (10th–20th).

OUTDOOR ACTIVITIES

Walking: Route GR 52, several circuits and trails, including in the Parc National du Mercantour • Fishing • Kayaking • Canyoning • Mountain biking: several trails.

FURTHER AFIELD

• Breil-sur-Roya (7 miles/11 km).
• La Brigue (8 miles/13 km).
• La Vallée des Merveilles and prehistoric paintings at Tende (18½ miles/30 km).
• Menton (28 miles/45 km).
• Apricale and Perinaldo, Italy (28 miles/45 km).

Alpes-Maritimes (06)
Population: 450
Altitude: 1,047–8,793 ft. (319–2,680 m)

TOURIST INFO—MENTON, RIVIERA, ET MERVEILLES
04 83 93 70 20
menton-riviera-merveilles.fr
TOWN HALL
04 93 04 51 23

Sare
Frontier traditions

The Rhune and the Axuria, legendary mountains of the Basque Country, tower over this village, which is famous for both its tradition of hospitality and its festivals. Ringed by mountains separating it from the Bay of Biscay and from Spanish Navarra, Sare honors vibrant Basque Country traditions. In particular, the tradition of the *Etxe*—the Basque house—finds full expression here. Among the eleven scattered parts of this former shepherds' village, the Ihalar neighborhood is one of the oldest, and here houses date from the 16th and 17th centuries. Ortillopitz is an authentic residence from 1660, restored by a local family keen to keep their history and the significance of the Basque home alive for future generations; the house allows visitors to experience "L'Etxe où bat le coeur des hommes" (The house where human hearts beat). Numerous chapels and shrines contain votive offerings of thanks for survival in storms at sea—reminders that Sare inhabitants were also seafarers.

 HIGHLIGHTS

Grottes de Sare (prehistoric caves): Multimedia show tour about the geology of the site, and the Basque people (05 59 54 21 88).
Ortillopitz, la Maison Basque de Sare (1660): Presentation of the Labourd architecture of the *Etxe*, or traditional Basque house, its authentic furniture, and Basque family life (05 59 85 91 92).
Musée du Gâteau Basque (Maison Haranea): Museum dedicated to the *gâteau basque* (filled cake). Tours led by a pastry chef; tastings (06 71 58 06 69).
Etxola animal park: All types of domestic animal (06 15 06 89 51).
Village: Guided tours in Jul.-Aug.; all year round by appt. for groups (05 59 54 20 14).
La Rhune tourist train (2,969 ft./905 m altitude): 35-minute climb to the top of La Rhune (05 59 54 20 26).
Ligarrieta: Nature site, with three signposted footpaths leading to the forest and ancient mines, dove shooting.

 ACCOMMODATION & EATING OUT

Hotel-restaurants
♥ Arraya**** (05 59 54 20 46).

 **LOCAL SPECIALTIES**

Food and Drink
Gâteau basque • Cider • Farm produce • Cheeses • Honey.
Art and Crafts
Textiles and Basque designs • Art gallery.

 EVENTS

Market: Farmers' and craft market Thurs. 8 a.m.-1. p.m. (May-Sept.); summer craft market Mon. 8 a.m.-1 p.m.
Aug.: Cross des Contrebandiers, cross-country race (last Sun.).
Sept.: Sare festival (2nd week, Sat.-Wed.).

 OUTDOOR ACTIVITIES

Wild salmon river fishing • Horseback riding • Basque pelota • Walking: Routes GR 8, GR 10, "Le Tour du Labourd," 8 marked trails, and hikes across the Spanish border • Mountain biking: 3 trails.

 FURTHER AFIELD

• Old farms in Ihalar, Istilart, Lehenbiskaï, and Xarbo Erreka (1 mile/1.5 km).
• Xareta: Urdax; Zugarramurdi (5-6 miles/8-10 km).
• Saint-Jean-de-Luz (9½ miles/15 km).
• Biarritz; Bayonne (12½-15 miles/20-24 km).

 MBVF NEARBY
• Ainhoa (5½ miles/9 km).

Pyrénées-Atlantiques (64)
Population: 2,700
Altitude: 243 ft. (74 m)

TOURIST INFO—PAYS BASQUE
05 59 54 20 14
en-pays-basque.fr

Sarrant

From antiquity to the Middle Ages

Located on the ancient Roman road between Toulouse and Lectoure, Sarrant puts its antique and medieval origins to use to promote art and culture. A stopover that appears on maps of the Roman Empire under the name "Sarrali," Sarrant developed around a *castrum* (fort) established in the 13th century, and expanded thanks to the "charter of customs" and privileges it was accorded by Philippe Le Bel in 1307. The main entrance to the village is a 14th-century vaulted gate cut into a massive square tower—a vestige of the old protective walls. The ramparts, blocked off by the houses embedded in them, have in part disappeared, and the moats have been filled in. Around the Église Saint-Vincent, rebuilt and enlarged after the Wars of Religion, the heart of the village forms two concentric circles lined with stone houses, some of which have upper floors adorned with wattle-and-daub half-timbering.

 HIGHLIGHTS

Église Saint-Vincent (13th, 16th, and 19th centuries): Furniture, reliquary.
Chapel (17th century): Exhibitions.
Town tower-gate: Illumination workshop.
Medieval garden: Free entry.
Maison de l'Illustration: Exhibitions and workshops (05 42 54 25 24).
Micro-Folie de Sarrant: Digital museum and virtual-reality space (06 73 69 09 03).
Medieval village: Self-guided tour with audio guide (QR code on information panels). Tourist info center in summer.

 **ACCOMMODATION & EATING OUT**

sarrant.com

 **LOCAL SPECIALTIES**

Art and Crafts
Illuminator • Wood turner and carver • Bookbinder • Bookstore • Engraver, silkscreen printer, typographer.

EVENTS

Jul.: Les Estivales de l'Illustration, illustration festival (Wed.–Sun., after 14th).
Aug.: Pottery market and classical concert (1st weekend); local festival (last weekend).
Nov.: Trail des Farfadets, running race (2nd weekend).

 **OUTDOOR ACTIVITIES**

Donkey and carriage rides • Walking and mountain biking.

FURTHER AFIELD

• Brignemont: Windmill (3 miles/5 km).
• Cologne; Mauvezin; Beaumont-de-Lomagne, fortified villages (4½–9½ miles/7–15 km).
• Château de Laréole (7 miles/11 km).

Gers (32)
Population: 380
Altitude: 410 ft. (125 m)

TOURIST INFO—BASTIDES DE LOMAGE
05 62 06 99 30
tourisme-bastidesdelomagne.fr
TOWN HALL
05 62 65 00 34
sarrant.com

Sauveterre-de-Rouergue

A royal *bastide* rich in arts and crafts

The fortified village of Sauveterre-de-Rouergue, halfway between Albi and Rodez, is driven by the passion and expertise of its craftspeople. The village's medieval past can be seen in its original 1281 street plan, the Saint-Christophe and Saint-Vital fortified gates, the rectilinear streets, and the central square complete with forty-seven arcades. The history of this centuries-old, lively site is told through its superbly corbeled stone and half-timbered houses, its 14th-century collegiate church of Saint-Christophe and its furnishings, and its coats of arms and stone carvings adorning the façades. Proud of its illustrious past as an important center for artisanal skills, the village was given a second wind a few decades ago by pioneering modern artists. Officially recognized as a hub for arts and crafts with the label "Ville et Métiers d'Art," Sauveterre continues to showcase its cultural heritage, passion for beauty, and commitment to excellence.

 HIGHLIGHTS

Collégiale Saint-Christophe (14th century): Southern Gothic style; 17th-century altarpiece.
L'Ancre – Pôle des Métiers d'Art du Pays Ségali museum, library, and boutique: Exhibitions on arts and crafts, artisans' boutique; workshops by appt. (06 98 61 74 64).
Atelier Max Capdebarthes: Leather craft workshop labeled "Entreprise du Patrimoine Vivant"; tour of workshop by appt. (05 65 47 06 64).
Village: Guided tours by appt., at tourist info center; braille guides; spoken-word tour of the village narrated by its inhabitants, art tour (05 65 72 02 52).

 ACCOMMODATION & EATING OUT

Hotel-restaurants
♥ Le Sénéchal**** (05 65 71 29 00)

 LOCAL SPECIALTIES

Food and Drink
Duck and foie gras • *Échaudés* (Aveyron cakes) • Goat cheeses.
Art and Crafts
Painters • Jeweler • Ceramist-engraver • Bladesmiths • Glassmakers • Cabinetmaker • Leather goods • Parchment sculptor • Landscape watercolorist • Photographer • Luthiers.

 EVENTS

Market: Sun. 9 a.m.–1 p.m.; summer market, Fri. 6–10 p.m, Place des Arcades.
Aug.: Fête et Détours de la Lumière, festival of lights (1st week).
Sept.: Fête du Melon, melon eating and accordion festival (1st Sun.).
Oct.: Fête de la Châtaigne et du Cidre Doux, chestnut and cider festival (last Sun.).

 OUTDOOR ACTIVITIES

La Gazonne leisure park: Swimming, disc golf: 18 baskets • Walking and mountain biking: Marked trails • "Mystère à Sauveterre" treasure hunt.

 FURTHER AFIELD

• Pradinas: Wildlife park (6 miles/10 km).
• Château du Bosc, home of Toulouse Lautrec (9½ miles/15 km).
• Rodez (21½ miles/35 km).

 MBVF NEARBY
• Belcastel (17 miles/27 km).
• Monestiés (23 miles/37 km).

Aveyron (12)
Population: 750
Altitude: 1,575 ft. (480 m)

TOURIST INFO—PAYS SÉGALI
05 65 72 02 52
tourisme-aveyron-segala.fr
sauveterre-de-rouergue.fr

Séguret

The vineyards of Montmirail

At the foot of the Dentelles de Montmirail, Séguret offers sweeping views of the Rhône valley from the Haut Comtat Venaissin. Set on a hillside and surrounded by vineyards, Séguret is overlooked by the tower of its medieval château. Inhabited since prehistoric times, the village gained prominence during the Gallo-Roman period before being developed in the 10th to 12th centuries. A Papal State until the French Revolution, Séguret was annexed to France in 1792. The town has preserved much of its built heritage, including *calades* (decorative cobblestones), the Reynier gate, the 15th-century bell tower, the Romanesque Église St-Denis, the Chapelle Notre-Dame-des-Grâces, and the 17th-century Fontaine des Mascarons. The Place des Arceaux and the Place de L'Église offer views over the Comtadine plain, all the way to the Rhône river and the Cévennes mountains. Séguret upholds its traditions, and, each Christmas, the village celebrates the *Mystère des Bergers*, a play that has been handed down orally through the generations since the Middle Ages.

HIGHLIGHTS

Chapelle Notre-Dame-des-Grâces (17th century): Painting of the Virgin Mary and depictions of the Annunciation and Visitation on the walls (17th–18th centuries).
Chapelle Sainte-Thècle (18th century): Exhibitions of paintings and santons (crib figures).
Église Saint-Denis (12th–13th centuries): 18th-century paintings.
Village: Signposted walk.

ACCOMMODATION & EATING OUT

village-seguret.fr

 LOCAL SPECIALTIES

Food and Drink
AOC Côtes du Rhône and local wines • Olive oil.
Art and Crafts
Santons (crib figures) • Art gallery • Sculptor • Jewelry designer • Painter.

EVENTS

Market: Thurs. 5– 8 p.m., Place Jean Moulin (Jun.-Aug.).
Jul.: Local saint's day (3rd weekend).
Aug.: Book fair (15th).
Dec.: *Bergié de Séguret,* mystery play (24th); Journée des Traditions, heritage fair (3rd Sun.).

OUTDOOR ACTIVITIES

Fishing • Cycle routes • Rock climbing in the Dentelles de Montmirail • Botanical trail • Walking: Route GR 4.

FURTHER AFIELD

- Vaison-la-Romaine (5 miles/8 km).
- Orange (13½ miles/22 km).
- Carpentras (14½ miles/23 km).

MBVF NEARBY
- Grignan (20 miles/32 km).
- Venasque (20½ miles/33 km).

Vaucluse (84)
Population: 847
Altitude: 886 ft. (270 m)

TOURIST INFO—VAISON VENTOUX PROVENCE
04 90 36 02 11
vaison-ventoux-tourisme.com
village-seguret.fr

Ségur-le-Château

A safe haven between the Limousin and Périgord

Rising proudly from a rocky outcrop on a meander of the Auvezère river, the old castle still reigns supreme over a village steeped in history. Ségur, meaning "safe place," was the birthplace of the viscounts of Limoges. In the late 10th century, the only heir to the viscount of Ségur married her cousin, Guy I of Limoges. The marriage brought the two viscountcies together for several centuries, making the castle at Ségur one of the Limousin's major strongholds. In the early 15th century, the king allowed the viscount, Jean de l'Aigle, to establish a court of justice known as a *cour des appeaux*. From this prosperous period, there remain noble houses with turrets or half-timbering, carved granite mullioned windows, towers with spiral staircases, and enormous hearths. The village's other noteworthy buildings include the watchtower, the tower of Saint Laurent, and Maison Henri IV.

 HIGHLIGHTS

Église Saint-Léger (19th century): Stained-glass window by contemporary artist Vincent Corpet, symbolizing Saint Léger's torture.
Castle (12th–15th centuries): Remains of the ancient Roman fortress of Ségur.
Village and castle: Guided tours Mon., Wed., and Fri., 11 a.m., Jun.–Aug.; by appt. offseason for groups (20 people minimum): 05 55 73 39 92.

 ACCOMMODATION & EATING OUT

Guesthouses
♥ La Ruche (05 55 73 07 26).

 LOCAL SPECIALTIES

Food and Drink
Trout • Honey • *Cul noir* (black-bottomed) farm pigs • Wine.
Art and Crafts
Terra-cotta sculptures and models • Porcelain painter.

 EVENTS

Market: Festive local farmers' market Mon. 5– 8 p.m., Place du Foirail (Jul.-Aug.).
Jun.: La Nuit Romantique (Sat. after summer solstice).
Aug.: Fête des Culs Noirs, pig festival (1st Sun.); flea market/outdoor rummage sale (2nd Sun.); street artists' fair (3rd Fri.).

 OUTDOOR ACTIVITIES

Fishing • Walking: 3 marked trails • Mountain biking.

 FURTHER AFIELD

• Château de Pompadour and stud farm (6 miles/10 km).
• Vaux: Ecomuseum of local heritage; paper maker (7 miles/11 km).
• Saint-Yrieix-la-Perche (9½ miles/15 km).
• Château de Jumilhac le Grand (15½ miles/25 km).

 MBVF NEARBY
• Saint-Robert (17 miles/27 km).

Corrèze (19)
Population: 205
Altitude: 886–1,083 ft. (270–330 m)

TOURIST INFO—PAYS DE SAINT-YRIEIX
05 55 73 39 92
tourisme-saint-yrieix.com

Seillans

Tradition and innovation in a Provençal village

Seen from below, Seillans resembles a huge staircase, its tall façades scaling the slope in steps. Gathered at the top, as if on a throne, are the Sarrasine gate, a medieval castle, a former priory of monks from Saint-Victor Abbey in Marseille, and the 11th-century church of Saint-Léger. Inside its three consecutive walls, Seillans is a patchwork of light and shade, an enticing maze of streets still echoing to the sound of horses' hooves, steeply sloping cobbled alleys, vaulted passageways, and shady corners in which fountains tinkle musically. In the valley below, where pines, olive trees, and vineyards jostle for space, the chapel of Notre-Dame-de-l'Ormeau houses an altarpiece that is unique in Provence. The recipient of the "Ville et Métiers d'Art" label acknowledging it as a center for artisanal excellence, Seillans is full of artists and craftspeople who bring its streets to life all year round.

 HIGHLIGHTS

Chapelle Notre-Dame-de-l'Ormeau (12th century): Roman stele, remains of early Christian chancel, ex-votos, 16th-century Baroque altarpiece, unique in Provence. Guided tours Thurs. 4:30 p.m., by appt. (04 94 76 01 02).

♥ **Maison Waldberg**: Collection of lithographs by surrealist artists Max Ernst and Dorothea Tanning and paintings by Stan Appenzeller. Self-guided tours Tues.–Sat. in May–Sept., and Thurs. in Oct.–Apr. Guided tours Thurs. 2:30 p.m. by appt. (04 94 76 01 02).

Village: Guided tour by appt., Thurs. 10:30 a.m., in front of the tourist info office (04 94 76 01 02).

 ACCOMMODATION & EATING OUT

paysdefayence.com

 LOCAL SPECIALTIES

Food and Drink
Honey • AOC Côtes de Provence wine • Olive oil • Farm produce • Goat cheese.

Art and Crafts
Art galleries and studios • Ceramists • Painters • Engraver • Model maker • Wrought ironwork • Soapmaking • Silk screening • Sculptor • Picture framer • Lithographer • Jewelry designer.

EVENTS

Market: Local farmers' and artisans' market, every 2nd Sun. (May to Sept.).
May: Salon de Mai, art exhibition (all month).
Jul.: Aïoli des Selves, dinner and dance (1st weekend); village festival (last weekend).
Aug.: Musique Cordiale, music festival (1st fortnight); pottery market (15th).

OUTDOOR ACTIVITIES

Leisure park with multisports area • Horseback riding • Walking: 15 marked trails and GR de Pays • Cycling: "La Méditerranée à Vélo" circuit.

FURTHER AFIELD

- Gorges de la Siagnole (9½–12½ miles/15–20 km).
- Lac de Saint-Cassien (12½ miles/20 km).
- Mont Lachens (15½ miles/25 km).
- Grottes de Saint-Cézaire, caves (18½ miles/30 km).

MBVF NEARBY
- Bargème (20½ miles/33 km).

Var (83)
Population: 2,800
Altitude: 1,201 ft. (366 m)

TOURIST INFO—PAYS DE FAYENCE
04 94 76 01 02
paysdefayence.com

Semur-en-Brionnais

Cluny history in Burgundy

Birthplace of Saint Hugh, one of the great abbots at the powerful monastery of Cluny, Semur is the historic capital of the Brionnais region, in the depths of Burgundy. Founded on a rocky spur, in the 10th century Semur-en-Brionnais became a defensive site ruled by the counts of Chalon. The Château Saint-Hugues is considered one of the oldest fortresses in Burgundy, and its keep is still intact. Inside, a collection of posters evokes the French Revolution, during which time the guards' rooms functioned as a prison. The Romanesque church dedicated to Saint Hilaire was erected by Geoffroy V in the 12th and 13th centuries. Its gate shows the saint defending the Catholic orthodoxy against Arians at the Council of Seleucia. The main square contains the 18th-century law courts (now the town hall), 16th-century men-at-arms' houses, and the salt store, with a ceiling decorated with allegorical paintings. The rampart walk still exists, as does the postern gate.

Château Saint-Hugues (10th century): Keep, towers, medieval warfare room; French Revolution poster collection; family tree of Hugh of Semur, abbot of Cluny (03 85 25 13 57).
Collégiale Saint-Hilaire (12th–13th centuries): Important Romanesque church; polychrome wood statues.
Église Saint-Martin-la-Vallée (11th–12th centuries): 12th–16th-century wall paintings.
Prieuré Saint-Hugues: Chapel, reception hall, cultural exhibitions (03 85 25 15 64).
Maison du Chapitre: Hall with ceiling and fireplace painted late 16th century; exhibition on local Romanesque art.
Salt store: Building where salt tax was paid; ceiling decorated with allegorical paintings from late 16th century.
Village: Guided group tour Mar.–Nov. (Les Vieilles Pierres association, 03 85 25 13 57).

 ACCOMMODATION & EATING OUT

brionnais-tourisme.fr

 LOCAL SPECIALTIES

Food and Drink
Brionnais wines.
Art and Crafts
Leather • Art bookbinder • Dressmaking • Flea market and interior decoration.

 EVENTS

Jun.–Sept.: Concerts organized by Les Amis de la Collégiale.
Jul.: Fête de la Madeleine (1st weekend after 14th).

 OUTDOOR ACTIVITIES

Walking • Mountain biking: Greenway with marked trails.

 FURTHER AFIELD

•Marcigny (3 miles/5 km).
•Saint-Christophe-en-Brionnais (5 miles/8 km).
•Rural villages: Oyé; Sarry; Saint-Didier-en-Brionnais; Fleury-la-Montagne (6–9½ miles/ 10–15 km).
•Romanesque churches: Anzy-le-Duc; Iguerande; Montceaux-l'Étoile; Saint-Julien-de-Jonzy; Varennes-L'Arconce (6–12½ miles/10–20 km).
•Historic towns: Charlieu; Paray-le-Monial; Charolles; La Clayette (12½–15½ miles/ 20–25 km).

Saône-et-Loire (71)
Population: 610
Altitude: 1,299 ft. (396 m)

TOURIST INFO—MARCIGNY-SEMUR
03 85 25 39 06
brionnais-tourisme.fr
semur-en-brionnais.fr

Talmont-sur-Gironde

Fortified village on an estuary

The Talmont promontory, girded by ramparts and crowned by its Romanesque church, seems to rise above the waves, in defiance of the waters of the Gironde. This walled town was built in 1284 on the orders of Edward I of England, who also ruled Aquitaine. On a promontory encircled by the Gironde estuary, Talmont has kept its original medieval street plan. The streets and alleyways are punctuated by flowers, dotted with monolithic wells and sundials, and enlivened by craftspeople and traders. Streets lead to the tip of the promontory, where the 12th-century church of Sainte-Radegonde watches over the largest estuary in Europe. From the Romanesque church, a stop on one of the routes to Santiago de Compostela, the rampart walk follows the cliff to the port, still used by traditional skiffs. Unmissable features of Talmont's landscape and heritage are the stunning panorama over the bay, the port, the village, the estuary, and the fishermen's huts.

 HIGHLIGHTS

Église Sainte-Radegonde (12th–14th centuries).
Musées Historique et de la Pêche: Local history museum on the site's geology; the church; the construction of the fortified town by Edward I, king of England; the American port built in 1917; and fishing in the lower Gironde estuary (06 85 50 77 81).
Naval cemetery: Numerous historiated memorials.
Village: Guided tour by appt. (05 46 08 21 00).

 ACCOMMODATION & EATING OUT

royanatlantique.fr

LOCAL SPECIALTIES

Food and Drink
Charente produce • Wines.
Art and Crafts
Jewelry • Clothing • Interior decoration • Painters and illustrators • Pottery • Soap making • Leather.

 EVENTS

May: Festival du Vent, kite festival (Ascension Thurs – Sun.).
Jul.–Aug.: Village tour by candlelight (shops remain open), Tues. 9 p.m.
Aug.: Talmont village fair (2nd Sun.).

 OUTDOOR ACTIVITIES

Fishing • Mountain biking and hybrid biking • Walking: Route GR 36 and path to Caillaud cliff.

 FURTHER AFIELD

• Barzan: Fâ, Gallo-Roman site (1 mile/2 km).
• Arces-sur-Gironde: 12th-century Église Saint-Martin (2½ miles/4 km).
• Meschers-sur-Gironde: troglodytic caves; beaches; estuary walks (3 miles/5 km).
• Royan (10½ miles/17 km).

 MBVF NEARBY
• Mornac-sur-Seudre (18 miles/29 km).

Charente-Maritime (17)
Population: 101
Altitude: 16 ft. (5 m)

TOURIST INFO— DESTINATION ROYAN ATLANTIQUE
05 46 08 21 00
royanatlantique.fr

Tournemire

Volcanic castles

Set in the Volcans d'Auvergne regional nature park, Tournemire dominates the Doire river valley. In medieval times, two families fought for control of this village of tufa stone, which stretches down as far as the Château d'Anjony. In the Middle Ages the Tournemire family built a fortress on the tip of the Cantal massif, but a rivalry with the Anjony family, whose own castle, built in 1435, was close to the keep at Tournemire, signaled destruction for this fortress—nothing but ruins remain today. However, the Château d'Anjony, with its square body and four corner towers, remains intact, as does the low wing added in the 18th century. Inside, the building still has its vaulted lower hall at basement level. The chapel and knights' hall are decorated by 16th-century frescoes. Flanked by 14th- and 15th-century houses, the 13th-century village church is characteristic of the Auvergne Romanesque style.

 HIGHLIGHTS

♥ **Château d'Anjony** (15th century): Guided tour, concerts (04 71 47 61 67).
Church (12th century): Wood carvings, reliquary of Sainte Épine brought back from the Crusades by Rigaud de Tournemire.
Village: Guided tour with resident author and amateur historian M. René Tible (06 71 58 84 08).
Cascade de Lavergne (waterfall): 33-foot (10-m) cliff located at La Faurge (forge), a highly original rock shelter (semi-troglodytic construction).
Grottes (caves): The oldest trace of a settlement in the village.
Calvaire (Calvary): Crosses of Christ and the two thieves, on the rocky spur of Roquerouge. View of the Doire river valley.

 ACCOMMODATION & EATING OUT

Hotels
♥ La Borie d'Hélipse**** (04 71 43 39 26).
♥ Auberge de Tournemire*** (04 71 47 61 28).
Restaurants and tea rooms
♥ La Petite Grange (04 71 43 39 26).

 LOCAL SPECIALTIES

Food and Drink
Traditional Auvergne produce • Bread baked in a wood-fired oven.
Art and Crafts
Byzantine icon writing workshop • Photographer.

 EVENTS

Market: Local produce market, Wed. 7 p.m., at the town hall (Jul.-Aug.).
Late Mar.-early Apr.: European Artistic Craft Days.
Jun.: La Nuit Romantique (Sat. after summer solstice).
Dec.: Christmas market with original artisanal creations (2nd Sun.).

 OUTDOOR ACTIVITIES

Walking.

 FURTHER AFIELD

• Col de Legal (7½ miles/12 km).
• Aurillac (15½ miles/25 km).
• Puy Griou and Puy Mary, volcanoes (21½ miles/35 km).

 MBVF NEARBY
• Salers (17½ miles/28 km).

Cantal (15)
Population: 130
Altitude: 2,625 ft. (800 m)

TOURIST INFO—PAYS DE SALERS
04 71 40 58 08
salers-tourisme.fr

Tournon-d'Agenais

A royal *bastide* in Lot-et-Garonne

Originally a Celtic fortified town and later a royal *bastide*, Tournon-d'Agenais has cultivated the good life in Lot-et-Garonne. Founded in 1271 by Philippe III, the son of Louis IX, on the borders of Agenais and Quercy, Tournon d'Agenais bears witness to the passing centuries in its architecture. Built on a spur overlooking two valleys between the Lot and the Garonne, the village's ramparts, tall, pale houses, and well-ordered streets are typical of the "new towns" that were built in the 12th century. Also surviving from this period is the Maison de l'Abescat, the residence of the bishop of Agen, which became a church in the 17th century and was recently converted into a concert venue. Invigorated by its inhabitants and the "Amis de la Bastide" association, Tournon d'Agenais continues to write its own history while perpetuating local traditions, such as the May 1st flower festival and the Foire de la Tourtière celebrating the delicious dessert.

 HIGHLIGHTS

Église Saint-André-de-Carabaisse (12th century): Painted vault depicting the symbols of the Four Evangelists.

Église Saint-Barthélémy-de-Tournon: Early church rebuilt in the 19th century; 20th-century bell/water tower.

Belfry: 17th-century belfry with a moon phase clock on its bell tower.

Village: Guided tours with a local storyteller (06 86 12 02 56).

 ACCOMMODATION & EATING OUT

Hotel-restaurants
♥ Les Voyageurs*** (05 53 40 70 28).

 **LOCAL SPECIALTIES**

Food and Drink
Tourtière (fruit pie) • Truffles • Honey.

Art and Crafts
Photographer • Ceramic sculptures • Art gallery.

EVENTS

Market: Sun. 8 a.m.–1 p.m.; evening market Fri. 5–8 p.m., Place de l'Hôtel de Ville. (Jul.–Aug).
May: Flower festival (1st).
Aug.: Foire à la Tourtière, pie festival (15th); Fête des Rosières (last weekend).
Sept.: Wine fair (2nd weekend).

OUTDOOR ACTIVITIES

Walking • Fishing • Mountain biking • Trail running.

FURTHER AFIELD

•Château Fort de Bonaguil, medieval fort (12½ miles/20 km).

 MBVF NEARBY

•Penne-d'Agenais (11 miles/18 km).
•Lauzerte (15½ miles/25 km).
•Monflanquin (17½ miles/28 km).
•Pujols-le-Haut (18 miles/29 km).

Lot-et-Garonne (47)
Population: 800
Altitude: 699 ft. (213 m)

TOURIST INFO—FUMEL VALLÉE DU LOT
05 53 71 13 70
05 53 71 67 63
tourisme-fumel.com

Tourtour

In the skies above Provence

Perched on a plateau high above Provence, with vineyards to the south and lavender fields to the north, Tourtour exudes the perfume of thyme and olive trees. Tourtour was fortified in the early Middle Ages to protect itself from frequent Saracen attacks. From this long-distant and precarious past, it has retained some of its fortifications and its layout, with streets encircling the old castle. The narrow alleyways of the medieval village boast buildings of old stone and curved tiles, and they accommodate a traditional oil mill—a symbol of this region. Intertwined streets surround the two castles—a medieval one with two towers, and a 17th-century one with four towers. The church stands high above both village and landscape; built in the 11th century and remodeled in the 19th, it provides an exceptional view of inland Provence, from Sainte-Baume and Mont Sainte-Victoire as far as the Maures massif and the Mediterranean.

 HIGHLIGHTS

Église Saint-Denis (11th century).
Théâtre de Verdure: Concerts in the summer.
Traditional olive oil mill: In operation Nov.–Feb.; art exhibitions mid-May–mid-Sept. (04 94 76 35 47).
Castle: Permenant exhibition of Ronald Searle's drawings (04 98 10 25 25).
Village: Guided group tour all year round by appt. (04 94 76 35 47).

 ACCOMMODATION & EATING OUT

lacs-gorges-verdon.fr

 **LOCAL SPECIALTIES**

Food and Drink
Organic produce (fruit, vegetables, fruit juice) • Olive oil.
Art and Crafts
Interior decoration • Art galleries and artists' studios • Fashion.

 EVENTS

Market: Wed. and Sat. 8 a.m.–1 p.m., Place Annabel et Bernard Buffet.
Easter: Fête de l'OEuf, Easter festival (Sun. and Mon.).
Jun.: Poetry festival (last weekend).
Aug.: Village festival (1st Sun.).

 FURTHER AFIELD

• Villecroze: Park, caves, and waterfalls (4½ miles/7 km).
• Salernes; Sillans-la-Cascade; Draguignan; Châteaudouble: Gorges (6–12½ miles/10–20 km).
• Lac de Sainte-Croix (18 miles/29 km).
• Abbaye du Thoronet; Sainte-Roseline chapel (19 miles/31 km).

MBVF NEARBY
• Cotignac (17½ miles/28 km).

Var (83)
Population: 585
Altitude: 2,133 ft. (650 m)

TOURIST INFO—LACS ET GORGES DU VERDON
04 94 76 35 47
lacs-gorges-verdon.fr

Turenne

A powerful dynasty in Limousin

Located at the foot of an old citadel bearing still-impressive remains, Turenne was, for ten centuries, the seat of an important viscounty. The Caesar and Trésor towers, on top of a limestone mound (an outlier of the Causse de Martel), mark the site of the earlier fortress of the viscounts of Turenne, who ruled the Limousin, Périgord, and Quercy regions until 1738. Along its narrow streets and on its outskirts, the village has kept a remarkably homogeneous architectural heritage from this period of history. There are mansions from the 15th to 17th centuries, sporting turrets and watchtowers, and simple houses-cum-workshops too, all topped by *ardoise* (slate) tiles and presenting spotlessly white façades to the hot sun in this southern part of Limousin. They rub shoulders with the collegiate church of Saint-Pantaléon, consecrated in 1661, and the 17th-century Chapel of the Capuchins.

HIGHLIGHTS

Castle: César and Trésor towers, and garden (05 19 31 02 68).
Village: Historical tours, interactive costumed tours, and evening tours in summer; group tours available (05 55 24 08 80); tourist train or shuttle bus (06 37 66 13 43).

ACCOMMODATION & EATING OUT

turenne.fr

LOCAL SPECIALTIES

Food and Drink
Walnut oil • Honey • Farmhouse bread.
Art and Crafts
Jewelry designer • Lighting designer • Ceramist • Glassmaker • Toys and wooden objects • Leather.

EVENTS

Mar. or Apr. (Maundy Thurs.): Foire aux Boeufs, cattle show.
Aug.: Outdoor rummage sale (3rd weekend).

OUTDOOR ACTIVITIES

Fishing • Walking: Routes GR 46, GR 480, and 6 marked trails.

FURTHER AFIELD

• Gouffre de la Fage, cave (4½ miles/7 km).
• Brive-la-Gaillarde (9½ miles/15 km).
• Lac du Causse (10 miles/16 km).

MBVF NEARBY

• Collonges-la-Rouge (6 miles/10 km).
• Vallée de la Dordogne: Martel (10½ miles/17 km); Curemonte (11 miles/18 km); Carennac (15 miles/24 km).

Corrèze (19)
Population: 809
Altitude: 886 ft. (270 m)

TOURIST INFO—BRIVE AGGLOMÉRATION
05 55 24 08 80
brive-tourisme.com
turenne.fr

Usson

A gilded cage for Queen Margot

To the west of the regional nature park of Livradois-Forez, Usson clings to its volcanic mound, which was once topped by a fortified castle where Margaret of Valois lived during her exile. Overlooking the Limagne plain, the village offers an exceptional view of the volcanic massifs of the Auvergne and the Chaîne des Puys, a UNESCO World Heritage Site. From 1586 to 1605, the Château d'Usson housed the exiled Margaret of Valois, daughter of Catherine de' Medici and wife of the future Henri IV, compromised in the political and religious quarrels of the period. For nineteen years, Margaret, who was dubbed "La Reine Margot," led a courtly, intellectual, and religious life. Demolished in 1633 by order of Richelieu in a bid to weaken the power of the dukes of Auvergne within the kingdom, the fortress nevertheless retains vestiges of its four outer walls, including the "Porte de France" and the Église Saint-Maurice, adjoined by the Queen's chapel.

 HIGHLIGHTS

Église Saint-Maurice (12th-16th centuries): 17th-century tabernacle, statues, paintings (04 73 71 05 90).
Basalt columns: Situated above the village.
Old forge: Restored with all its tools (hearth, bellows, anvil, etc.).
Village: Guided group tour of the village and church, by appt. (04 73 89 15 90).
Exhibition on the history and culture of Usson (at the Usson tourist info center).

 ACCOMMODATION & EATING OUT

issoire-tourisme.com

 **LOCAL SPECIALTIES**

Art and Crafts
Painter • Stone carver.

 EVENTS

May: Pilgrimage to Notre-Dame-d'Usson (Ascension Thurs.).
Jun.: Les Médiévales d'Usson, medieval festival and archery tournament (2nd weekend).
Jul.-Aug.: Rencontres Culturelles d'Usson, music, history and heritage festival.

 OUTDOOR ACTIVITIES

Fishing • Walking: 4 marked trails, including 2 discovery trails "Géologie, Volcanisme et Paysages" (geology, volcanism, and landscapes) and "En Suivant la Salamandre" (Follow the salamander).

 FURTHER AFIELD

•Château de Parentignat (5 miles/8 km).
•Issoire: Abbey church (7 miles/11 km).
•Nonette and Auzon, hilltop villages (9½-15½ miles/ 15-25 km).
•Clermont-Ferrand (28 miles/45 km).

 MBVF NEARBY

•Montpeyroux (15 miles/24 km).

Puy-de-Dôme (63)
Population: 300
Altitude: 1,772 ft. (540 m)

TOURIST INFO—AUVERGNE PAYS D'ISSOIRE
04 73 89 15 90
issoire-tourisme.com

Venasque

The taste of Provence

Facing Mont Ventoux, Venasque stretches the length of a steep, rocky outcrop in the Vaucluse mountains. At the mouth of the Gorges de la Nesque and overlooking a Roman road, the village rises above vineyards and cherry orchards. Occupied in Neolithic times and during the Roman period, in the 13th century this naturally defensive site was reinforced to the south by a rampart with three towers and a moat 6½ feet (2 m) deep. Siffredus of Carpentras, who was bishop here in 542, is believed to have built the foundations of the Église de Notre-Dame-de-Venasque and a church dedicated to Saint John the Baptist. North of Notre Dame, and connected to it, is a baptistery in the form of a Greek cross containing marble columns from Roman buildings. Along the steep alleyways, the light-colored façades of houses built in the 14th and 17th centuries echo the old hospice on Rue de l'Hôpital. The village, proud of its terroir, is a major producer of cherries labeled "Mont de Venasque."

 HIGHLIGHTS

Baptistery (6th century, altered in the 13th century): Greek cross floorplan with semicircular apses and blind arcades (04 90 66 62 01).
Église Notre-Dame-de-Venasque (13th century): Avignon school painting of the Crucifixion from 1498, processional cross from the same period in the treasury.
Village: Information panels.

ACCOMMODATION & EATING OUT

Gîtes and vacation rentals
♥ La Planette****
(06 62 45 82 24).

LOCAL SPECIALTIES

Food and Drink
Cherries and dessert grapes • Heirloom vegetables • Lamb • Olive oil.
Art and Crafts
Ceramists • Painters • Potters • Sculptor • Weaver •

Pillows and comforters made from organic sheep wool.

 EVENTS

Market: Fri. 8 a.m.–1 p.m., Place des Tours (May–Oct.).
Jun.: Festival de la Cerise, cherry festival (early Jun.); Comic book festival (mid-Jun.).
Jul.: Jazz festival (23rd–24th).
Aug.: Local saint's day (14th–15th).
Sept.: Antique and second-hand book fair (1st Sun.).

 OUTDOOR ACTIVITIES

Rock climbing • Walking • Walks with a donkey • Cycle touring.

 FURTHER AFIELD

•Le Beaucet and La Roque-sur-Pernes, hilltop villages (3 miles/5 km).
•Carpentras (7 miles/11 km).

 MBVF NEARBY
•Gordes (9½ miles/15 km).
•Ménerbes; Roussillon (15 miles/24 km).

Vaucluse (84)
Population: 1,054
Altitude: 1,050 ft. (320 m)

TOURIST INFO—VENTOUX PROVENCE
04 90 66 11 66
ventouxprovence.fr
venasque.fr

Veules-les-Roses

Beach resort in the Pays de Caux

In the hollow of a valley located on the Caux plateau that ends in a cliff overlooking the Côte d'Albâtre, Veules-les-Roses is bursting with charm, nestled between land and sea. Inhabited since the 4th century, it takes its name from the ancient Saxon word *well*, meaning "water source." Water is everywhere in the local landscape and has shaped the village's history since its foundation. The sea brought prosperity to this village of fishermen in the Middle Ages, and in the 19th century prompted the development of one of the first beach resorts to be frequented by famous artists and writers. Other tales speak of the Veules, the "shortest river in France," which powered weaving and flour mills, and irrigated the still-active watercress beds. Veules-les-Roses still presents visitors with a variety of architecture and landscapes, from the sea front with its beach huts and fishermen's houses, to its villas and thatched cottages with flower gardens.

 HIGHLIGHTS

Église Saint-Martin (13th-16th centuries): Painted murals in the choir vault; polychrome statuary from the 15th–17th centuries. **Route along the "shortest river in France"**: Route along the Veules to discover the local nature and architecture of the village and the beach resort (cliff, mills, religious buildings, cress beds, drinking troughs, thatched cottages, villas). Self-guided tours; guided group tour all year round by appt., and in Jul.–Aug. for individuals (02 35 97 00 63).

 ACCOMMODATION & EATING OUT

Hotels
♥ Douce France (02 35 57 85 30).

 LOCAL SPECIALTIES

Food and Drink
Cress • Veules oysters • Gin (Looda) • Jams (Soizette).
Art and Crafts
Artists' galleries • Upholsterer • Interior designer • Ceramists.

 EVENTS

Market: Wed. a.m., Rue Victor Hugo; Sun. p.m.: sale of watercress (from source of the Veules river, under the thatched roof). On the seafront: sale of fish every morning and oysters every weekend.

Apr.: Cress festival.
Jun.: Rose en Fête, rose and garden festival (weekend of Father's Day).
Jul.: Linen festival (2nd weekend).
Jul.-Aug.: Evening markets, Rue du Dr. Pierre Girard.

 OUTDOOR ACTIVITIES

Swimming (beach) • Water sports • Fishing: Sea and shore • Walking: 4 circuits.

 FURTHER AFIELD

•Saint-Valery-en-Caux: Maison Henri IV (4½ miles/7 km).
•Sainte-Marguerite-sur-Mer: Vasterival gardens (9½ miles/15 km).
•Tourville-sur-Arques: Château de Miromesnil (10 miles/16 km).
•Varengeville-sur-Mer: Church and sailors' cemetery; Bois des Moutiers ornamental gardens (12½ miles/20 km).
•Dieppe (16 miles/26 km).

Seine-Maritime (76)
Population: 523
Altitude: 260 ft. (79 m)

TOURIST INFO—LA CÔTE D'ALBÂTRE
02 35 97 00 63
cote-albatre-tourisme.fr
TOWN HALL
02 35 97 64 11
veules-les-roses.fr

Vézelay

The hill where the spirit soars

Gazing at the Monts du Morvan, Vézelay sits on a steep hill surmounted by the basilica of Sainte-Madeleine. Built in the 12th century in honor of Mary Magdalen, whose relics are believed to lie there, the abbey was both a pilgrimage destination and a departure point for Compostela. The arrival in 1146 of the abbot and reformer Bernard de Clairvaux subsequently made it an important Christian center. Beautiful Romanesque and Renaissance residences survive from this thriving era, rubbing shoulders with charming winegrowers' houses in a symphony of stone façades and rooftops, all covered with the flat, brown tiles typical of Burgundy. The basilica was restored in the 19th century by architect Viollet-le-Duc, and both it and Vézelay hill were listed as UNESCO World Heritage Sites in 1979. The basilica is renowned for its Romanesque art and the recently restored tympanum is one of its most imposing yet delicate elements. The Maison Jules-Roy, Cité de la Voix, and Maison Romain-Rolland demonstrate the village's artistic and literary commitment.

 **HIGHLIGHTS**

Basilique Sainte-Madeleine (12th–19th centuries): Guided visits for individuals or groups by the Fraternités de Jérusalem (03 86 33 39 50).
Maison du Visiteur: Multimedia exhibition on the world of the 12th-century builder (03 86 32 35 65).
Musée de l'OEuvre-Viollet-le-Duc: Romanesque capitals and fragments deposited by Viollet-le-Duc during his restoration work at the basilica (03 86 33 24 62).
Maison Jules-Roy: House and gardens of the writer; exhibitions and literary soirées (03 86 33 35 01).
Musée Zervos – Maison Romain-Rolland: Modern art collection (1925-65) bequeathed to the commune by art critic and publisher Christian Zervos (03 86 32 39 26).
Village: Guided tours for individuals and groups; guided tours of the village and basilica by accredited lecturer-guides; audio guides for those with vision impairment (03 86 33 23 69).

 ACCOMMODATION & EATING OUT

destinationgrandvezelay.com

 **LOCAL SPECIALTIES**

Food and Drink
Honey • Heritage bread • AOC Vézelay wines • Chablis wines • Craft beers.
Art and Crafts
Illuminator • Earthenware pottery • Metal, stone, and fabric crafts • Painter-sculptors • Potter • Monastic products • Weaver • Jewelry • Candles • Leather goods.

 EVENTS

Market: Wed. 8 a.m.–12 p.m., Place du Champ de Foire (Apr.-Dec.).
Jul.: Sainte-Madeleine Pilgrimage (22nd).
Aug.: Rencontres Musicales de Vézelay, music festival (late Aug.).

 OUTDOOR ACTIVITIES

Canoeing, kayaking, and rafting • Horseback riding • Fishing • Walking: Routes GR 13, GR 654, and 4 circular marked trails • Mountain biking: 5 circular trails.

 FURTHER AFIELD

•Château de Bazoches-du-Morvan ; Avallon ; Château de Chastellux ; Grottes d'Arcy-sur-Cure, caves (6–12½ miles/10–20 km).

 MBVF NEARBY
•Noyers (25 miles/40 km).

Yonne (89)
Population: 450
Altitude: 991 ft. (302 m)

TOURIST INFO—GRAND VÉZELAY
03 86 33 23 69
destinationgrandvezelay.com

Villefranche-de-Conflent

A defensive site

Villefranche-de-Conflent owes its reputation as a commercial center to its founder, Guillaume Raymond, count of Cerdagne, and its fortifications to the works of Vauban. Lying in a deep valley where the Cady and Têt rivers meet, the village occupied a strategic site since its foundation at the end of the 11th century; it later became the capital of the Conflent region. The belfry tower of La Viguerie was the administrative center, and the many shops are reminders that Villefranche was a commercial center. In the 17th century, the military engineer Vauban strengthened its role as military capital of this border region by adding his fortifications to the medieval ramparts, today listed as a UNESCO World Heritage Site. The Liberia Fort, linked to the village by the Mille Marches steps built up the mountainside, is an ingenious network of galleries equipped with twenty-five cannon ports. Inside the village, the buildings and finest residences sport stunning pink marble façades.

 HIGHLIGHTS

Église Saint-Jacques (11th–14th centuries): 12th-century Romanesque carved portal, Baroque furniture (altarpiece by Joseph Sunyer, 1715) (04 68 05 87 05).
Ramparts (04 68 05 87 05).
Fort Liberia (17th century): Tours of Vauban's site (04 68 96 34 01).
Grottes des Grandes Canalettes: Caves with stunning geological features and multimedia show (04 68 05 20 20).
Dinopédia (prehistoric grotto): Cave fortified by Vauban.
Village: Guided tour (sensory tour, audio guides, Braille and large-print guidebooks available: 04 68 05 41 02); tour by torchlight Mon. and Wed. 9 p.m. in Jul.–Aug. (04 68 05 87 05).

 ACCOMMODATION & EATING OUT

tourisme-canigo.com

 **LOCAL SPECIALTIES**

Food and Drink
Artisanal ice creams, pastries, and Catalan confectionery.
Art and Crafts
Artisanal leather goods • Ceramist • Cabinetmaker • Wrought ironworker • Lapidary studio • Wax painting • Pottery • Witch doll maker • Soaps and candles.

 EVENTS

Easter: Fêtes des Géants, Easter festival (Sun.); Aplec, pilgrimage to Notre-Dame-de-Vie (Mon.).
Jun.: Fête de la Saint-Jean (23rd)
Jul.: Fête de la Saint-Jacques (4th weekend); Fête de la Sorcière, witch festival (2nd Sun.).
Oct.: Fête du Champignon, mushroom festival (1st Sun.).

 OUTDOOR ACTIVITIES

Adventure park • Canyoning • Spelunking • Via ferrata-souterrata • Walking.

 FURTHER AFIELD

• Saint-Michel-de-Cuxa (5 miles/8 km).
• Saint-Martin-du-Canigou (5 miles/8 km).

 MBVF NEARBY

• Eus (7½ miles/12 km).
• Évol (8 miles/13 km).
• Castelnou (23 miles/37 km).

Pyrénées-Orientales (66)
Population: 200
Altitude: 1,417 ft. (432 m)

TOURIST INFO—CONFLENT-CANIGÓ
04 68 05 41 02
tourisme-canigo.com

Villeneuve

A medieval and contemporary stopover in the Aveyron

Located between the Lot and Aveyron valleys, the medieval town of Villeneuve spans the centuries with a modern spirit. Founded in the 11th century, Villeneuve was originally a *sauveté*: a rural town built around a monastery and placed under the church's protection. In the 13th century, the count of Toulouse added a *bastide*, one of the many "new towns" designed on a grid pattern that were built throughout the southwest at a time when the kingdoms of France and England were engaged in a struggle for influence. The dual nature of the village's design is visible today in its layout and rich heritage, notably the high gate and the Tour Savignac, both vestiges of the old fortifications; the market square lined with arcades; and the Église du Saint-Sépulcre, whose frescoes serve as a reminder of Villeneuve's position on the Saint James's Way pilgrimage route. The residents of this still-bustling merchant town enjoy blending time periods, in evidence at the Galerie Jean-Marie Perrier, where visitors are invited to step back into the 1960s.

 HIGHLIGHTS

Église du Saint-Sépulcre (11th–14th centuries): Polychrome murals depicting the miracle of the hanged pilgrim, 16th-century stall, 17th century Baroque altar (05 36 16 20 00).
Château de Ginals: Fortified castle and medieval keep. Self-guided tour (leaflet available); guided tour with an accredited lecturer-guide (06 16 79 61 73).
Pre-Romanesque Église de Toulongergues (10th century): Polychrome frescoes. Guided tour Wed. 3 p.m. in Jul.–Aug., all year round by appt. (05 36 16 20 00).
Galerie Jean-Marie-Perrier: Permanent exhibition of 180 photographs of celebrities from the 1960s; audio guide with the photographer's own commentary (05 65 81 53 04).
Village: Guided group tour of the church and village all year round; torchlit tours by appt.; sensory tour (reservation recommended) to feel, touch, and play (05 36 16 20 00).

ACCOMMODATION & EATING OUT

Restaurants
♥ Art et Galets
(06 25 59 41 06).

LOCAL SPECIALTIES

Food and Drink
Goat cheese • Medicinal and aromatic plants.
Art and Crafts
Glassmaker • Organ builder.

EVENTS

Market: Sun. a.m., Place des Conques.
Jul.: Medieval festival (3rd weekend).
Aug.: Festival en Bastides, street arts festival (early Aug.).

OUTDOOR ACTIVITIES

Walking • Mountain biking • Walks with a donkey or pony.

FURTHER AFIELD

• Foissac: Prehistoric cave (5½ miles/9 km).
• Villefranche-de-Rouergue, royal *bastide* (7 miles/11 km).
• Martiel: Abbaye de Loc Dieu (11 miles/18 km).
• Gorges de l'Aveyron (18½ miles/30 km).

MBVF NEARBY

• Capdenac (14½ miles/23 km).
• Belcastel (19½ miles/31 km).
• Najac (20½ miles/33 km).

Aveyron (12)
Population: 1,974
Altitude: 1,345 ft. (410 m)

TOURIST INFO—BASTIDES & GORGES DE L'AVEYRON
05 36 16 20 00
bastides-gorges-aveyron.fr

Villeréal

Royal *bastide* and artistic center

Overhanging the Dropt valley, on the borders of Lot-et-Garonne and the Dordogne, the fortified town of Villeréal combines a vibrant history with a gentle pace of life and an artistic vocation. Founded in 1267 by Alphonse de Poitiers, the *bastide* of Villeréal tells the tale—as do a number of its neighbors—of how Aquitaine was fought over at this time by England and France. The village has the classic arrangement of streets at right angles lined with half-timbered houses, but is also unique in having two squares. As is typically the case, the Place aux Cornières has a remarkable early 16th-century covered market hall in its center, whose upper story is supported by impressive oak pillars; since 1269 it has teemed with life during the weekly market. Not far away, the 13th-century church overlooks the second square. Its massive silhouette, crenellated rampart walk, and two towers with pointed roofs linked by a gallery are reminders that this religious building also had a defensive role.

 HIGHLIGHTS

Église Notre-Dame de Villeréal (13th century): Fortified church with crenellated rampart walk (05 53 36 43 84).
Village: Guided tour of the *bastide* (05 53 36 09 65), geocaching trail (Tèrra Aventura app.).

 ACCOMMODATION & EATING OUT

Gîtes and vacation rentals
♥ Jeancel ♙♙♙ (06 33 77 11 37).

 LOCAL SPECIALTIES

Food and Drink
Products from southwest France • Flour.
Art and Crafts
Ceramist.

EVENTS

Market: Sat. 8 a.m.–1 p.m.; Wed. 8 a.m.–1 p.m. (Jul.-Aug.); farmers' market Mon. 6–11 p.m. (early Jul.–mid-Sept.); flea market 2nd Sun. each month, Place de la Halle.
May: Antiques/flea market (1st).
Jul.: Un Festival à Villeréal, theater festival (1st week); Feria la Grande Bodega, music festival (last Sun.).
Aug.: Rummage sale (3rd Sun.).
Sept.: Horse festival (last Sun.).

 OUTDOOR ACTIVITIES

Walking: 2 circuits • Cycling: Tour of the *bastide*.

 FURTHER AFIELD

•Château de Biron (7½ miles/12 km).
•Issigeac (9½ miles/15 km).

 MBVF NEARBY
•Monflanquin (7½ miles/12 km).
•Monpazier (9½ miles/15 km).
•Belvès (19½ miles/31 km).

Lot-et-Garonne (47)
Population: 1,307
Altitude: 338 ft. (103 m)

TOURIST INFO—COEUR DE BASTIDES
05 53 36 09 65
coeurdebastides.com
mairie-villereal.fr

Vogüé

A castle in the Ardèche

Nestled in an amphitheater at the foot of a cliff, Vogüé dips its toes in the almost Mediterranean-like waters of the Ardèche river. The riverside roads dotted with arched passageways lead to the castle that dwarfs the village. This ancestral home of the Vogüés, one of the most illustrious families in the region, was rebuilt in the 16th and 17th centuries. It has a tower at each corner, and façades decorated with mullioned windows. It is now managed by the Vivante Ardèche association and houses collections on the region's history and architecture, the works of Ardèche engraver Jean Chièze (1898-1975), and contemporary art. In the old village streets, medieval houses roofed with curved tiles are interspersed with arcades. Their stepped terraces overflow with flowers, and in the Midi sunshine everything radiates a Mediterranean air.

 **HIGHLIGHTS**

Castle (17th century): 12th-century state room, keep, and kitchen, Jean Chièze room, Vogüé room, chapel, hanging garden; temporary art and craft exhibitions. Guided tour for individuals and tours for groups by appt.; costumed tour Tues. and Wed.; gourmet and recreational soirées in summer (04 75 37 01 95).
Église Sainte-Marie (17th century): Vault of the three lords of Vogüé.
Chapelle Saint-Cérise "la Gleysette": Located on the cliff, above the castle. Collection of statues and view of the Ardèche valley.
Art studios: Studios in the cellars of the former presbytery, with garden, gallery and craftsmen's boutique (ceramists, glassmakers, etc.).
Village: Storytelling tour, Tues. a.m. (04 28 91 24 10).

 ACCOMMODATION & EATING OUT

gorges-ardeche-pontdarc.fr

 LOCAL SPECIALTIES

Food and Drink
Honey • Nougat • Coteaux de l'Ardèche wines.
Art and Crafts
Artisanal cosmetics • Art gallery.

 EVENTS

Market: Mon. 8 a.m.-12 p.m, Vogüé train station (Jul.-Aug.); farmers' market Thurs. 6-9 p.m., Place du Château (Jun.-Sept.).
Jul.: Les Cordes en ballade, classical music festival (1st fortnight); dance and fireworks (14th).
Jul.-Aug.: Cinéma Sous les Étoiles, open-air cinema festival.
Aug.: Flea market (1st Sun.); open-air theater.

 OUTDOOR ACTIVITIES

Canoeing and kayaking • Rock climbing • Walking • Cycling: Via Ardèche greenway.

 FURTHER AFIELD

• Sauveplantade: Church; Rochecolombe; Lanas (1-2½ miles/2-4 km).
• Aubenas (6 miles/10 km).
• Ruoms (9½ miles/15 km).
• Gorges de l'Ardèche; Vallon-Pont-d'Arc; Grotte Chauvet 2 (12½ miles/20 km).

 MBVF NEARBY
• Balazuc (4½ miles/7 km).

Ardèche (07)
Population: 1,305
Altitude: 486 ft. (148 m)

TOURIST INFO—GORGES DE L'ARDÈCHE - PONT D'ARC
04 28 91 24 10
gorges-ardeche-pontdarc.fr

Art and Crafts

Painting studios • Ceramics • Jewelry and clothing.

 EVENTS

May: Fêtes des Plantes, plant festival (3rd weekend).
May–Sept.: Festival International d'Orgue, organ festival.
Jul.: Rummage sale (1st Sun.).

 OUTDOOR ACTIVITIES

Fishing • Walking • Mountain biking • Carriage rides.

 FURTHER AFIELD

•Mervent; Forêt de Vouvant-Mervent, forest (4½ miles/7 km).
•Fontenay-le-Comte (10 miles/16 km).
•Marais Poitevin (18½ miles/30 km).
•Puy-du-Fou, theme park (28 miles/45 km).

Vouvant

Nature and mystery in the Vendée

Deep in the forest of Vouvant-Mervent, the Mère river winds through a landscape that has inspired both art and mystery. William V, duke of Aquitaine (969–1030), discovered the site of Vouvant while hunting. Struck by its strategic position, he built a castle, a church, and a monastery here in the 11th century. In the Romanesque church of Notre-Dame, the 12th-century portal and apse, and the 11th-century crypt are all well worth seeing. The castle has retained only its keep, the Mélusine Tower, sections of the ramparts, and a 13th-century postern gate, which was used by Saint Louis (King Louis IX). A Romanesque bridge straddles the river Mère, linking the two riverbanks and offering an exceptional view of the ramparts. Two figures have marked the village's history: the Père de Montfort, known for his mystic predictions, and the fairy Mélusine, whose legend is still well known in France today.

 HIGHLIGHTS

Église Notre-Dame (11th–13th centuries): Organ built in 2020; sound and light show on the church portal at dusk in summer.
Nef Théodelin (11th century): Exhibition center.
Tour Mélusine (13th century): 115-ft. (35-m) tower; views over the village and the Vendée landscape.
For access contact tourist info center (02 51 00 86 80).
Village: Guided tours for individuals and groups by appt. (02 51 00 86 80 / 02 51 69 44 99).

 ACCOMMODATION & EATING OUT

vouvant-vendee.fr

 LOCAL SPECIALTIES

Food and Drink
Brioches • Foie gras, duck confit • Honey.

Vendée (85)
Population: 860
Altitude: 361 ft. (110 m)

TOURIST INFO—FONTENAY-VENDÉE
02 51 00 86 80
02 51 69 44 99
fontenay-vendee-tourisme.com
TOWN HALL
02 51 00 80 21
vouvant-vendee.fr

Yèvre-le-Châtel

(Commune of Yèvre-la-Ville)

A medieval inspiration for modern artists

On the boundary between the regions of Beauce and Gâtinais, Yèvre-le-Châtel is a happy blend of medieval heritage, floral displays, and contemporary art. The fortress of Yèvre, built in the 13th century under King Philip Augustus, commands the Rimade valley and a wide horizon. Its high ramparts and four round towers dominate the Romanesque church of Saint-Gault and the unfinished nave of Saint-Lubin. There is a circular walk around the curtain wall and, from the top of the towers, there are stunning views over the surrounding landscape, as far as the forest of Orléans. All along the flower-bedecked streets, old houses and gardens hide behind limestone walls. The village seduced many 20th-century painters, including Maria Vieira da Silva, Árpád Szenes, and Eduardo Luiz; today, contemporary works of art enhance the visitors' tour of the village, as they wander through the lanes and squares.

 HIGHLIGHTS

Castle (13th century): Medieval fortress, botanical gardens, and collection of 150 aromatic and medicinal plants (02 38 34 25 91).
Église Saint-Gault (12th century).
Église Saint-Lubin (13th century).
Roseraie Marcel Robichon: Rose garden devoted to the varieties created by M. Robichon, renowned rose grower and predecessor of André Eve.
Village: Classed as "remarkable" by the Ministry of Culture. Guided tour by appt. (02 38 34 25 91).

 **ACCOMMODATION & EATING OUT**

yevre-la-ville.fr

LOCAL SPECIALTIES

Food and Drink
Farmhouse produce (oil, honey, saffron, cider, wine, jam).

Art and Crafts
Art gallery.

 EVENTS

Market: Sun. a.m., Place du Bourg.
May 1st, mid-Jul., and last Sun. of Sept.: Large local produce market (80 local producers and artisans).

 **OUTDOOR ACTIVITIES**

Walking: Route GR 655 and Rimarde valley trail.

 **FURTHER AFIELD**

•Pithiviers (3½ miles/6 km).
•Montbarrois: Jardins de la Javelière, gardens (classed as "remarkable" by the Ministry of Culture; 11 miles/18 km).
•Château de Chamerolles (12½ miles/20 km).
•Malesherbes: Musée de l'Imprimerie, printing museum (15½ miles/25 km).

Loiret (45)
Population: 231
Altitude: 361 ft. (110 m)

TOURIST INFO—GRAND PITHIVERAIS
02 38 30 50 02
grandpithiverais.fr
yevre-la-ville.fr

Yvoire

Medieval reflections in the waters of Lake Geneva

Known as the "pearl of Lake Geneva," Yvoire combines the pleasures of a lakeside village with its medieval heritage as a sentry overlooking an important waterway. Its strategic position between the Petit Lac and the Grand Lac inspired the count of Savoy, Amadeus V the Great, to begin important fortification works here in 1306, at the height of the Delphino-Savoyard war. He built the castle on the site of a former stronghold and surrounded it with a fortified village. Castle, ramparts, gates, ditches, and medieval houses have miraculously survived an extremely stormy past. The village is overflowing with flowers in all colors of the rainbow, with exceptional displays that change with the seasons, which makes for a wonderful sight against the stone squares and façades. The serenity imparted by the waters of Lake Geneva, which instinctively draws the eye, is pleasantly disturbed by pleasure boats or a few fishermen.

 HIGHLIGHTS

Le Jardin des Cinq Sens: Sensory garden classed as "remarkable" by the Ministry of Culture; plant maze, modeled on medieval garden design (04 50 72 88 80).
Le Domaine de Rovorée-La Châtaignière: Nature reserve of 59 acres (24 ha); signposted walking trails (04 50 72 80 21).
La Châtaignière: Mansion featuring 20th-century architecture typical of the lakeside. Exhibitions, artist residencies.
Village: Guided tours with guides from Patrimoine des Pays de Savoie; guided tour by lantern in peak season (04 50 72 80 21).

 ACCOMMODATION & EATING OUT

destination-leman.com

 **LOCAL SPECIALTIES**

Food and Drink
Lake Geneva perch •
Artisanal ice creams and cookies • Savoy produce.
Art and Crafts
Wooden craft objects • Crystal artist • Basketmaker • Glassmaker • Contemporary fashion and jewelry designers.

 EVENTS

Jul.: Yvoire Jazz Festival (1st weekend); Fête du Sauvetage, festival organized by the Yvoire Lifesavers association (last Sat.).
Aug.: Venetian parade (3rd weekend).

 OUTDOOR ACTIVITIES

Boat trips on Lake Geneva • Walking.

⚲ **FURTHER AFIELD**

• Nernier (1 mile/2 km).
• Château d'Allinges (9½ miles/15 km).
• Thonon-les-Bains; Ripaille: castle; Évian-les-Bains (10–15½ miles/16–25 km).
• Geneva (17 miles/27 km).
• Nyon (20 minutes by boat).

Haute-Savoie (74)
Population: 1,084
Altitude: 1,181 ft. (360 m)

**TOURIST INFO—
DESTINATION LÉMAN**
04 50 72 80 21
destination-leman.com

Index of Villages

Photographic Credits

HEMIS

4: Lods © BLANCHOT Philippe; 6: Polignac © RIEGER Bertrand; 20: Aiguèze © GUIZIOU Franck; 21: Ainhoa © JACQUES Pierre; 23: Ansouis © CAVALIER Michel; 26: Ars-en-Ré © ZYLBERYNG Didier; 27: Aubeterre-sur-Dronne © LENAIN Hervé; 29: Auvillar © AZAM Jean-Paul; 34: Baume-les-Messieurs © LENAIN Hervé; 35: Les Baux-de-Provence © GUIZIOU Franck; 39: Belvès © BARRERE Jean-Marc; 41: Beuvron-en-Auge © RIEGER Bertrand; 45: Bonneval-sur-Arc © JACQUES Pierre; 47: Brouage © LENAIN Hervé; 50: Camon © GUIZIOU Franck; 51: Candes-Saint-Martin © LEROY Francis; 53: Cardaillac © LEROY Francis; 56: Castelnau-de-Montmiral © LENAIN Hervé; 59: Charroux © LENAIN Hervé; 60: Château-Chalon © GUIZIOU Franck; 62: Châtillon-en-Diois © MOIRENC Camille; 63: Coaraze © BLANCHOT Philippe; 64: Collonges-la-Rouge © GARDEL Bertrand; 65: Conques © AZAM Jean-Paul; 66: Cordes-sur-Ciel © MORANDI Tuul and Bruno; 69: Crissay-sur-Manse © LENAIN Hervé; 71: Domme © BODY Philippe; 74: Estaing © DEGAS Jean-Pierre; 75: Eus © LEROY Francis; 77: Flavigny-sur-Ozerain © OLART Fabien; 80: Fourcès © SUDRES Jean-Daniel; 81: La Garde-Adhémar © COLIN Matthieu; 83: Gargilesse-Dampierre © LENAIN Hervé; 87: Gourdon © JACQUES Pierre; 89: Hell-Bourg © imageBROKER; 90: Hunawihr © MATTES René; 91: Hunspach © CAVIGLIA Denis; 92: Lagrasse © LEROY Francis; 94: Lautrec © AZAM Jean-Paul; 95: Lauzerte © BARRERE Jean-Marc; 97: Lavardin © LENAIN Hervé; 98: Lavaudieu © RIEGER Bertrand; 99: Lavoûte-Chilhac © MATTES René; 101: Locronan © RIEGER Bertrand; 102: Lods © LENAIN Hervé; 104: Lourmarin © CAVALIER Michel; 106: Lyons-la-Forêt © LENAIN Hervé; 111: Minerve © GUIZIOU Franck; 112: Mirmande © MONTICO Lionel; 113: Mittelbergheim © MATTES René; 114: Moncontour © PASQUINI Cédric; 117: Monpazier © ESCUDERO Patrick; 118: Montbrun-les-Bains © GUIZIOU Franck; 119: Montclus © JACQUES Pierre; 122: Montrésor © BODY Philippe; 123: Montsoreau © CHICUREL Arnaud; 124: Mornac-sur-Seudre © BLANCHOT Philippe; 125: Mortemart © LEROY Francis; 126: Moustiers-Sainte-Marie © MONTICO Lionel; 127: Najac © DEGAS Jean-Pierre; 129: Noyers © MATTES René; 130: Oingt © MONTICO Lionel; 131: Olargues © LENAIN Hervé; 135: Penne-d'Agenais © BRUSINI Aurélien; 134: Pérouges © GUIZIOU Franck; 135: Pesmes © MATTES René; 136: Peyre © JACQUES Pierre; 138: Le Poët-Laval © SUDRES Jean-Daniel; 142: Pujols-le-Haut © LENAIN Hervé; 143: Puycelsi © DENIS-HUOT Mixhel and Christine; 144: Riquewihr © MATTES René; 145: Rocamadour © Jon Arnold Images; 146: Rochefort-en-Terre © MATTES René; 151: La Roque-sur-Cèze © JACQUES Pierre; 152: Roussillon © CAVALIER Michel; 153: Saint-Amand-de-Coly © CAVIGLIA Denis; 154: Saint-Antoine-l'Abbaye © GUIZIOU Franck; 156: Saint-Bertrand-de-Comminges ©TARDY Hervé; 157: Saint-Céneri-le-Gérei © LENAIN Hervé; 159: Saint-Côme-d'Olt © LENAIN Hervé; 160: Saint-Guilhem-le-Désert © JACQUES Pierre; 162: Saint-Jean-Pied-de-Port © GUIZIOU Franck; 163: Saint-Léon-sur-Vézère © ROY Philippe; 164: Saint-Quirin © CAVIGIA Denis; 165: Saint-Robert © GUY Christian; 166: Saint-Suliac © STICHELBAUT; 167: Saint-Véran © MONTICO Lionel; 168: Sainte-Agnès © CEGALERBA-SWEMBERG; 171: Sainte-Eulalie-d'Olt © LENAIN Hervé; 172: Sainte-Suzanne © BODY Philippe; 173: Salers © GUY Christian ;175: Sant'Antonino © CAVALIER Michel; 177: Sare © MORANDI Tuul and Bruno; 179: Sauveterre-de-Rouergue © LENAIN Hervé; 180: Séguret © GUIZIOU Franck; 181: Ségur-le-Château © LENAIN Hervé; 183: Semur-en-Brionnais © CAVIGLIA Denis; 184: Talmont-sur-Gironde © LEROY Francis; 187: Tourtour © SONNET Sylvain; 188: Turenne © GUY Christian; 190: Venasque © MATTES René; 192: Vézelay © CHICUREL Arnaud; 193: Villefranche-de-Conflent © AZAM Jean-Paul; 194: Villeneuve © AZAM Jean-Paul; 195: Villeréal © LEROY Francis; 196: Vogüé © GUIZIOU Franck; 197: Vouvant © LENAIN Hervé; 199: Yvoire © JACQUES Pierre; 200: Hell-Bourg © Jon Arnold Images.

Les Plus Beaux Villages de France association

8: Beynac-et-Cazenac © A. BARBALAT; 22: Angles-sur-l'Anglin © Kazutoshi Yoshimura; 24: Apremont-sur-Allier © P. BERNARD; 25: Arlempdes © Kazutoshi Yoshimura; 28: Autoire © Kazutoshi Yoshimura; 30: Balazuc © Kazutoshi Yoshimura; 31: Barfleur © P. BERNARD; 32: Bargème © Kazutoshi Yoshimura; 33: La-Bastide-Clairence © P. BERNARD; 36: Beaulieu-sur-Dordogne © P. BERNARD; 37: Le Bec-Hellouin © P. BERNARD; 38: Belcastel © Office de Tourisme de Belcastel; 40: Bergheim © Pamella Rodrigues; 42: Beynac-et-Cazenac © A. BARBALAT; 43: Blangy-le-Château © D. and M. DUPERRAY; 44: Blesle © P. BERNARD; 48: Brousse-le-Château © René-Pierre Delorme; 49: Bruniquel © Sylvain Pradal; 52: Capdenac-le-Haut © Cyril Novello; 54: Carennac © D. Viet; 55: Le Castellet © Alisa Descarpentries; 57: Castelnaud-la-Chapelle © P. BERNARD; 58: Castelnou © P. BERNARD; 61: Châteauneuf © Carte postale; 67: Cotignac © P. BERNARD; 70: Curemonte © Y. LEMAITRE; 72: Eguisheim © P. BERNARD; 73: Entrevaux © P. BERNARD; 76: Evol © OT Conflent Canigo; 78: La Flotte © P. BERNARD; 79: Fontevraud-l'Abbaye © PBVF; 82: La Garde-Guérin © P. BERNARD; 84: Gassin © P. BERNARD; 85: Gerberoy © A. GOUVERNEL; 86: Gordes © P. BERNARD; 88: Grignan © P. BERNARD; 93: Larressingle © Kazutoshi Yoshimura; 96: Lavardens © Y. LEMAITRE; 100: Limeuil © Y. LEMAITRE; 103: Loubressac © Kazutoshi Yoshimura; 105: Lussan © Bruno Bouvart; 107: Le Malzieu-Ville © Pascal Philippot; 108: Marcolès © PBVF; 109: Martel © P. BERNARD; 110: Ménerbes © Kazutoshi Yoshimura; 116: Monestiés © Kazutoshi Yoshimura; 116: Monflanquin © Antoine Dominique; 120: Montpeyroux © Pierre-Alain Heyde; 121: Montréal © M. Laffargue; 128: Navarrenx © Olivier Robinet; 132: Parfondeval © Isabelle Chrétien; 137: Piana © Kazutoshi Yoshimura; 139: Polignac © Jean-Marc Guérin; 140: Pradelles © P. BERNARD; 141: Prats-de-Mollo-la-Preste © P. BERNARD; 147: La Roche-Guyon © P. BERNARD; 148: Rodemack © P. BERNARD; 149: La Romieu © Herve Leclair Aspheries; 150: La Roque-Gageac © Youcef Benbrahim; 155: Saint-Benoît-du-Sault © Soledad Alonso; 158: Saint-Cirq-Lapopie © P. BERNARD; 161: Saint-Jean-de-Côle © PBVF; 169: Sainte-Croix-en-Jarez © P. BERNARD; 170: Sainte-Enimie © Westend61; 174: Sancerre © PBVF; 176: Saorge © P. BERNARD; 178: Sarrant © Maxime Dallemagne; 182: Seillans © PBVF; 185: Tournemire © Jean-Michel Peyral; 186: Tournon d'Agenais © Lucas Frayssinet; 189: Usson © P. BERNARD; 191: Veules-les-Roses © ALC Veul'Images; 198: Yèvre-le-Châtel; © Pascal Philippot.

Acknowledgments

Flammarion wishes to thank the Les Plus Beaux Villages
de France association (Alain Di Stefano, Anne Gouvernel,
Cécile Varillon, Pascal Bernard, and Sophie Damblé),
as well as Editerra (Sophie Lalouette).

Les Plus
Beaux Villages
de France®

Become a Friend of the Association

Are you a fan of Les Plus Beaux Villages de France?

Whether you are enthusiastic about heritage or looking for fresh travel experiences, you can support our work by becoming an "Ami," or friend, of the association. You will receive the network's latest news by way of our electronic newsletter *Vivons l'Exception !* (information for the general public) and our internal newsletter *PointCom*.

By supporting the Les Plus Beaux Villages de France association, you contribute to an initiative that began over forty years ago, with the goal of encouraging the development of sustainable tourism in French villages by promoting cultural, built, and environmental heritage; maintaining businesses and activities for local residents; and ensuring a quality of life for all.

Les Plus Beaux Villages de France are for everyone. So, join the adventure!

Become a member by clicking on "Le Label," and then "Rejoignez-nous," on our website:

les-plus-beaux-villages-de-france.org